BABYLON

PAUL KRIWACZEK

BABYLON

Mesopotamia and the
Birth of Civilization

Thomas Dunne Books
St. Martin's Press
New York

THOMAS DUNNE BOOKS.
An imprint of St. Martin's Press.

BABYLON.
Copyright © 2010 by Paul Kriwaczek.
All rights reserved.
Printed in the United States of America.
For information, address
St. Martin's Press, 175 Fifth Avenue, New York, N.Y. 10010.

All maps and line drawings © Jeff Edwards

www.stmartins.com

ISBN 978-1-250-05416-6

First published in Great Britain by Atlantic Books,
an imprint of Grove Atlantic Ltd

First U.S. Edition: April 2012

CONTENTS

ACKNOWLEDGEMENTS

My thanks are due to my brother, Frank Kriwaczek, for his help in accessing documents and journals that would otherwise have been unavailable to me, and as ever to my literary agent and good friend Mandy Little, for her invaluable support and wise guidance.

LIST OF ILLUSTRATIONS

Maps

These maps are purely indicative and omit many lines and landmarks for the sake of clarity.

List of Photographic Illustrations

History which does not inform present-day concerns amounts to little more than self-indulgent antiquarianism

Quentin Skinner, Regius Professor of Modern History at Cambridge University, Inaugural Lecture, 1997

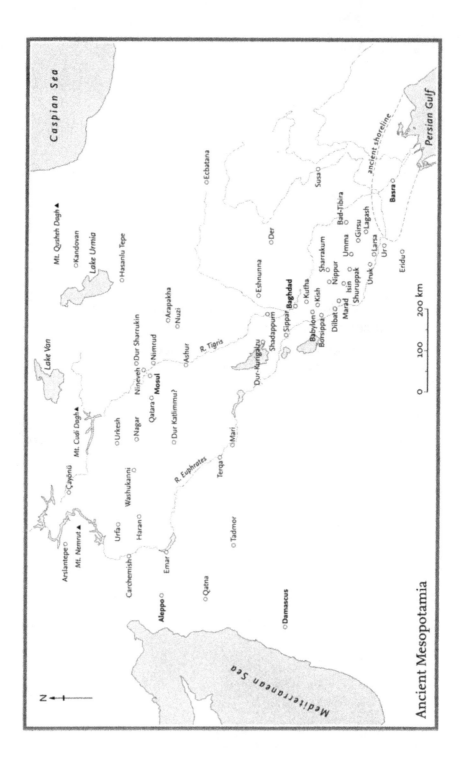

Ancient Mesopotamia

1

Lessons from the Past:
An Introduction

They hanged Saddam Hussein on the first day of the Feast of the Sacrifice, 'Eid ul-Adha, 30 December 2006. It was not a dignified execution. Reading the newspaper reports of that grisly – and botched – act of barbarism, more revenge than justice, and seeing the mobile-phone video images distributed immediately afterwards, I cannot have been the only one to feel that the language of daily journalism was inadequate to encompass such extravagant, larger-than-life events.

The cruel tyrant's army crumbles away. He himself escapes, disappears from sight for a time, but is eventually discovered, filthy and heavily bearded, cowering like an animal in a hole in the ground. He is taken captive, publicly humiliated, held in solitary confinement for a thousand days and put on trial before a tribunal whose verdict is a foregone conclusion. Hanging him, his exultant executioners almost tear off his head.

As in biblical times, God took to speaking to men again, instructing the makers of history. At a secret meeting between senior army officers in Kuwait during the run-up to the First Gulf War, Saddam had explained that he had invaded Kuwait on heaven's express instructions: 'May God be my witness, that it is the Lord who wanted what happened to happen. This decision we received almost ready-made from God... Our role in the decision was almost zero.'

In a BBC documentary, broadcast in October 2005, Nabil Sha'ath, Foreign Minister of the Palestinian authority recalled that 'President Bush said to all of us: "I'm driven with a mission from God. God would tell me,

'George, go and fight those terrorists in Afghanistan.' And I did; and then God would tell me 'George, go and end the tyranny in Iraq...' And I did. And now, again, I feel God's words coming to me."'

It would have come as no real surprise had the conflict begun with a voice booming out from heaven, crying 'O President Saddam,' and continuing, as in the Book of Daniel, 4:31: 'to thee it is spoken; The kingdom is departed from thee. And they shall drive thee from men, and thy dwelling shall be with the beasts of the field.' It takes the language of the Old Testament, the Book of Kings perhaps, to depict the details of Saddam Hussein's end in their full, almost mythic, dimensions. Thus:

> It was the morning of the Sabbath, before the sun rose. And they brought him into the city, even unto the place of execution.
>
> And they bound his hands and his feet as was the custom among them in the way of execution. And they reviled him saying, how are the mighty fallen, and may you be cursed by the Lord.
>
> And they placed the rope about his neck and they reviled him again, praising the names and titles of his enemies, and saying, may God curse you, may you go down to hell.
>
> And he replied, saying, Is this your manhood? This is a gallows of shame.
>
> And again they spoke unto him, saying, prepare to meet God. And he prayed to God, saying, there is no God but the Lord.
>
> And so they hanged him. And a great shout went up in the place of execution and in the streets and in the markets. It was the morning of the Sabbath, as the sun rose over the walls of Babylon.

Seeing George W. Bush's Iraq War through biblical eyes is not just a writer's conceit, the reaction of someone like me, introduced as a child to Middle-Eastern history by the Bible. Saddam too saw himself as a successor to the rulers of antiquity. He particularly modelled himself on Nebuchadnezzar II (605–562 BCE), conqueror and destroyer of Jerusalem and its temple, describing him, in a multiple anachronism, as 'an Arab from Iraq', who fought, like Saddam himself, against Persians and Jews. (Nebuchadnezzar was not an Arab but a Chaldean, there would be no Iraq for another two and a half millennia, and Judaism as we know it did not yet exist.) The emblem of the 1988 Babylon International Festival showed Saddam's profile superimposed on Nebuchadnezzar's; according to a *New York Times* journalist, the outline of his nose was lengthened to make him resemble the Mesopotamian king more closely. Saddam also honoured Hammurabi (c.1795–1750 BCE), the ruler of the Old Babylonian Empire renowned for his eye-for-an-eye legal code, and named the most powerful strike-force in the Iraqi army the Hammurabi Republican Guard Armoured Division; another unit was the Nebuchadnezzar Infantry Division.

The Iraqi leader was, said the BBC's John Simpson, 'an inveterate builder of monuments to himself', undertaking great construction projects in conscious emulation of his illustrious predecessors. Giant images of the Iraqi leader showed him, like an ancient Sumerian monarch, carrying a building-worker's basket on his shoulder, although the ancients would have been pictured bearing the first load of clay for brickmaking, while Saddam was represented bearing a bowl of cement. He began a massive reconstruction of the site of ancient Babylon, although his rebuilding, said one architectural historian, was 'poor quality pastiche and frequently wrong in scale and detail… ' Like the monarchs of antiquity, Saddam had the bricks inscribed with his name; thousands bore the rubric: 'The Babylon of Nebuchadnezzar was rebuilt in the era of the leader President Saddam Hussein'. Never one to display unnecessary good taste, he had the text written in modern Arabic rather than Babylonian cuneiform.

The political reasons for Saddam Hussein's concern to connect with the far distant, pre-Muslim, past of his country are plain. As in the case of the Shah of next-door Iran, who in 1971 famously declared his kinship with Cyrus the Great, founder of the first, Achaemenid, Persian Empire, any pitch for leadership of the Middle East demands that the pretender first neutralize the claims of holy Mecca and Medina in Saudi Arabia, the cities of the Prophet, to be the sole ultimate source of Islamic legitimacy.

There is much irony in the fact that Anglo-American Middle East policy, from Operation Ajax, the deposing of democratically elected, socialist, secularist Prime Minister Mohammad Mossadeq in Iran in 1953, to Operation Iraqi Freedom, the overthrow of secular nationalist dictator Saddam Hussein in 2003, has served in fact, if not intention, to ensure the continuing hold of Islam over nearly all the countries of the region. Thus inevitably boosting the claim of Salafi Islam, which looks to the immediate successors of the Prophet for its political models, to provide the only authentic principles on which to build a legitimate political system.

Perhaps Saddam – whatever else he might have been, he was neither stupid nor unperceptive – also recognized another, even greater, truth of Middle-Eastern power-politics. Our way of life and understanding of the world may have changed utterly since ancient times, but we flatter ourselves unduly if we think that our behaviour is in any way different, or that human nature has altered much over the millennia.

History tells us that the region the Greeks called Mesopotamia, because it lay 'between the rivers' Tigris and Euphrates, was fought over by Romans and Parthians, by Byzantines and Sassanians, by Muslims and Magians, until rank outsiders, Mongols and Turks, conquerors from distant Central Asia and beyond, created a desert and called it peace. Nobody with even a passing acquaintance with the history of the land could have been surprised at its reversion to confusion after the heavy Ottoman yoke was lifted from Iraq's neck in the 1920s, or the collapse into chaos after the deposition of the modern Ba'ath tyranny that held together the three former Ottoman provinces, mutually antagonistic and seemingly united only by the League of Nations to allow the great powers to extract oil.

But the attempts to grab control over the fertile Mesopotamian plain go back much further even than Roman times. Twice as far, in fact. And while the ancient powers who vied for sovereignty have long since crumbled to dust, their clashes still ring faintly in the air.

The bustling, thriving town now called Shush in south-west Iran, where the foothills of the Zagros Mountains run down on to the Mesopotamian Plain, is no more than 55 kilometres from the Iraqi border, another 70 from the Tigris. The streets are strung out either side of a slackly flowing branch of the Karkheh River, the air tinged grey-blue by the exhausts of the poorly maintained cars, which fight for space with crowds of pedestrians, bicycles, and men pushing heavily laden carts. Shush, ancient Susa, is the setting for the biblical Books of Nehemiah, Esther and Daniel: 'I was in Shushan the palace,' states the account of his visions in Daniel 8:2, '... and I saw in the vision that I was by the river Ulai.' Stand today on the main street that runs parallel to the river and you cannot escape reminders of the place's great antiquity.

In front of you, between the road and the river-bank stands the reputedly ancient tomb of Daniel himself – nothing Hebraic about it, but an unremarkably Islamic building topped out with an unusual spiral cone rendered in white plaster. (Daniel's story was supposed to take place some time in the sixth century BCE, and this sepulchre dates from 1871.) The shrine is greatly honoured by local Shi'a Muslims; visitors enter the building in a steady stream, to fall on their knees, recite prayers and kiss the elaborate gilded metal grille that protects the sarcophagus.

Across the street rises the gigantic mound that is the site of the ancient city, bearing at its top the fragmented stone remains of the Persian Achaemenid kings' winter capital. Walk around the ruins and you crunch over fragments of brick and pottery that may be as much as 5,000 years old, for Susa is one of the oldest continuously inhabited settlements anywhere in the world, probably founded not much later than 5000 BCE. From the middle of the second millennium BCE it was the capital of a state called Elam, master of this part of Iran long before the advent of the Persians, and founded by a people who may just possibly, from the linguistic evidence, have been related to the speakers of Dravidian languages like Kannada and Malayalam, Tamil and Telugu, languages now found almost exclusively in southern India.

Right beside you, were you visiting as I did in 2001, you would have found erected along the pavement at the foot of the mound a long single-storied temporary building. This housed a gruesome exhibition detailing the sufferings of the town in the course of the Iran–Iraq War, the long struggle that started with an assault on Iran launched by Saddam Hussein in 1980, and ended when the Ayatollah Khomeini reluctantly accepted a cease-fire in 1988, an act which he equated to 'drinking poison'. The *New York Times* reported that the final exchange of prisoners of war took place only on 17 March 2003 – a mere six days before the next catastrophe: the assault by the 'coalition of the willing' on Saddam Hussein. Imagine the experience of the ex-prisoners, free after so many years of bitter incarceration, only immediately to have to face US 'shock and awe'.

Shush, although never taken by Iraqi forces, was at one time a little over three kilometres from the front line in the brutal conflict, which seemed to repeat the worst and cruellest excesses of the 1914–18 European war: trench warfare, bayonet charges, suicidal assaults, and the indiscriminate use by one side of chemical weapons. To which new grotesque specialities were added Iran's human-wave attacks, and her use of young volunteer martyrs as living minesweepers. There were well over a million military casualties; tens of thousands of civilians were wounded or killed.

Iranian culture has a gift for celebrating a sense of sacred martyrdom. The exhibition on Shush's main street preserved one of the defensive trenches dug when it was feared that the city would fall to Saddam's forces. In 2001 it was still littered with the detritus abandoned when it was struck by the direct hit of an artillery shell: a grotesquely dented steel helmet, a shredded, bloodstained boot, and a crushed and twisted assault rifle. A show of unspeakably shocking photographs of Shushite casualties reminded western visitors of cultural differences in what horrors are acceptable for public presentation. The displays aiming to recreate the realities of the First World War in London's Imperial War Museum are dreadful enough; they cannot compare with the grisliness of this temporary exhibition, with its depictions of the gruesome bloodletting that had taken place here little more than ten years earlier. By the exit was an account of the conflict, explaining how Saddam had attempted to conquer the provinces of Khuzestan, Ilam and Kermanshah to incorporate as part of his blasphemous Ba'ath empire; how Iran had bravely resisted, and then turned the tables by striking with great military success into Iraq, until graciously accepting, for humanitarian reasons, a UN ceasefire.

Had you just come down, as I had, from the site of the ancient city atop the great mound, you could not help but recall the equally long account of its history painted on a large peeling sign near the entrance ticket office, detailing the attempts by the kings of Elamite Susa to dominate the city-states and empires of Mesopotamia. There was even a list of artefacts carried off as loot by Elamite raiders, including the famous stele inscribed with the law code of Hammurabi, eventually to be unearthed in Susa by modern European archaeologists. The struggle for power was brought to an end in the most dramatic way when Susa was destroyed by the Assyrian Emperor Ashurbanipal in the seventh century BCE.

*

Much later, having thought to explore Mesopotamia's history in greater detail, I would read the conqueror's own description of that action, written on a clay tablet dug up from the ruins of Nineveh by Sir Austen Henry Layard:

> *Susa, the great holy city, abode of their Gods, seat of their mysteries, I conquered. I entered its palaces, I opened their treasuries where silver and gold, goods and wealth were amassed... I destroyed the ziggurat of Susa. I smashed its shining copper horns. I reduced the temples of Elam to naught; their gods and goddesses I scattered to the winds. The tombs of their ancient and recent kings I devastated, I exposed to the sun, and I carried away their bones toward the land of Ashur. I devastated the provinces of Elam and on their lands I sowed salt.*

And in the British Museum I would examine the alabaster bas-relief illustrating the conquest: Assyrian sappers demolishing the walls with crowbars and pickaxes as flames flicker from the main gate and over the tall city towers, a stream of captives and soldiers carrying their rich booty through the surrounding forest.

Here was evidence that the Iran–Iraq War was no isolated clash, initiated by a vicious modern dictator running amok, and contingent on local, personal and temporary factors. Instead it was the most recent act in a millennia-long violent dispute played out over centuries – and one which will no doubt continue long into the future – over the control of Mesopotamia. That is, should the Tigris–Euphrates Valley be mastered from the west or from the east.

The location of the land, squeezed between Arabia and Asia, between the desert and the mountains, between Semites and Iranians, inheriting from and owing allegiance to both, has shaped the region's destiny from the very beginnings of its recorded history.

It turned out to be no easy task to delve deeper into the details of the distant past. I soon discovered that anyone wishing to improve their understanding of contemporary geopolitics by reading up on ancient times is immediately faced with the sheer profligacy of Mesopotamian scholarship. Since 1815, when Claudius Rich, the young British Resident in Baghdad, published his *Memoir on the Ruins of Babylon*, an instant best-seller which triggered a burgeoning interest across Europe in the remains of the vanished world, academic as well as popular books, monographs, pamphlets, articles, and scholarly papers written for peer-reviewed journals have streamed off the presses, and new titles are being added nearly every day. For in spite of everything that is already known about life on the ancient Tigris–Euphrates plain, in actual fact far more still remains unknown. Only a minor proportion of long-recognized archaeological sites has been explored; only limited sections of these have been excavated; only a fraction of the million or so documents, now distributed among museums and private collections all over the world, has been fully studied, deciphered and translated; many times that number must be waiting to be brought up into the light. In 2008, an inscribed clay cone that had languished, forgotten since the 1970s, in a shoebox on a shelf at the University of Minnesota, was found to record the reign of a previously unknown king of ancient Uruk.

This is a field of knowledge that is constantly changing. Not so long ago almost all cultural change was attributed to invasion and conquest. Now we are far less sure. Four decades ago it was still assumed that the first attempt at empire, by Sargon of Akkad, who flourished some time around 2300 BCE, represented the conquest by Semitic people of the indigenous Sumerians. Most evidence now proposes that the two communities had lived together peacefully in the region from time immemorial. Names may be given different readings. A well-known Sumerian king c.2000 BCE was first read as Dungi, more recently as Shulgi; the one Sumerian name popularly recognized today, Gilgamesh, first appeared in 1891 misread as Izdubar. Texts may come to be translated quite differently, even reversing their meaning. The verdict in a murder trial before the Assembly of Nippur in the twentieth century BCE, has been read by one scholar as condemning one of the defendants to death, while by another as absolving her of all guilt.

Dates are constantly being revised. The ancient Mesopotamians had their own dating systems – although their accounts cannot necessarily be believed, for example the impossibly long reigns ascribed to some of their kings – but it is still very hard to work out the equivalent in our own calendar. It helps that the accurate observation of the heavens was one of the first sciences established in ancient times, and that a strong belief in omens and portents ensured that unusual celestial phenomena were carefully recorded. Since our own Newtonian astronomy allows us to state exactly when, according to our calendar, such predictable events as solar and lunar eclipses occurred, it should be possible to put an accurate date on ancient reports.

And yet the texts are often so enigmatic, and our ability to understand their language – even after a century and a half of study – so incomplete, that it can be difficult to make out exactly what is being described. Thus the report apparently detailing a solar eclipse, on a tablet unearthed in Ras Shamra, Syria, in 1948: 'The day of the Moon of Hiyaru was put to shame. The Sun went in with her gatekeeper, Rashap.' (Rashap may be a name for the planet Mars.) One pair of scholars has linked this account to a solar eclipse known to have occurred on 3 May 1375 BCE; another, later, academic duo re-dated the occurrence to 5 March 1223. More recently, the text has been associated with the solar eclipses of the 21 January 1192 and 9 May 1012. Yet other, equally reputable, researchers have cast doubt on whether the tablet actually refers to an eclipse at all.

As a result of such disagreements, the reign of the famous law-giver Hammurabi, King of Babylon, has been variously dated to 1848–1806 BCE (long chronology), 1792–1750 BCE (middle chronology), 1728–1686 BCE (short chronology) and 1696–1654 BCE (ultra-short chronology).

This is not just a recent issue. Already in 1923, the editor of Punch magazine, Sir Owen Seaman, was protesting loudly, in verse, that his mental equanimity had been disturbed when the British Museum's cuneiform expert Cyril Gadd shifted the date of the final fall of Assyrian Nineveh back – by as far as six years!

> But still I counted on the Past,
> Deeming it steady as a rock;
> History, I said, stands fast;
> And it has been a horrid shock,
> A bitter, bitter blow to me
> To hear this news of Nineveh.
>
> They taught us how in six-o-six
> (B.C.) that godless town fell flat;
> And now the new-found records fix

A date anterior to that;
It fell, in fact, six-one-two,
So what they taught us wasn't true.

The gentleman who worked it out,
He got it from a slab of clay,
And it has seared my soul with doubt
To see the old truths pass away;
Such disillusionment (by GADD)
Might surely drive a fellow mad.

If we smile with Sir Owen at those, like Cyril Gadd, to whom noting a difference of six years in more than 2,500 is important, who devote their entire working lives to amassing precise details, abstruse minutiae, of a world long since disappeared, researchers pursuing with the dedication of Soviet Stakhanovite quota-busters an activity that many would find irrelevant to any modern interest, we must also recognize that without data, there can be no knowledge and without knowledge there can be no understanding. And any understanding of how human beings have lived together in the past must bear in some way on both the present and the future.

Getting to grips with the sweep of history is proverbially a matter of balancing one's perception of the trees against gaining a view of the whole wood. In the case of ancient Mesopotamia, although details may change, and change radically, although knowledge may yet have far to grow, a pattern is still recognisable. The trees may constantly be shifting, but you can still make out the wood. At first only faint and shadowed, none the less a shape, an outline representing a self-contained story of the ancient Middle East, does emerge out of what has been assembled by the indefatigable intellectual labour, inextinguishable enthusiasm and irrepressible industry of a century and a half of scholars and students of Assyriology – misnamed, really, because Assyria is but one of the protagonists of the narrative.

I find the form that takes shape surprising, remarkable, extraordinary and astonishing.

I find it surprising for its longevity. If history, as by most definitions, begins with writing, then the birth, rise and fall of ancient Mesopotamia occupies a full half of all history. What would evolve into the script called cuneiform, wedge-shaped signs impressed by reed stylus into clay tablet, first appeared in the last centuries before 3000 BCE. That was the start, the *terminus a quo*. Independent Mesopotamia vanished from history upon the conquest of Babylon by Cyrus the Great of Persia in 539 BCE. That was the end, the *terminus ad quem*. In round numbers, its duration was 2,500 years. From 500 BCE to the present is the same distance in time. From today's perspective the Persian emperor's victory is as far back in our past as was Cyrus from the origin of the civilization he both vanquished and inherited.

I find it remarkable for its continuity. Throughout all that time – the same span as takes us from the classical age of Greece, through the rise and fall of Rome, of Byzantium, of the Islamic Khalifate, of the Renaissance, of the European empires, to the present day – Mesopotamia preserved a single civilization, using one unique system of writing, cuneiform, from beginning to end; and with a single, continuously evolving literary, artistic, iconographic, mathematical, scientific, and religious tradition. To be sure, there were cultural differences between different places and different times. A Sumerian from 3000 BCE transplanted to the Assyria of the seventh century would of course have experienced profound bewilderment and culture shock. None the less, although one of the civilization's two languages, Sumerian, ceased early to be spoken on the streets and the other, Akkadian, divided into different dialectical varieties before finally giving way to the speech of incoming Arameans, yet both continued to be written and understood to the very end. The last great Assyrian emperor, Ashurbanipal (685–627 BCE), took pride in being able to read 'the cunning tablets of Sumer, and the dark Akkadian language which is difficult rightly to use; I took my pleasure in reading stones inscribed before the flood'.

I find it extraordinary for its creativity. In the course of its two and a half millennia, the cuneiform-based tradition invented or discovered almost everything we associate with the civilized life. Beginning in a world of Neolithic villages, largely self sufficient and self-sustaining subsistence farming communities, and ending with a world, not only of cities, and empires, and technology, and science, and law, and literary wisdom, but even more: with what has been called a world system, a linked web of nations, communicating and trading and fighting with each other, spread across a large part of the globe. Such was the achievement of the writers of cuneiform.

I find it astonishing for its non-ethnicity. The bearers of this ground-breaking tradition were not one nation or one people. From the start at least two communities, Semitic and non-Semitic, inhabited the land, one originally from the deserts of the west and the other just possibly from the mountains of the north. To these ethnic foundations were added the genetic contribution of many invaders and conquerors, Gutians, Kassites, Amorites and Arameans among them, who, in almost every case, assimilated to Sumerian–Akkadian language and culture, and in most instances contributed with gusto to the further advance of their adopted way of life. Those who did not were always remembered with scorn. Both of Saddam Hussein's heroes, Hammurabi, an Amorite, and Nebuchadnezzar, a Chaldean, as well as many other commanding figures in Mesopotamian history, came from outsider families, from immigrant stock.

Thus the civilization that was born, flourished and died in the land between the rivers was not the achievement of any particular people, but the result of the coming together and persistence through time of a unique combination of ideas, styles, beliefs and behaviours. The Mesopotamian story is that of a single continuous cultural tradition, even though its human bearers and propagators were different at different times.

One further unexpected feature strikes me powerfully. Because that story is so long over, and because we can observe it from a sufficient distance, one cannot help but note how much ancient Mesopotamian civilization behaved both like a living organism and as if it were governed by natural laws. It is rather like watching one of those speeded-up time-lapse film sequences you sometimes see in nature programmes on TV: a seed germinates, the shoot becomes a seedling, the plant grows, bushes up, flowers, sets seed, propagates itself, withers and dies – all in the space of half a minute or so.

But are not societies, empires and civilizations human constructs, the products of arbitrary, contingent and essentially unpredictable decisions by independent intelligent actors, and far from the result of some kind of mathematical determinism? Perhaps less so than we may think. It is not hard to see that if one found a way to plot Mesopotamian civilization's energy, creativity and productivity as a graph, it would look like a long bell-shaped curve, rising at first imperceptibly from the baseline, growing exponentially to a high point, maintaining its vigour and vitality over considerable time – though with fluctuations – and then without warning declining swiftly, before finally flattening out to approach ever more slowly the zero base line. Thus: birth, growth, maturity, decline, senescence and final disappearance.

Starting about 10,000 BCE, very soon after the final melting of the continental glaciers, though quite slowly at first, people began to adopt a more settled way of life, grouping together in village communities, and, rather than merely exploiting the opportunities offered by nature, they started to control the plants and animals on which they subsisted. Crops were planted, herds were corralled, the flora and fauna essential to people's survival were genetically modified by selective breeding, the better to serve their human purposes.

Into this relatively uniform, mostly undifferentiated, largely homogeneous world of subsistence farmers and peasant hamlets, the idea of civilization was born: in a single place, at a single time. From there and from then the concept spread at remarkable speed to conquer the world.

Yet not all communities took up the opportunity. What held the refusers back may have been the very comfort and effectiveness of their village life with its well-established routines and well-honed survival skills. As in many other fields of human endeavour, it seems to have taken the recalcitrance of the awkward reality of the Mesopotamian alluvial plain, the resistance of these unwelcoming surroundings, the difficulty of making a living in this unpropitious place, to provide the grit in the oyster, the nucleus around which the great leap forward of humanity crystallized.

Farming the new land of the Mesopotamian plain, potentially fertile but actually desolate and barren because of very low annual rainfall, required that people get together to organize systems of irrigation. The German–American writer and thinker Karl Wittfogel coined the term 'hydraulic civilizations' for societies in which the need to control water demanded collective action, so stimulating the development of an organizing bureaucracy, which led inevitably, in his view, to typical oriental despotic rule. This idea, though highly influential in the earlier twentieth century, is no longer much respected by scholars, who accuse Wittfogel of not allowing the facts to stand in the way of an attractive theory. Yet it cannot be denied that the riverine environment around the two great Middle Eastern streams did demand collaboration in irrigation works to ensure its settlers' survival. And that somehow this led to the invention of city life.

The rest is history, as the cliché has it. From its mysterious, shadowy beginnings until its final, well-documented end, ancient Mesopotamia acted as a kind of experimental laboratory for civilization, testing, often to destruction, many kinds of religion, from early personifications of natural forces to full-blown temple priesthood and even the first stirrings of monotheism; a wide variety of economic and production systems, from (their own version of) state planning and centralized direction to (their own style of) neo-liberal privatization, as well as an assortment of government systems, from primitive democracy and consultative monarchy to ruthless tyranny and expansive imperialism. Almost every one of these can be paralleled with similar features found in our own more recent history. It sometimes seems as if the whole ancient story served as a dry-run, a dress rehearsal, for the succeeding civilization, our own, which would originate in the Greece of Periclean Athens after the demise of the last Mesopotamian empire in the sixth century BCE, and which has brought us to where we stand today.

Though the experimenters of antiquity are long dead, their names largely forgotten, their homes buried, their possessions scattered, their fields barren, their temple towers ruined, their cities interred under mounds of dust, their empires remembered, if at all, by name only, their story still promises to teach us much about how we arrived at the way we live now. History may not repeat itself but, as Mark Twain said, it does rhyme.

2

Kingship Descends from Heaven:
The Urban Revolution

Before 4000 BCE

Eridu

Leave the modern traffic, the bicycles, the cars and delivery lorries fuming along St Giles' and Beaumont Street in Oxford, and pass through the Ashmolean Museum's rather overblown neoclassical façade. In a glass case in one of the galleries you will find a baked clay object, square in cross-section, dull in colour, partly broken, and covered in what at first sight look like birds' footprints. You may have to look hard to find it, because it is only about 20 cm high and 9 cm wide.

It doesn't look like an object of any great importance, yet it is. Look at it closely, and it will draw you back through time to the origins of civilization. It is called the Weld-Blundell Prism, after the benefactor who bought it during a visit to Mesopotamia in the spring of 1921. Victorian architects like C. R. Cockerell, who in 1841 based the Ashmolean's design on the Temple of Apollo at Bassae, thought that they were celebrating the ultimate roots of our culture. But the prism directs us much further back, long before the Greeks, long before King Solomon, long before Moses, long before Abraham the Patriarch, even before Noah and his flood, to the time when cities were first imagined.

The bird-scratchings are writing: two columns of closely written text on each of its four faces, encoding an early version of the Sumerian King List, a long and exhaustive enumeration of the dynasties of different Mesopotamian cities, and the regnal years of their rulers. Some are wildly improbable, like Alulim who reigned for 28,800 years and Alalgar for 36,000, but the list tracks the kingship from Eridu to Bad-tibira, to Larsa,

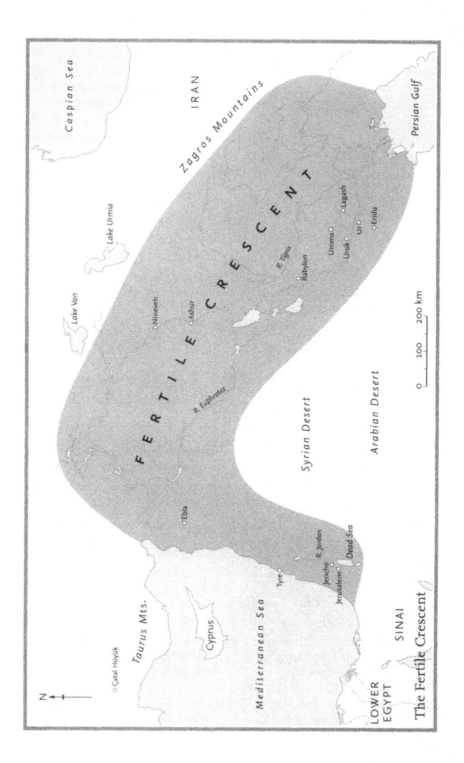

The Fertile Crescent

to Sippar, to Shuruppak, 'and then the flood swept over.' The written marks were impressed on to the prism by an unnamed scribe in the city of Larsa in Babylonia in about 1800 BCE.

Cuneiform texts may look colourless and unexciting, but there is actually something wonderfully intimate about them. These marks, I cannot help thinking, were made by a person, probably with a family, a wife (scholars think that scribes were mostly male) and children, whose experience of life – stroppy teenagers, arguments with the boss – cannot have been so very different from our own, even in such a different society at such a different time. If we were familiar enough with cuneiform, as much at home with it as the ancient scribes were, we should surely be able to recognize individual styles of handwriting. Sadly, that degree of familiarity is far beyond most of us. Cuneiform is extremely hard to read. But at least scholars have been able to work out what this tablet says. It begins: 'After kingship was lowered down from heaven, the kingship was in Eridu.'

The Larsa scribe did not invent this. The oldest known version of the King List was almost certainly compiled rather earlier, from oral traditions, by a senior official in the court of the self-styled 'Lord of the Four Quarters of the Earth', King Utu-hegal of Uruk, in Sumer, southernmost Mesopotamia, the first true city in the world, some time not very much before 2100 BCE. Its point was, presumably, political. King Utu-hegal of Uruk had led the campaign to expel the Gutians, barbarian occupiers from the Iranian mountains to the east with no understanding of, or appreciation for, civilization, who had plunged southern Mesopotamia into a century-long dark age. Utu-hegal was now anxious to establish that there had only ever been one legitimate ruling city in all Sumer, and that he and Uruk were the rightful inheritors of kingship over the entire region. It was a fiction, of course, but one that contained a grain of truth. For all ancient Mesopotamians knew that civilization had begun at Eridu in the deep south, on the shores of the Southern Sea (to us the Persian or Arabian Gulf) at a place today called Abu Shahrein, and now some 190 kilometres from the water.

Two thousand years after Utu-hegal's time his civilization died. Eridu was forgotten, its location lost, until, in 1854, John Taylor, the Hon. East India Company's agent and British vice-consul in Basra, began fossicking among what he called the Chaldean Marshes on behalf of the British

Museum. There he found a collection of mounds and 'a ruined fort, surrounded by high walls with a keep or tower at one end,' topping a hillock near the centre of a dried-out lake. The place was half-hidden in a valley about 25 kilometres wide, which opened, at its northern end, on to the Euphrates River. Much of it, he wrote, was 'covered with a nitrous incrustation, but with here and there a few patches of alluvium, scantily clothed with the shrubs and plants peculiar to the desert.' Taylor also found nearby faint traces of an ancient canal, 5.5 metres wide, to the northwest. He knew that he had come across important remains because, as a later excavator described it, 'a peculiar characteristic of Shahrein is the 'fan' of detritus that extends around the mounds, and has carried with it, out on to the desert, thousands of objects belonging to the lower strata of the mounds themselves ... The loose sandy mounds are torn every winter by rain-floods ... carrying with them remains of all ages.'

A career diplomat, untrained in archaeological technique, Taylor dug a few desultory pits, but was disappointed not to find the sort of spectacular artefacts he had hoped to send home to the Museum. And one find – a 'handsome carved lion in black granite' – was left behind for want of transport. But he did find several bricks inscribed with cuneiform writing. It had become possible to read some of these signs only a few years previously, but enough was already understood to know that Taylor had rediscovered the famous and ancient sacred city of Eridu, the place where Utu-hegal's King-List Compiler, like all ancient Mesopotamians, knew that civilization had begun.

Abu Shahrein (it means Father of Twin Moons, perhaps from ancient bricks found there stamped with crescents, symbols of a moon god) looks a very unlikely location for humanity to have taken such a momentous step. Dry, dusty and deserted, the tan-coloured mounds look as rumpled as a slept-in bed. Around them, boundless and bare, the lone and level sands stretch far away. There is nothing within sight that speaks of life, of humanity, of progress, of achievement. Even the river that once made Eridu habitable is now distant and out of sight.

To understand the history of this place you have to imagine a very different scene. You have to turn back the clock nearly 7,000 years, until you see the salt swell of the Gulf just to the south, bringing sea-going vessels from (today's) Bahrain, Qatar and Oman, the ocean waters infiltrating the land to form extensive sea-marshes teeming with enough fish, flesh and fowl to support a thriving human population. Back until the desert sands of modern Iraq's al-Muthanna province revert to a grassy and shrubby steppe supporting tribes of sheep- and goat-herders who travel a migratory path to and from the sparkling lakes of what is today the great an-Nafud sand sea of Saudi Arabia. Back until the well-beaten track that carried trade goods to southern Mesopotamia from the highlands of Iran in the east even at this early date, is once again patiently trodden by men bearing huge loads on their backs, clustered together in groups for protection against wild animals and human marauders. (The domestication of beasts of burden, even the donkey, let alone the camel and the horse, is still in the future.) Back until the hillock in the centre of the 6-metre depression below the surrounding river silt, alluvium, looking like the focal point of a meteorite-impact crater, rises again above the sweet waters of a great swampy lake, full of fish and freshwater mussels, attracting humans and animals from all around. This the Sumerians called the Apsu, and thought it an upwelling of the freshwater ocean on which the very earth itself floats. Back until the great river Euphrates, which constantly shifts its sinuous course across the plain, depositing its heavy load of silt over a terrain that slopes less than 6 cm in every kilometre, runs close by once again, bringing down with it, perhaps by boat, pioneers from the north, already experienced in building dykes and canals to control the waters.

Their skills were much needed. The Euphrates is no mild and friendly river like the Nile, with a late summer inundation, regular as clockwork, that prepares the ground for planting winter wheat. The Sumerians called the Euphrates the Buranun (a folk-etymology, attractive but unsupported, suggests the name derives from Sumerian words meaning 'Great Rushing Flood'). It breaks its banks erratically and unpredictably in the spring, when the seed, already in the ground, must first be protected from drowning beneath the floodwaters, and then later from drying out under a blazing sun that evaporates more than half the river's flow before it reaches the sea.

So the people who first set up home here, who built their reed huts by the water's edge, who created fields to grow their wheat and barley, and gardens to plant their vegetables and date palms, taking their animals out to graze on the steppe, were not choosing the path of least resistance. If they had wanted an easy life, they would have established their settlements where sufficient annual rainfall makes farming simple, behind the invisible line which demarcates the area where more than 200 mm of rain falls each year – called by geographers the 200 mm isohyet. This line curves in a great semicircle from the foothills of the Zagros Mountains in the east, past the Taurus mountains in the north, and on to the Mediterranean coast in the west, a shape that prompted the American archaeologist James Henry Breasted to name it the Fertile Crescent. In southern Mesopotamia, well inside the curve, hardly any rain falls for most of the year. Here the newcomers had only the rivers to water their crops, and to do even that they had first to reshape the very land itself, with levees, dykes, ditches, reservoirs and canals.

Elsewhere in the world, for several thousand years men and women had happily led lives of subsistence agriculture, finely attuned to their needs and desires, a lifestyle that would hardly change in its essentials until nearly our own times. Indeed in many places it continues right up to the present day. That was not enough for the pioneers of the Mesopotamian plain. They had not run out of land suitable for traditional farming. Human populations were tiny and widely dispersed, leaving ample room for new agricultural settlements. But those who came here were apparently not interested in doing as their ancestors had done, adapting their manner of living to fit into the natural world as they found it. Instead they were determined to adapt their environment to suit their way of life.

This was a revolutionary moment in human history. The incomers were consciously aiming at nothing less than changing the world. They were the very first to adopt the principle that has driven progress and advancement throughout history, and still motivates most of us in modern times: the conviction that it is humanity's right, its mission and its destiny to transform and improve on nature and become her master.

From before 4,000 BCE, over the next ten to fifteen centuries, the people of Eridu and their neighbours laid the foundations for almost everything that we know as civilization. It has been called the Urban Revolution, though the invention of cities was actually the least of it. With the city came the centralized state, the hierarchy of social classes, the division of labour, organized religion, monumental building, civil engineering, writing, literature, sculpture, art, music, education, mathematics and law, not to mention a vast array of new inventions and discoveries, from items as basic as wheeled vehicles and sailing boats to the potter's kiln, metallurgy and the creation of synthetic materials. And on top of all that was the huge collection of notions and ideas so fundamental to our way of looking at the world, like the concept of numbers, or weight, quite independent of actual items counted or weighed – the number ten, or one kilo – that we have long forgotten that they had to be discovered or invented. Southern Mesopotamia was the place where all that was first achieved.

The scribe who wrote the text on the Ashmolean's prism, like the palace official in King Utu-hegal's court, knew how this great leap forward had come about: kingship had been lowered to earth from heaven. That is not far from the proposals of wildly wayward modern commentators, like Erich von Däniken and Zechariah Sitchin, who put it all down to aliens from outer space. Others concluded, with the prejudices of their own times, that the upheaval was caused by the coming together of different races, each with its own character and abilities. The Marxist tradition has unsurprisingly emphasized social and economic factors. I. M. Diakonoff, one of the greatest Soviet Assyriologists, subtitled one of his books, 'the birth of the most ancient class societies and the first centres of slave-owning civilization'. Currently the environmental idea is fashionable: that climate change, epochs of hotter and drier weather alternating with wetter and cooler periods, prompted humans to adapt their way of living. Still others see the emergence of civilization as an inevitable consequence of evolutionary changes in human mentality since the end of the last ice age.

However, on one thing both ancients and moderns agree. They all treat people as passive objects, recipients of outside influences, targets of the workings of external forces, compliant tools of outside agencies. But we humans aren't really like that; we don't react so unthinkingly.

The actual story would have to allow for the everlasting conflict between progressives and conservatives, between the forward and backward looking, between those who propose 'let's do something new' and those who think 'the old ways are best', those who say 'let's improve this' and those who think 'if it ain't broke, don't fix it'. No great shift in culture ever took place without such a contest.

This had already happened at least once before.

The Neolithic Revolution that took our ancestors from hunting and gathering in small kinship-based bands to a settled, communal village life of subsistence agriculture was the greatest ever mass-destroyer of skills, cultures and languages in human history. Tens of thousands of years of accumulated knowledge and elaborate tradition were swept aside. Recent studies of this pivotal period of human history concur: no band of hunter-gatherers can have simply given up all they knew and settled down to sedentary farming without engaging in a giant battle of ideas.

Hunting and gathering had provided a relatively easy living. The new ways were, on the face of it, much harder and less rewarding than those that had served humanity so well for so long.

To the author of Genesis, the Neolithic Revolution signified the fall of man: 'Cursed is the ground for thy sake; in sorrow shalt thou eat of it all the days of thy life. Thorns and thistles shall it bring forth to thee; and thou shalt eat of the herb of the field. In the sweat of thy face shalt thou eat bread.' The same message was recently updated by science-writer Colin Tudge: 'Farming in Neolithic times was obviously harsh: the first farming peoples were less robust than the hunter-gatherers who had preceded them, and suffered nutritional, traumatic and infectious disorders that their forebears had been spared.' In this light it seems that the momentous change to agriculture as the basis of life can only have been driven by the spread of a powerful new ideology, necessarily in those days expressed in the form of a new religion, propagated with, as the distinguished prehistorian Jacques Cauvin put it in his book *The Birth of the Gods and the Origins of Agriculture*, 'messianic self-confidence'.

The next great shift of values and ideals was the one that ultimately led from village farming to our own city civilization. The urban revolution was not quite as destructive of the old ways as the change from hunting and gathering to farming had been. But those who chose this path still had to give up a great deal, including their autonomy, their freedom and their very identity as self-reliant and independent actors. It must have been a very powerful belief that persuaded them to follow a dream whose full working-out was both unforeseeable and unforeseeably far ahead, a belief that could persuade men and women that the sacrifice was worth making: that city living offered the possibility of a better future, indeed that there was such a thing as the Future, which could be made different from what had gone before. This was, above all, an ideological choice.

The beginnings of that ideology are buried under the sands at Eridu. Here, if anywhere, we might be able to observe the processes that brought the ancient city into being.

The God of Progress

With the end of World War II, preparations were made for British control of Iraq to come to an end. This was to be a momentous event for the region. After being ruled by Achaemeneans, Greeks, Romans, the Muslim Khalifs, the Mongols, the Iranian Safavids, the Ottomans and the British, Mesopotamia was to become truly free and independent for the first time in some two and a half millennia – since the conquest of Babylon by the Persian Cyrus the Great in 539 BCE.

More than 4,000 years ago, after the expulsion of the Gutians, King Utu-hegal of Uruk had reasserted Sumerian independence and the legitimacy of his own rule by ordering the Sumerian King List to be compiled, starting with the heaven-decreed kingship of Eridu. In the twentieth century the Directorate General of Antiquities in Iraq chose to mark the country's forthcoming independence by ordering a scientific excavation of Abu Shahrein, to demonstrate 'the strong thread of continuity that runs throughout the past of Iraq.'

As the archaeologists dug into John Taylor's gigantic 'ruined fort', which they were now able to date to the twenty-first century BCE, they uncovered a much earlier and smaller building under one corner, dating from nearly 2,000 years before that. Beneath this they found yet another sixteen levels of habitation, going right back to the beginning of the fifth millennium BCE, when they finally reached 'a dune of clean sand' on which had first been erected 'a primitive chapel', a little over ten feet square, constructed of sun-dried brick, with a votive pedestal facing the entrance and a recessed niche, perhaps for a sculptured image.

The layering fascinated the archaeologists who could now follow the history of the site in detail through the several thousand years of its history. But it also tells us something important about the people who built here. Sun-dried brick demands constant maintenance if it is not to recycle itself back into the ground – it was lack of repair, not destruction, that crumbled most of the ancient cities of Sumer into mounds of dust. Yet the architects of ancient Eridu were never satisfied with restoring or refurbishing. Every building they erected on top of the reverently preserved remains of the previous one was bigger and more elaborate. Starting with the simple 'chapel', 3.5 by 4.5 metres, they ended, a millennium later, with a temple of monumental proportions: its innermost chamber, the cella, was 15 metres long. These people were, unlike the others of their time, never slaves to tradition, never satisfied with what had gone before, but aiming for constant improvement. In the course of some ten centuries, they tore down and rebuilt these constructions eleven times, an average of once every ninety years or so, displaying an impatience with the old and a welcome of the new on an almost modern American scale.

The Eridu temple was the symbol of a community who believed in – perhaps one might even say invented – the ideology of progress: the belief that it was both possible and desirable continually to improve on what had gone before, that the future could and should be better – and bigger – than the past. The divine power celebrated and honoured here was the expression, embodiment and personification of that idea: no less than the God or Goddess of Civilization.

How did the deity of progress who helped lay the foundations of the modern world come to be first envisaged here, in this now desolate place? It happened before the invention of writing – necessarily so, for writing was itself one of the later products of the progressive ideology. All we have is the mute evidence dug up by archaeologists.

They found all too little. There was pottery, naturally, both broken and whole: the elegant, thin-walled, beautifully decorated ware found over much of Mesopotamia in this era. This was not everyday crockery, but fragile and expensive, presumably crafted for an elite. A few inconsequential beads, trinkets, amulets and terracotta figurines were also found. But mostly they found fish-bones and ashes, ashes and fish-bones, in vast quantities: under the floors, behind the walls, on the altars, even collected in rooms of their own. Examination of the bones showed that the fish had been eaten. It would seem that sacred fish suppers played an important role in whatever religious rites were performed here.

The first worshippers would have come from many miles around to the edge of the Apsu, the lagoon of Eridu. There must have been something that attracted travellers, something recognized as a kind of spiritual force, a supernatural influence, what the Greeks called *numen* – a Nod from God. Egyptologist Anthony Donohue has shown that several, perhaps most, of the great religious centres of ancient Egypt were built at sites where the Egyptians recognized images of their gods in natural formations of the landscape. There are no rocks at Eridu, only sand, silt and salt. But perhaps an event of some kind occurred here, maybe a great storm with a giant bolt of lightning, visible across the entire Euphrates Valley, or perhaps even a meteorite struck the surface with a roar like thunder, breaking through the thick crust to release as if by a miracle salt-free groundwater from below. Such an impact has been conjectured by a research group in South Africa. Or could the miracle have been just that upwelling of cool, sweet, fresh water that gainsaid the pitiless burning sun of the salt marshes? We might imagine that the visits were at first occasional, timed to coincide with the brief season of high water, when the swamp became a sizeable lake, as it sometimes still does. The visitors would have been drawn from many different social groups, people who spent the rest of their year wide-ly separated from each other, maintaining different cultures, maybe even speaking different languages and certainly leading very different lives. Even today, anybody familiar with a country where the old ways still hold sway, like Mali in West Africa, will know how quickly the distant sound of drumming from a village masked dance can attract hundreds from the surrounding areas to the banks of the Niger: farmers speaking Bambara, fishermen Bozo, herders Fulani, traders Songhay.

It is easy to guess that those who came to the sacred Apsu would have joined together in ritually feasting on the rich harvest of the marsh; great shoals of freshwater mussel shells have been found among the earliest layers of the site. To our forebears, food never lost its ritual significance (as it still hasn't to the religious-minded of our own day). Here at Eridu, with its numinous associations, the sacred meal would have been a seri-ous, although not necessarily solemn, occasion. And from this regular event, perhaps yearly, perhaps monthly, by the holy marsh at the edge of the sea, would slowly have grown an entirely new group identity: 'those who come to the Apsu'. Drawn from the pioneer settlers in southernmost Mesopotamia, their very presence and survival demonstrated a commitment to changing the face of the land and to securing a different and better future. The religious rites they performed at the water's edge would forever associate the divine spirit of the Apsu with that belief.

One day – after how long is impossible to say, centuries perhaps – it was decided that a permanent shrine to their watery spirit of progress should be built, in the form of a small chapel. Its permanence would be strikingly unusual for the location. While 'those who came to the Apsu', like everyone else in southern Mesopotamia and like the local Marsh Arabs today, lived in houses built of bundled and woven reeds, their monument was to be constructed of brick. That decision signalled the beginning of a new phase in history.

Culture, as the distinguished British archaeologist Colin Renfrew has pointed out, need not be seen as something that merely reflects social reality; instead it can be the process by which that reality comes into being. In his book *Prehistory, the Making of the Human Mind*, Renfrew considers what happens when a permanent monument is first conceived as a project.

> *In order to bring this about, the rather small group of occupants of the territory in question would need to invest a great deal of their time. They might also need to invoke the aid of neighbours in adjoining territories, who were encouraged no doubt by the prospect of feasting and local celebration. One can imagine that when the monument was completed it might itself have become the locus for further, annual celebrations and feast days. It served henceforth both as a burying place and as a social focus for the territory.*

So the monument becomes the centre of what soon emerges, as a direct result of these activities, as a living community.

Moreover, in this corner of the world, where sand frequently blows in from the desert to obliterate all familiar features, where the courses of rivers constantly change, and where calamitous flooding often undoes every mark that humans try to make on the landscape, a permanent monument is particularly significant. Suddenly introduced into the ever-shifting kaleidoscope of everyday experience, it provides a sense of continuity and, by extension, a sense of history and of time. A person can look at the construction, reflect that 'my ancestor helped build this', and feel a sense of connection to roots, lineage and the otherwise vanished past. And the repeated enlargement and elaboration of the building, while always carefully preserving the relics of the old under or within its structure, acts as a symbol, visible from afar, of that belief in progress and development of which it is the physical consequence.

The message is not lost on Eridu's neighbours. This first monument, in what will be the land of Sumer, will serve as an inspiration, an example, a model for other groups to emulate. Over the years new communities of worshippers will form nearby, and other temples to other gods will be planted like broadcast seed across the entire area where the Tigris and Euphrates Valleys ran down to the Southern Sea.

There are still vague memories of that era in the version of history disguised, romanticized and politicized in the very much later myths that the Sumerians and their successors spun about their origins and their deities. Forever after, as long as Mesopotamian civilization lasted, they would remember that every city had been inspired and founded by its own particular divinity as his or her earthly home. City names were written with a sign denoting 'god', a sign for the name of the god, and the sign for 'place': Nippur was written GOD.ENLIL.PLACE, and Uruk GOD.INANNA.PLACE. (Sumerian cuneiform word-signs, or logograms, are conventionally represented in upper case in the roman alphabet.)

And forever after, the divinity celebrated at Eridu would be remembered as the inspirer and instigator of the arts of civilization. In one unexpected way, he is remembered still.

Topographical names, toponyms, what we call the rivers, hills and valleys in the landscape, are among humanity's most conservative and archaic relics. In England, the rivers Humber and Ouse have been so called, in an unknown language, since Neolithic times; in France the area named Paris memorializes the Iron Age Celtic tribe of the Parisii.

What is true on the ground is yet more so in the sky, which changes less over time. The names by which we know the constellations and the signs of the zodiac mostly go back to the Greeks; some, like Leo the lion and Taurus the bull, we have inherited from the Babylonians. And one is probably even more ancient: a distant, very faint, but still persistent echo of a story the ancients told about the god whose house was built at Eridu.

If you live in the northern hemisphere and go out with a star map between nine and ten o'clock of a cloudless September evening, looking towards the southern horizon you will see a group of faint stars arrayed around a triangle. They make up the constellation Capricorn. It is not easy to make out, but by applying some imagination to the pattern you should be able to see it as a sea-goat, upper half caprid and lower half fish. It is arguably the earliest constellation to have been noted, perhaps because in ancient times the winter solstice, the shortest day of the year, occurred when the sun was in Capricorn. And maybe also because the image outlined by the stars was from the start identified with Eridu's god of progress.

One of the magical things about ancient Mesopotamian history is that it sheds light on the origins of so much that characterizes our own world, in this case religious myth. That is, of course, not to say that religion first began here on the alluvial plain at the head of the Gulf. Religion is certainly as old as humanity itself, and almost as certainly even older, dating back to the time when our pre-human ancestors began to bury their dead with ceremony. But here, in this new land, with their new lives, the settlers had mostly to start again and repeat the process of religious creation. We can thus witness how at least some stories about the gods came to be. We can see how many of the Mesopotamians' divinities first sprang from the human imagination as personifications, hypostases, of the forces of nature.

'I do not know much about gods; but I think the river / Is a strong brown god – sullen, untamed and intractable', wrote T. S. Eliot. Thorkild Jacobsen, one of the geniuses of twentieth-century Sumerian studies, gave as an example the god Ningirsu, 'Lord of Girsu', the major township of the Lagash city-state, a deity associated with war and destruction. 'One must realize,' he said,

> that Ningirsu was the yearly flood of the river Tigris personified. Each year when the winter snows begin to melt in the high mountains of Iran they pour down through the foothills in numerous mountain streams to swell the Tigris. This was experienced theologically as the deflowering of the virgin foothills, Nin-hursag, Lady Foothills, by the great mountains, Kur-gal, farther back; the waters of the flood being his semen. Kur-gal, whose other

name was Enlil, *is thus* Ningirsu's *father.* Ningirsu's *mother is* Nin-
hursag, *Lady Foothills, and the reddish-brown colour of the flood waters
which comes from the clay picked up by the water in passing through the
foothills is seen as due to blood from his deflowering.*

The flood to which all this refers, the god Ningirsu *himself, is awesome
indeed. I have seen the Tigris at Baghdad filling the wide valley in which
it flows, rising to a height of more than that of a four story house – a sight
not easily forgotten.*

Or consider the bird known as Zu, Anzu or Imdugud. The sun beats down
remorselessly on the plain of Sumer for much of the year. But occasionally, a sudden storm arrives. An inky black cloud first appears over the
southern horizon and spreads remarkably swiftly until it darkens the
entire sky and assaults the land beneath with thunder, lightning and
torrential rain. Then, just as quickly, it disappears in the opposite direction. It is not hard to understand why the Sumerians chose to imagine
this storm cloud as a great and terrifying thunderbird, lion-headed and
eagle-winged.

These images are more than mere personifications. Interpreting
the phenomena of nature in such detail as the activities of gods demonstrates a powerful imagination and a poetic sensibility of the highest
order, underscoring the perception that religions are the greatest of all
humanity's collectively created works of art. In time, of course, as with
all metaphors, freshness fades; the lively form in which the gods were
first visualized becomes degraded into mere emblem. The god celebrated
at Eridu, the constructive, creative and imaginative potential inherent in
the fertilizing waters, 'the numinous inner will-to-form in the Deep,' as
Thorkild Jacobson wrote, 'came to be seen as a gigantic ibex, the antlers
of which showed above the water as reeds.' Thus the Capricorn, a horned
goat above the water-line, a fish below it (also reflecting, I like to think, his
genesis among fishers and herders) the image through which his memory
was passed down to posterity. Remembered too was the Apsu, the sacred
lake from which he emerged, referenced by a basin of fresh water installed
in every later Mesopotamian temple – and perhaps also, long after, still
remembered in the *Wudu*, or washing, pool of the Islamic mosque and
maybe even in the baptismal font of the Christian church.

In later days the god of Eridu was pictured in seal engravings as wearing a flounced woollen robe and the horned crown of divinity, with two streams of fish-filled water, perhaps representing the Euphrates and the Tigris rivers, flowing from his shoulders. When eventually Sumerian scribes came to write down their myths some 2,000 years after the founding of the temple, his name is revealed. The texts register that Eridu was the home of the god Enki, 'Lord Earth', 'King of Eridu', 'King of the Apsu'. Even later yet Genesis 4:17–18 makes him the son of Cain: 'And unto Enoch [Enki] was born Irad [Eridu]'.

Mesopotamians recognized Enki as the god who brings civilization to humankind. It is he who gives rulers their intelligence and knowledge; he 'opens the doors of understanding'; he teaches humans how to construct canals and plan temples, 'putting their foundation pegs in exactly the right places'; he 'brings forth abundance in the shining waters'; he is not the ruler of the universe but the gods' wise counsellor and elder brother; he is 'Lord of the Assembly'; he is *Nudimmud*, 'the shaper', the fashioner of images, the patron of artisans and craftsmen. And, prefiguring the story of the Tower of Babel, it was he who divided the speech of mankind – an interpretation surely of the multiplicity of languages spoken by his first devotees.

> *Enki, the Lord of abundance, of trustworthy commands,*
> *The Lord of wisdom, who understands the land,*
> *The leader of the gods,*
> *Endowed with wisdom, the Lord of Eridu*
> *Changed the speech in their mouths, [brought] contention into it,*
> *Into the speech of man that had previously been one.*

Most importantly, Enki was the custodian of the '*Me*', perhaps pronounced something like *Meh*, an untranslatable Sumerian expression which the great Assyriologist Samuel Noah Kramer explained as the 'fundamental, unalterable, comprehensive assortment of powers and duties, norms and standards, rules and regulations, relating to... civilized life'. (One might more tersely define them as the basic principles of civilization: it shows how self-consciously aware the ancient Mesopotamians were of the difference between civilization and all other ways of living – and its superiority – that they expressed it with an entirely new cognitive concept, for which we have no equivalent in our way of thinking.) When listed long after by Babylonian mythographers, the '*Me*' include matters of governance such as: high-priesthood, divinity, the noble and enduring crown, the throne of kingship, the exalted sceptre, the staff, the holy measuring rod and line, the high throne. There are matters relating to war like weapons, heroism, the destruction of cities, victory and peace. The '*Me*' encompass human abilities and qualities like wisdom, judgement, decision-making, power and enmity. They delineate strong emotions like fear, strife, weariness and the troubled heart. And there are arts and crafts like those of the scribe, the musician, the metalworker, the smith, the leather worker, the builder and the basket weaver, as well as numerous different priestly offices, varieties of eunuch and musical instruments.

Mesopotamians never forgot the role the god of Eridu played in founding civilization, even though the details of his story evolved over time. Some 4,000 years after the building of the first chapel by the Apsu, when Greeks ruled in the Near East, a Babylonian priest called Berosos wrote a history of his country in which he described how a creature, an intermediary between god and his human devotees, came out of the water to teach civilization to humanity: 'He taught them to construct cities, to found temples, to compile laws, and explained to them the principles of geometrical knowledge. He made them distinguish the seeds of the earth, and showed them how to collect the fruits; in short, he instructed them in everything which could tend to soften manners and humanize their lives. From that time, nothing material has been added by way of improvement to his instructions.'

The City and Sex

The pioneer settlers of southern Mesopotamia, discovering new gods in their new home, did not entirely abandon their earlier religious traditions. Sixty-five kilometres from Eridu, on the other, sunrise, side of the fickle Buranun River, another settlement grew around another temple. It first became known as Unug, later Uruk in the land of Sumer, which the Hebrews would one day call Erech in the land of Shinar (and some think gave Iraq its present name). Unug's shrine was dedicated to an aspect of the Great Goddess, she whose ultimate origins lie back in the Old

Stone Age, an expression of the threefold divinity of womanhood: virgin, mother, whore.

As mother, she was the nurturing cow, 'the beautiful cow to whom the moon god in the form of a strong bull sent healing oils', says one hymn. Her divine milk was the nourishment of royalty; an Assyrian text proclaims, 'Little wast thou Ashurbanipal, when I delivered thee to the [the Great Goddess] Queen of Nineveh; weak wast thou when thou didst sit upon her knees; four teats were set in thy mouth.' She was protector of the pastures where the sacred herd grazed, like the ones often illustrated on engraved seals and pictured in an early temple frieze now in the British Museum. Her presence was symbolized by the door of the holy cowshed and the gate of the sacred cattle pen: the sublime porte of ancient Mesopotamia. The paired reed-bundles that framed the entrance, with loops at the top to hold a pole from which once hung a reed-mat door, became the goddess's symbol in images and later in Sumerian cuneiform. Long, long after, the sacred stall would be remembered as the *Bucolium*, the ox-shed, in which, according to Aristotle, the symbolic marriage between the Athenian ruler's wife and the god Dionysus took place every year. The Queen of Heaven of the Christian church would one day give birth to her baby saviour in a distant but direct descendant of the mother-goddess's cow-byre.

At Unug, the Great Goddess was celebrated under the name Inanna. But here it was her harlotry, her aspect as whore, that was most strongly emphasized. Necessarily so, for cities were always, until modern times, greater consumers rather than producers of humanity. Densely packed together in unsanitary conditions, the people who thronged the narrow lanes between high walls, cheek by jowl with the poultry and livestock from which most human epidemics spread, did not live long. We have no records from ancient Sumer, but in Roman Oxyrhynchos in Egypt, a city of probably equivalent size to Uruk, 'one-third of all babies perished before their first birthday; half of all children died before they turned five; roughly one-third of the population was under 15; fewer than 10 per cent were over 55... up to one-third of children lost their fathers before reaching puberty; over half before the age of 25; the average ten-year-old had only a one in two chance of having any grandparents alive.' In southern Mesopotamia, the slow-moving or stagnant waters of the marshes, canals and ditches must have kept the prevalence of mosquito-borne disease, malaria and swamp-fever, at a constant high.

Historians have not much discussed infection as a determinant of ancient history. Archaeologists report that Sumerian cities were sometimes abandoned for years, or decades, occasionally for centuries, before eventually being reoccupied. Aside from warfare, the cause is usually ascribed to change in the local environment: a shift of a river's course, a rise or fall of the water-table, an encroachment of the desert, even general climate change. But I wonder if we should not also consider it possible that disease and pestilence sometimes wiped out such a large proportion of the inhabitants that the intricate organization of city life, in which every citizen was a necessary cog in the urban machine, could no longer be sustained.

Whether that is true or not, the colossal death rate certainly put huge reproductive pressure on both women and men. Libido, the urge for sex, was of paramount importance in maintaining the population. The powers of Inanna, who controlled the compulsion to copulate, whom in these more decorous days we describe as the Goddess of Love, was all that stood between survival and extinction. Make babies, was the rule, or disappear. When Inanna absented herself from the living world, disaster ensued:

> *No bull mounted a cow, no donkey impregnated a jenny,*
> *no young man impregnated a girl in the street;*
> *the young man slept in his private room;*
> *the girl slept in the company of her friends.*

Inanna was herself personally irresistible. When she preened herself and 'went out to the shepherd, to the sheepfold,... her genitals were remarkable. She praised herself, full of delight at her genitals.' Nobody, not even another god, could withstand her charms. And to the myth-makers of Sumer who wrote down the story of Inanna's relations with Enki, that sexual charm was as important to the foundation of their civilization as Enki's ideology of progress.

Sumerian myths, at least as we find them related in the cuneiform texts, are very different from most other ancient stories, particularly the tales of the Bible. They have an appealingly mundane and down-to-earth quality; their complicated plotlines and use of direct speech are far more reminiscent of modern soap opera than the lofty pronouncements of the ancient Hebrew poets. The tale of Inanna and Enki is no exception.

Inanna decides to travel from her house in Unug: 'I shall direct my steps to Enki,' she says to herself, 'to the Apsu, to Eridu, and I myself shall speak coaxingly to him, in the Apsu, in Eridu.' The first few lines of the text are missing, so we do not know what her initial aim was, but it soon becomes clear that she wants something from him. 'I shall utter a plea to Lord Enki,' she says. Enki, in turn, 'he of exceptional knowledge, who knows the divine powers in heaven and earth, who from his own dwelling already knows the intentions of the gods... even before holy Inanna had approached within six miles... knew all about her enterprise.' He issues his servant with careful instructions: 'Come here, my man, listen to my words... When the maiden Inanna has entered the Apsu and Eridu... offer her butter cake to eat. Let her be served cool refreshing water. Pour beer for her, in front of the Lion Gate, make her feel as if she is in her girl-friend's house, make her welcome as a colleague. You are to welcome holy Inanna at the holy table.' The servant does as he is told, and soon Enki and Inanna are drinking beer together in the Apsu, enjoying the taste of sweet date wine. 'The bronze cups are filled to the brim,' and the two of them start a drinking competition.

The next section of the story is missing but from what follows it is clear that, as they get drunker, Inanna, no doubt deploying her sexual charms, manages to wheedle out of Enki more than a hundred of his 'Me' – what Kramer, who first translated the epic, here described as the 'divine decrees which are the basis of the culture pattern of Sumerian civilization.' When Enki eventually wakes from his drunken stupor he looks around and sees that Inanna has gone. Enki turns to his minister Isimud.

'Isimud, my minister, my Sweet Name of Heaven!'

'Enki, my master, I am at your service! What is your wish?'

'Since she said that she would not yet depart from here... can I still reach her?'

But holy Inanna had gathered up the divine powers and embarked on to the Boat of Heaven. The Boat of Heaven had already left the quay. As the effects of the beer cleared from him who had drunk beer... King Enki turned his attention to Eridu.

He looks around and notices to his consternation that his 'Me' are missing; they seem to be envisaged as physical objects, perhaps inscribed tablets of some kind.

> 'Where are the office of en priest, the office of lagar priest, divinity, the great and good crown, the royal throne?'
> 'My master has given them to his daughter.'
> 'Where are the noble sceptre, the staff and crook, the noble dress, shepherdship, kingship?'
> 'My master has given them to his daughter.'

Enki goes through the entire list of 'Me' and is appalled to find that he has given them all away. So he orders his minister, accompanied by several terrifying monsters, to pursue Inanna in her Boat of Heaven and persuade her to give the 'Me' back: 'Go now! The *enkum* monsters are to take the Boat of Heaven away from her!'

And so we cut to the chase.

> The minister Isimud spoke to holy Inanna: 'My lady! Your father has sent me to you… What Enki spoke was very serious. His important words cannot be countermanded.'
> Holy Inanna replied to him: 'What has my father said to you, what has he spoken? Why should his important words not be countermanded?'
> 'My master has spoken to me, Enki has said to me: 'Inanna may travel to Unug, but you are to get the Boat of Heaven back to Eridu for me'.'
> Holy Inanna spoke to the minister Isimud:
> 'How could my father have changed what he said to me? How could he have altered his promise as far as I am concerned? How could he have discredited his important words to me? Was it falsehood my father said to me, did he speak falsely to me? Has he sworn falsely by the name of his power and by the name of his Apsu? Has he duplicitously sent you to me as a messenger?'
> Now as these words were still in her mouth, he got the enkum monsters to seize hold of the Boat of Heaven.

But Inanna manages to get away. Six more times Enki sends Isimud and the monsters, including 'the Fifty Giants of Eridu' and 'all the great fish together', to take the Boat of Heaven away from Inanna. And six more times 'Inanna gets hold again of the divine powers which had been presented to her, and the Boat of Heaven.'

As the Boat of Heaven nears Uruk,

> 'her minister Ninshubur spoke to holy Inanna:
>
> 'My lady, today you have brought the Boat of Heaven to the Gate of Joy, to Unug. Now there will be rejoicing in our city.'
>
> Holy Inanna replies:
>
> 'Today I have brought the Boat of Heaven to the Gate of Joy, to Unug. It shall pass along the street magnificently. The people shall stand in the street full of awe... The king shall slaughter bulls, he shall sacrifice sheep. He shall pour beer from a bowl... The foreign lands shall declare my greatness. My people shall utter my praise.'

Sadly it is in the nature of clay tablets for the edges, particularly the top and bottom, to most readily crumble away. Just as we wonder how this dispute between two powerful gods is all going to end, the text becomes fragmentary and then peters out altogether. We can tell that Enki and another god have something conciliatory to say. A festival is proclaimed. A number of places in Unug are commemoratively named: 'Where the boat came to dock at the quay, she named that place with the name White Quay'. But until another, more complete, copy of the text of the myth is found, or at least one that preserves the currently missing sections, we shall never know any more than we do now.

What are we to make of this story? At first glance it seems to be simply an account of how Uruk learned the arts of civilization from Eridu, to the eternal glory of the goddess Inanna. But the account it gives leaves many questions unanswered. For example, why was Enki so reluctant to let the 'Me' go?

We ought to remember that this myth, as we have it, is not a sacred text, revealed to us from heaven. It is a work of literature, of human craft. It has to be true that whoever put these words together had a purpose in mind. It was clearly intended as praise for the Great Goddess, a demonstration of her superior cunning, possibly to be sung to instrumental accompaniment in her temple, which would explain the long passages that are repeated word for word, like the choruses of a song.

But perhaps it was also meant to emphasize that one cannot have civilization without a necessary degree of libertinism, to explain or justify the sexual laxity of city life – something of which country-dwellers have complained throughout history. They surely did so in ancient times too, when the cities were renowned for their courtesans and prostitutes, their homosexuals and transvestites, their 'party boys and festival people who change masculinity to femininity to make the people of Ishtar [another later name for the goddess] revere her.' In the famous Epic of Gilgamesh, one of the great literary compositions of the ancient world, it is a brazen harlot who seduces the archetypal primitive savage, the wild man Enkidu, 'whose birthplace was the mountain; with the gazelles he was accustomed to eat herbs, with the cattle to drink water'. She does so to tear him from his background and to civilize him, to teach him the ways of progress. He learns the lesson well, though he comes to regret it. The ancient Mesopotamians believed – as perhaps we still do – that sex and city living go together: that the sexually repressive and conservative morality of country-folk cannot help but crush those creative, imaginative and progressive impulses which offer to improve the human condition.

Every Mesopotamian knew that civilization had been born at Eridu, but its god Enki had kept its principles, the 'Me', hidden away in his Apsu, reserved for divine use, and unavailable to humans. By thus liberating them, the goddess Inanna, queen of sex, had acquired for her people the ideology of progress and development, and had made it possible for her city Uruk, on the sunrise side of the Great Rushing Flood, to become the world's first true city.

3

The City of Gilgamesh:
Temple Rule

Between c.4000 and 3000 BCE

Uruk

The outer wall shines in the sun like brightest copper;
the inner wall is beyond the imagining of kings.
Study the brickwork, study the fortification;
climb the great ancient staircase to the terrace;
study how it is made;
from the terrace see the planted and fallow fields,
the ponds and orchards.
One league is the inner city,
another league is orchards;
still another the fields beyond;
over there is the precinct of the temple.
Three leagues and the temple precinct of Ishtar
measure Uruk, the city of Gilgamesh.

Gilgamesh, legendary ruler of Uruk, famous drinker, womanizer and bat-
tler against monsters, was a King Arthur of Mesopotamian antiquity who
set out on a quest for the holy grail of immortality. He may well have been
based on a historic figure: excavators have found inscriptions proving
that other kings previously thought purely mythical, like Enmebaragesi
of the city of Kish, did once tread the earth. According to the epic, when
Gilgamesh died the citizens diverted the course of the Euphrates and buried him in the river-bed before letting the waters flow over the spot again
– the same tall tale that has been told about many others since, from the

Prophet Daniel to Attila the Hun, Alaric the Goth and Genghis Khan. In 2003 a team of German archaeologists, who had conducted a magnetic survey of the location, reported that 'in the middle of the former Euphrates River we detected the remains of a building which may be interpreted as a burial'.

I begin with Gilgamesh because his is probably the only Sumerian name at all familiar today, a remarkable consequence of the rediscovery of his story in clay tablets excavated in 1853 from the ruins of Assyrian King Ashurbanipal's library at Nineveh. These were late copies of a text first compiled by a scribal scholar called Sin-Leqi-Unninni in around 1200 BCE, working with materials dating back another 800 years or so. Yet if Gilgamesh really did live and rule Uruk, his reign would have been some time around 2600 BCE; and even this date followed centuries after his city had risen, flourished and then declined as the cultural powerhouse of the Sumerian world, and the originator of what might be called temple rule.

Towards the end of the fourth millennium BCE, at about the time that writing was being invented but before it is able to tell us much, Uruk had already spread over some 400 hectares, greater in size and population than Periclean Athens or republican Rome three millennia later. Surveys of the settlement pattern in southern Mesopotamia show that the number of village-dwellers in the area declined precipitously, while the urban population increased. Environmental historians guess that the great movement of people from the countryside into the cities was caused by a change of climate, which became drier at this time, making subsistence agriculture harder to sustain. But perhaps they exaggerate the stick and underrate the carrot. There was something about Uruk that was hugely attractive. We know cities in our own world which act as powerful magnets, irresistibly attracting incomers from near and far, where every new arrival has his or her unique individual reason for migrating, but all are summed up by the simple proposition: to improve the way I live. Maybe people came to Uruk too, just because that is where they most wanted to be.

To judge both by later accounts and the archaeological remains, Uruk was a place of intense activity, a city of vibrant public life, where coracles and punts laden with produce bumped along canals that did service for main streets, as if in an antediluvian Venice; where porters bearing giant loads on their backs elbowed their way through alleyways thronged with priests and bureaucrats, students, workers and slaves; where processions and celebrations vied for space with prostitutes and street gangs. From the remains of conduits and tanks built of waterproof kiln-baked bricks, some scholars believe there were also green and shady public gardens. Temples, public buildings, shrines and gathering-places clustered around the precinct called Eanna, the House of Heaven, known in later times as the earthly residence of the goddess Inanna – as also around a nearby secondary religious focus, where Anu, the sky god, was honoured. These were not closed and secretive places, like many temples would be in other parts of the ancient world, accessible only to priests and to the initiated. In her book *Mesopotamia, the Invention of the City*, Gwendolyn Leick notes that 'the overall impression of the Uruk monuments is of well-planned public spaces... designed for maximum accessibility, with great care being taken to ensure easy circulation.'

At times Uruk must have seemed like one gigantic building site, echoing with the banging and shouting of carpenters and scaffolders, of brick-makers and brick-layers, of plasterers and mosaic-artists, and of masons skilled in working the stone imported from 80 kilometres to the west. Large quantities of stone were used to erect some of the monuments of Uruk, and the technological solutions developed by her architects and builders remained unrivalled for centuries. The work must have been almost unceasing, for the Urukians too were driven by that passion for novelty, the compulsion to put the old behind them, to renew and innovate, that was the special signature of so much ancient Mesopotamian city life.

In the middle of the fourth millennium BCE a huge building, larger than the Parthenon in Athens, partly or wholly constructed of imported limestone, stood on a central platform in the Eanna quarter. The shrine was even more remarkable for the fact that its ground plan almost exactly anticipated, by 3,000 years, the layout of early Christian churches. There was a central nave, a crossways transept, a narthex or lobby, and an apse at one end flanked by the two rooms that in a Christian sanctuary would be called the *diaconicon* and the *prothesis*. A magnificent walkway leading to a wide public terrace ran alongside. The huge embedded pillars of the colonnade, 2 metres in diameter and built of sun-dried bricks internally reinforced with tightly bound bundles of reeds were protected from surface damage by a unique Mesopotamian invention: baked-clay cones, shaped like oversized golf tees and coloured red, white and black, hammered into the surface in tightly packed arrangements that mimicked the patterns on woven reed matting. Nearby another building, the 'stone cone temple', its walls decorated with coloured stones set into plaster, was constructed partly of limestone but also, notably, of a new synthetic material invented in a typical flash of Mesopotamian brilliance: cast concrete, prepared by mixing powdered baked brick with gypsum plaster.

The labour that went into the repeated reconstruction of these buildings was immense: many millions of work hours. Only a very powerful idea could have driven the Urukians to invest so much of themselves in their city. Yet though there are many texts from later times that describe Uruk and its famous king, the stories give no indication of what might have been the driving force underlying the spectacular innovations that made the city of Gilgamesh the first workshop of its world.

Uruk's city-wide and centuries-long building boom was not comparable to ancient Egypt's a little later, when monuments were dedicated to the glorification and immortality of dynasties of ruthless rulers. Unlike Uruk, Egyptian tombs and temples were built to last to the end of time. Here, by contrast, they were subject to that passion for repeated reconstruction that characterized all early Mesopotamian societies. And though powerful kings would reign in Mesopotamia in due course, all the signs for this era point to a society with no overly great distinctions of wealth or power.

We may yet learn more. Excavations have so far concentrated on the temple surroundings, and most of Uruk, today called Warka, still lies buried under the sands. To date two extraordinary images have been unearthed, created in the days when Uruk was the only true city on earth. One suggests a community of relative equals, united in worship of their supreme goddess and of the great idea which she represented. It is sculpted in low relief around a 1-metre-high alabaster vessel known as the Warka Vase: five tiers of carvings representing a procession on its way to bring offerings to the doorway of the goddess's temple. The other is, arguably, a portrait head of the goddess herself: the Warka Mask, also known as the Lady of Uruk.

The 5,000-year-old life-sized head of the Lady of Uruk was already damaged in antiquity: there are dark, blank holes where eyes looked out; the deep birds-wing groove across her forehead that once held inlaid eyebrows is empty; the wig that once covered the smoothed planes on her head is long gone; the tip of her nose is smashed. And yet, despite all that, and the fifty centuries that separate her time from ours, the expression on her face is as striking and engaging as ever. André Parrot, a leading French archaeologist, put it most poetically: 'We seem to catch a gleam of living eyes within the empty sockets and behind the forehead, patterned with smooth curves of hair, we sense an alert, lucid mind. The lips have no need to part for us to hear what she has to say; their undulation, complemented by the ripple of the cheeks, speaks for itself.' Even in her damaged state, the Lady of Uruk must count as one of the great masterpieces of world art.

The tiers of carvings in the Warka vase complement this image of the Great Goddess. This is a religious object, offering a symbolic moment in the yearly round of her temple, the place they called Eanna, in fourth millennium Uruk. Hence the sense of spirituality, of serious purpose, calm dignity and self-confident poise that is radiated by the exquisitely carved figures. In the distance, around the base, flows the wavy course of a waterway: presumably the wide Euphrates that gives life to the city. Above it are fields and orchards, stalks of barley alternating with date palms, the ultimate source of Uruk's wealth and well-being. Over these roams the sacred flock, fleecy sheep among bearded and wide-horned rams, creatures dedicated to the goddess of the sheepfold. Now comes a human procession: ten men shuffle forward, naked and shaven, each holding a basket, jug or pottery container heaped with the fruits of earth, tree and vine; priests, perhaps, or temple servants. On the top tier the parade arrives at the sacred site, signalled by the looped reed-bundles of its ceremonial doorway. A welcoming female figure, the high priestess who represents the goddess, stands outside wearing an ankle-length robe, holding out her right hand in a thumbs-up gesture of greeting or blessing. She receives a container of offerings from the hands of the leader of the naked men, behind whom once stood a figure whose image was broken away in antiq-uity. All that remains is a bare foot, the fringed hem of a garment and an elaborate tasselled belt held up by a formally clothed female retainer. We guess that he may have been a high priest or other senior dignitary, possi-bly the 'priest–king' imagined by some historians. Positioned around these figures are a pair of containers heaped with offerings and two platters of food. More mysteriously, there are also twin vases, a bull's head, a ram, a lion cub and two women holding unidentifiable objects – Gwendolyn Leick suggests that one of these is reminiscent of the later written sign for *En*, priest. All this would of course have been instantly recognisable to the people who worshipped here, just as in a Christian context we understand a lion to mean St Mark, an eagle St John and a calf St Luke. To us, however, without a key to unlock the symbolism of the Warka Vase, its meaning remains opaque.

Some maintain that the scene depicts the ruler of the city offering sacri-fice to its founding goddess. Some that it represents a seasonal harvest fes-tival. Others have speculated that it shows a stage in the mystic marriage, the *hieros gamos*, in which two humans, high-priest and high-priestess, couple with each other publicly, in emulation of the Great Goddess and her spouse. Yet even if we have no way of knowing what event is pictured here, the scene does tell us something about the people of Uruk and how they thought.

Homo Ludens

The Warka Vase shows a formal ceremony, different from the sponta-neity and improvisation of the masked dances and shamanic rites that would have been inherited from earlier times, though they too would have continued throughout this period and into the next. The naked men in the procession, uncircumcised but depilated, are stripped of all marks of individuality, status or position. Their faces are deadly serious. Their beardlessness, like that of many of the men who figure in statuettes and figurines of the period, suggests no shame in a return towards childhood innocence. Each character performs a set role in the proceedings, remind-ing us that a religious rite, like all ceremonies, is a kind of play, with actors carefully following a predetermined script, yet at the same time throwing themselves into the action with all the unselfconscious enthusiasm, the willing suspension of disbelief, of children. The British anthropologist Robert Marett has suggested that an element of 'acting out', of 'make-believe', was a feature of all early religions.

The Greek philosopher Plato went even further in *The Laws*, which he wrote in 360 BCE, where he proposed religious ritual as a model for the whole of life: 'Life must be lived as play, playing certain games, making sacrifices, singing and dancing, and then a man will be able to propitiate the gods, and defend himself against his enemies.'

In 1938, the Dutch historian and philosopher Johan Huizinga published *Homo Ludens, a Study of the Play Element in Culture.* (In Latin *Homo ludens* translates roughly as Man the Player.) Huizinga defined play as 'an activity which proceeds within certain limits of time and space, in a visible order, according to rules freely accepted, and outside the sphere of necessity or material utility', and he showed that play in the widest sense of the word is an essential element of most aspects of civilization. Law, he argued, is play, as are religion, the arts and the pursuit of knowledge. Even warfare has elements of play. Huizinga quotes II Samuel 2:14, when two military leaders, Abner and Joab, confront each other across the Pool of Gibeon:

> *And Abner said to Joab, Let the young men now arise, and play before us. And Joab said, Let them arise. And they caught every one his fellow by the head, and thrust his sword in his fellow's side; so they fell down together.*

(The Hebrew word 'play' is from the basic root *sachaq*: to play, to sport, to laugh, to rejoice, to make merry.) Even in World War I the officer class on both sides of the Western Front treated each other with respect and 'played by the rules', as did Indian and Pakistani officers during the series of wars that led to the independence of Bangladesh.

When Huizinga's book was republished in the 1960s it was taken up as a required text by the hippie thinkers of that most playful of decades. In 1970 the Australian writer Richard Neville, then a doyen of London's so-called underground press, published *Play Power.* The spirit of play newly reintroduced into western society, he argued, could change the face, and organization, of society out of all conservative recognition. If he was right, then thinking of play may cast some light on the rise of the City of

Gilgamesh, by prompting us to look in an unexpected place for a similar time of headlong progress and change.

Huizinga was a humanist academic, born in 1872, who had seen the world he knew, and in which he felt comfortable, destroyed in World War I. He believed that western civilization was being progressively ruined by the absence of play. 'The nineteenth century,' he wrote, 'seems to leave little room for play. Tendencies running directly counter to all that we mean by play have become increasingly dominant... These tendencies were exacerbated by the Industrial Revolution and its conquests in the field of technology.' But Huizinga was, I believe, quite wrong. Anyone who has ever watched children amuse themselves will recognize that the scientific and technological face of civilization is precisely the result of play in its purest form. Just as children are constantly exploring, experimenting, testing and trying things out, for no conscious purpose except the sheer enjoyment of the game itself, so pure science and applied technology play with ideas and toy with the principles and substance of the world; all the time wondering 'just suppose...' and asking 'what happens if...?'

Indeed far from being malign in its blinkered materialism as Huizinga believed, science is often criticized for its apparent irrelevance, for its lack of practical application. The British mathematician G. H. Hardy was rather proud of that fact. He famously wrote that much of science was quite useless: 'For my own part, I have never once found myself in a position where such scientific knowledge as I possess, outside pure mathematics, has brought me the slightest advantage.'

Those societies in which seriousness, tradition, conformity and adherence to long-established – often god-prescribed – ways of doing things are the strictly enforced rule, have always been the majority across time and throughout the world. Such people are not known for their sense of humour and lightness of touch; they rarely break a smile. To them, change is always suspect and usually damnable, and they hardly ever contribute to human development. By contrast, social, artistic and scientific progress as well as technological advance are most evident where the ruling culture and ideology give men and women permission to play, whether with ideas, beliefs, principles or materials. And where playful science changes people's understanding of the way the physical world works, political change, even revolution, is rarely far behind.

So although it may seem an unexpected, even bizarre, comparison, the nearest equivalent to the burst of creativity and development that took place in prehistoric Uruk during the fourth millennium BCE may well be the upheaval that changed the face of the globe near the end of the eighteenth century CE. In both cases a long-established and respected way of life was overturned; people streamed into the cities from the countryside; new inventions and materials followed hard on each others' heels; and the structure of society itself was reshaped in ways unseen before. As Andrew Sherratt, an important scholar of prehistory, once wrote: 'the insights to be gained from comparing episodes far separated in time are reciprocal ones: knowledge of the Urban Revolution informs interpretation of the Neolithic Revolution, and vice versa... Might not historians of the Industrial Revolution, in their turn, profit from learning of these earlier transformations?'

The reverse might be even more helpful, for the ideas behind the making of the modern world have been much studied while we know next to nothing about the details of the worship of the Great Goddess of Uruk. We are ignorant of the ideology that she represented in the minds of the Mesopotamians of the fourth millennium BCE. But we do know that their beliefs made possible the greatest explosion of social, material and technological progress known until the Industrial Revolution of our own era. The change seems to have happened as rapidly as ours. In the words of Professor Piotr Michalowski, one of today's most respected anthropologists: 'The complex social and political changes that took place in Mesopotamia in the late Uruk period toward the end of the fourth millennium represent a quantum leap of unprecedented dimensions and not a gradual evolutionary historical development.'

Could not such an extraordinary eruption of creativity and imagination be the result of recognizing play, in the word's widest sense, as a legitimate way of interacting with the world? There was probably much laughter in fourth millennium Uruk.

Go along to the Museum at Chicago University's Oriental Institute, or to its website, to confirm the importance of play in the ancient Mesopotamian world. Look at the charming pull-along toys dug from the sands of Tell al-Asmar, ancient Eshnunna. One is about 13 cm long, made of fired clay, with a tiny ram's head attached to a large cylindrical body. It is mounted on four thin wheels and in front is the hole through which a string was once threaded. This was never intended to look anything like a real animal; the ram's head is no more than a gesture. (Those who, like me, always thought that pull-along toys were shaped to imitate railway locomotives, will note that its hollow body is oddly reminiscent of Thomas the Tank Engine.) This is a toy pure and simple, made for the pleasure of a three- to five-year-old.

Though it was found in a temple's ruins and may have had a religious meaning, its form almost forces you to imagine it being dragged along behind a little boy through the dust of a shady courtyard or busy city street 5,000 years ago. As he plays, the adults around him are playing too: dreaming up the long, long list of new creations and inventions that now appear in the archaeological record for the first time in Uruk and its neighbours.

For most of the basic technology that supported human life until industrial production began to take over our world a bare two centuries ago, was first devised at this time and in this part of the world: at home the beer-brewer's vat, the potter's kiln and the textile loom; in the fields the plough, the seed-drill and the farm cart; on the rivers and canals the wind-vane and the sailing boat; in music the harp, lyre and lute; in building technology fired bricks, the vault and the true arch.

And everywhere – as on the Chicago Museum toy – in the streets, fields and canal-banks, the wheel: both emblem and enabler of human mobility.

Some inventions seem to demand a sudden flash of inspiration, a true *jeu d'ésprit*, for their conception. The wheel is one of them. Scholars have debated its origins with great energy and ingenuity. Some have concluded with certainty that wheels developed from the wooden rollers that had long been used to move heavy items on sledges over short distances. Others suggest that full rotary motion itself was the important new idea. Yet other historians persuasively point out that the principle of the roller and the wheel are conceptually different: rollers are really mobile extensions of the surface over which the weight is moved; wheels are part of the moving object itself. These writers suggest a different source for the idea: the turntable, pivoted at its centre and used to make perfectly round pots, which actually appears in the archaeological record before the wheel. If these scholars are right, then somebody, some day, must have picked up a turntable to move it and, naturally enough, rolled it along its edge. The great leap forward was to recognize that when turning, the central pivot of the disc always stayed the same height above the ground. Hence the inspired notion of attaching a set of turntables to the structure of a sledge, transferring the device from the domain of the potter to that of the haulier.

On the other hand, there are many developments that may well have come about by gradual evolution. To the careful makers of the handsomely decorated pottery of the time, uneven firing, and the smudges, smuts and smeeches left on their pots by burning wood during the process of baking in an open hearth, must have been disheartening. The obvious solution was to separate the vessels from the flames. Progressive trial and error would have led to the typical Mesopotamian beehive-shaped kiln, with a vent at the top and a perforated floor separating the fuel from the firing chamber.

Yet even gradual evolution had its surprises. It turned out, and surely not intentionally, that apart from protecting the carefully prepared ware from damage, kilns also allowed for a much higher firing temperature. And that made the humble potter's kiln into the principal laboratory instrument of the ancient Mesopotamian world. And just as the modern chemical industry was the result of accidentally discovering synthetic dye-stuffs, pretty rather than practical, so, true to the spirit of play, the first achievement of Uruk's experimenters was not utilitarian.

The blue-green rock called lapis lazuli was a prized gemstone in ancient times. It was made into seals and jewellery, beads and bangles, inlays and decorations on sculpture. In Sumerian literature, city walls are adorned with it: 'Now Aratta's battlements are of green lapis lazuli, its walls and its towering brickwork are bright red.' So were temples: 'He built the temple from precious metal, decorated it with lapis lazuli, and covered it abundantly with gold.' A goddess instructs King Gudea of Lagash: 'open up your storehouse and take out wood from it; build a chariot for your master and harness a donkey stallion to it; decorate this chariot with refined silver and lapis lazuli.'

But lapis lazuli is rare, obtainable only from a few places in Central Asia, notably the mountains of Badakhshan in the north of today's Afghanistan, 2,500 kilometres from southern Mesopotamia. It seems utterly astonishing that there could be a thriving trade across so vast a distance, in the days when the prized rock had to be carried on foot across a wilderness of wild mountain ranges and deadly deserts, to satisfy the vanity of Mesopotamian gods and kings. And yet the trade did flourish, to judge by the huge quantity of lapis lazuli objects found in excavations all over the Middle East.

Given the cost of the material, and the difficulty in procuring it, inventive minds were soon striving for a way to reproduce the lustrous blue colour artificially. They succeeded; and in doing so created the very first totally man-made material – not as the result of chance, or an accidental observation, but by thinking and by experimenting.

I myself have seen the 5,000 year old process devised by these pioneers of synthetic chemistry still in operation in the 1960s: artificial lapis lazuli (now miscalled Egyptian faience) being made in a workshop at the back of a mosque in Herat, Afghanistan. A filthy cavernous shack, filled with smoke and choking chemical fumes, thin shafts of sunlight bursting through breaks in the roof competing with the blinding glare of the white-hot furnace in the corner. A young boy in a large turban dreamily pumping air into the fire with a giant bellows. And the proprietor proudly showing me the result: beads and trinkets covered in a somewhat lumpy, deep blue-green glaze.

We can guess how the invention may have come about. Soft copper carbonate minerals, green malachite and blue azurite, had been used, probably since Old Stone Age times, to make pigments for decorating craft-ware. And faces too: ground to a powder and mixed with fat they make very serviceable eye-shadow. Hold a piece of either mineral in a fire and it will flare vividly blue or green. The ancients, unfamiliar with spectronomy or pyrochemistry probably thought that the heat was driving the colour out of the mineral into the flame. It would have seemed feasible to capture this colour and deposit it on to another object. But how to stop the colour dissipating into the air together with the smoke? The solution was to put the object to be coloured together with the ground-up mineral into a closed container and heat them in a kiln. The experimenters soon found that the process took a long time, a whole day, and a high temperature, not much less than 1,000° C was needed. But it worked – as in Herat it still does. The object emerged from the furnace with a hard, shiny, deep blue-green covering; not as fine as true lapis lazuli perhaps, but almost as good.

The realization that mixing minerals together and subjecting them to high temperatures could change their properties completely and create an entirely novel material would have far-reaching consequences. Homo Ludens must have tried the procedure on a great variety of rocks, stones and other materials. And it would happen – not often perhaps, but enough to encourage further experiment – that the result would lead to something completely new, like the method of salt-glazing bricks for which a much later Assyrian recipe instructs: 'Sand, alkali from the 'horned' plant, whiteweed. Pulverize and mix together. Lay in the cold kiln with four draught holes and then drive it between the draught holes. Burn a light smokeless fire. Bring it out, let it cool, pulverize it again, add to it pure salt. Place in the kiln. Burn a light smokeless fire. As soon as it appears yellow let it run upon the brick and the name is frit.'

Other discoveries were glass and cement, and the smelting of copper. Then it was found that adding tinstone to copper ore changed the properties of the resulting metal for the better. The alloy was harder, stronger, kept a sharp edge for longer and, most importantly, melted at a lower temperature, making it easier to cast. It would ultimately take the southern Mesopotamians out of the Stone Age and into the Bronze Age, with all the attendant profound cultural, social and political change.

The Smithy of the Gods

One episode in the Epic of Gilgamesh tells how Uruk received a message from King Aga of Kish threatening an attack:

> Gilgamesh laid the matter before the city elders, seeking a solution:... 'let us not submit to the house of Kish, let us wage war!'
>
> The convened assembly of his city's elders answered Gilgamesh: '... let us submit to the house of Kish, let us not wage war!'
>
> Gilgamesh,... placing his trust in the goddess Inanna, took no notice of what his city's elders said. He again laid the matter before the city's young men, seeking a solution: '... let us not submit to the house of Kish, let us wage war!'

The convened assembly of his city's young men answered Gilgamesh: 'To stand on duty, to sit in attendance, to escort the king's son – to hold a donkey by the hindquarters as they say – who is there that has breath for such? Let us not submit to the house of Kish, let us wage war!

'Uruk, the smithy of the gods, Eanna, house come down from heaven – the great gods it was who gave them shape... You are their king and their warrior! O crusher of heads, prince beloved of the god An, when he arrives why be afraid? Their army is small with a rabble at the rear, its men will not withstand us!'

Gilgamesh leads his young men out to fight, captures King Aga of Kish and then, in an unexpected display of generosity, sets him free to return to his home city.

This is literary epic, not history, though it might possibly reflect a real conflict between Uruk and Kish, a city about 150 kilometres to the north-west. It was written as long after the events it purports to describe as has passed between the days of King Arthur and his Round Table and our own. And, like the Arthurian romances, it says rather more about the time when it was written than about the era it describes.

None the less, it does give a distant glimpse of a moment in Uruk's story, as it moved gradually from the Stone Age towards the Metal Age ('the smithy of the gods'); from what Thorkild Jacobsen called primitive democracy, when a ruler still had to consult the people ('the convened assembly of his city's elders'), to kingship and autocracy, when the ruler did as he pleased without reference to anyone else's opinion; and from peaceful coexistence to a constant state of aggressive bellicosity ('let us wage war'). All of these changes, good and bad, were part of the move from village living to fully fledged civilization.

Village societies evolve and adapt naturally to their environmental and political circumstances. Civilizations, on the other hand, are designed. In Uruk the same experimental approach that was applied to the material world was also directed towards engineering the way people in the city lived together. The city was like a machine, and its citizens like the moving parts that made it work.

In the villages most families were relatively equal; in the city, there was a hierarchy of status. In the villages 'what do you do?' was never a necessary question; in the city it was important to know the answer. In the villages survival depended on being a member of a household, even if only as a slave; in the city, new ways of making a living suddenly became available. Instead of contributing to the subsistence of your own extended family, as had been the only option throughout all of the past, you might now work instead for the temple or the palace, and in return receive, not a place by the hearth, but a wage. Surviving relics suggest that many did so in the city of Gilgamesh.

The most characteristic objects found both whole and broken in the ruins of Uruk – up to half of all pottery finds – are crude and rather ugly earthenware containers known as bevelled-rim bowls, very different from the elegant and delicate painted pottery of the previous era. These vessels were made neither by coiling nor by turning the clay on a wheel, but instead show signs of having been made in simple moulds. (Similar vessels have recently been produced experimentally to test this analysis.) This may have been the very first application of the principle of mass-production to a consumer product. In agrarian villages pots had been made in the household to a high aesthetic standard and in styles and with designs that were traditional and that meant something to their users. They were often very beautiful. Mass-produced bevelled-rim bowls, by contrast, were turned-out in commercial workshops and invested with no more significance than their utility.

This change has been called the Evolution of Simplicity. As the city developed, manufacturing began to be restricted to a cadre of professional workers resulting in, as one historian describes it, 'the aesthetic deprivation of the non-elite.' Pottery was now judged only by its efficiency and economy: standardized containers may have been ugly but they were good enough and cheap enough to serve the new society's needs. The change was recognisably not unlike the switch from craft to industrial production in Victorian times, lamented and fruitlessly opposed first by the Romantic and then the Arts and Crafts movements. Perhaps some ancient Mesopotamians protested too.

How bevelled-rim bowls were made proved to be much easier to answer than what for and why. In shape, they resemble the containers piled high with produce carried in procession to the goddess's temple by the naked marchers on the Warka vase. But the vessels on the vase look rather elegant; the real things are so rough and ready that it is hard to imagine anyone eating from them, let alone presenting them to a goddess. They are porous, so of no use for water or beer. And they were, apparently, disposable, since as many have been found whole as have been recovered in fragments. (They have been likened to the polystyrene burger containers that today litter our streets and beaches.) While some scholars still believe that offerings were brought to the temple in bevelled-rim bowls, most think that they were probably used to distribute measured quantities of bread or grain as wages or rations. When writing first appeared, the symbol representing food, rations or bread looks very much like a bevelled-rim bowl.

Wages and rations imply a dependent workforce no longer looking after its own subsistence, as happened in the conversion of rural peasantry into urban proletariat in modern Europe. If that is what took place in Uruk, what was this new working class labouring on, and for whom? There was certainly building work to be done. The temples, similar to households, but on a grander scale, had their own fields, gardens and orchards which required seasonal labour as well as hydraulics workers, specialists in regulating and maintaining the flood-protection and irrigation systems. Then there were the herdsmen and women looking after the sheep, goats and oxen; there were those producing craftware, the textiles, baskets and pottery, including the bevelled-rim bowls themselves; not to mention the sculptors and jewellers, the experimenters, copper-smelters, metallurgists and metal-workers, of the Smithy of the Gods.

Unlike during the modern urban revolution, there were no independent entrepreneurs competing amongst each other. The world's first city developed around its temples, and only later did palaces play a role. Its view of the world was conditioned, as in all ancient societies, by totalitarian religious belief. So the picture that comes into focus is that of a theocratic command economy, hierarchically organized, centrally directed, and regulated according to an ideology propagated by a priesthood, playing the role that, 5,000 years later, Soviet Marxists would call 'the engineers of human souls'. Such was temple rule.

As a way of life, the economic and social system the priesthood supported was, for a long time, strikingly successful. During the latter part of the fourth millennium BCE, Uruk and other southern Mesopotamian cities flourished greatly and grew ever larger. Moreover, across the Mesopotamian world and well beyond it, settlements sprang up along the major trade routes, displaying the typical cultural signatures of the motherland. They too had Uruk-style temples, built with bricks of exactly the same dimensions and laid in precisely the same patterns, the walls often decorated with similar baked-clay cones; they showed similar food preferences; they used the same administrative technology; and they produced the same bevelled-rim bowls, with all that these implied about their social systems and working practices. The wide distribution of these typical Uruk inventions suggest that the Urukian political dispensation was actively exported from the southern plains to the entire region, even to far distant areas in today's Turkey, Syria and Iran, with no doubt the same 'messianic self-confidence', as Jacques Cauvin saw as having driven the Neolithic revolution.

Some of the outposts were entirely new settlements, built on virgin land as miniature replicas of their home cities. Others were long established large villages or small towns, where previously a Stone Age style of life had held sway, but where the Uruk culture now took over. Yet others were more like enclaves, town quarters where Urukians lived in their way while all around them the older traditions persisted.

To some scholars, the 'Uruk Expansion' indicated only one thing: a colonial empire aimed at exploiting natural resources not available in the south, an empire maintained by military domination. Yet it must be remembered that this situation arose *before* the introduction of those technologies which now appear to be prerequisite to holding together by force a far-flung empire: effective and rapid communications (writing was invented only towards the end of Uruk's era of dominance) and efficient transport using domesticated beasts of burden (the first, the donkey, arrived from north Africa nearer the period of Uruk's decline than its rise; the local equid, the Asiatic wild ass or onager, is famously untameable).

Other archaeologists have interpreted the evidence to imply peaceful trading-posts, or even waves of fleeing refugees, all these analyses based on the belief that the new Urukian settlements were populated by expatriates from the home city. However one should not underestimate the power of ideas to attract new converts to a modish way of life, without coercion. Our recent history clearly shows how a fashionable ideology like Marxism–Leninism can be widely and enthusiastically taken up and implemented in many self-styled and short-lived democratic socialist republics, without any coercion. Moreover, a belief in 'modernity' – western technology, western architecture, western clothing, western food – has spread rapidly across the world even to places that were never, or only briefly, part of any European empire. Today there is hardly anywhere on earth where western brands cannot be found, and it looks as if something similar happened back in the fourth millennium BCE too. It was to have consequences more profound than almost any other in history. For it ultimately gave rise to the invention of writing.

In February 2008 Dr David Wengrow, of University College London, made a splash in both the academic and business communities, when he published an article arguing that the Uruk civilization was the original inventor of the brand. With the advent of mass production – of textiles, ceramics, beverages and processed foodstuffs – consumers wanted to be assured of the origin and quality of the products they used. These commodities were given a mark that uniquely identified their origin and source. While our word brand derives from the practice of burning a symbol on to something to show its provenance, the Mesopotamians used lumps of clay instead, marked with easily identifiable signs, to seal baskets, boxes, jugs and other containers.

This might have begun with the amulets many wore, picturing religious or mythological themes. As a handmade product, each amulet was different, and was associated with the person who wore it, or for whom it was made. Stamped on to clay, the pattern made by the amulet immediately identified its owner.

The obvious next step was to make a die intended solely to be pressed into clay, with the design therefore engraved in reverse. These 'stamp seals' were the first ever form of printing. However, to create an image of reasonable size needed a large seal, perhaps inconvenient to wear, and it was soon realized that if the design was wrapped around a cylinder and then rolled over the clay, the resulting impression would be more than three times the cylinder's diameter. So was born the cylinder-seal, one of the most characteristic, and beautiful, of Uruk's inventions, which would continue in everyday use until the very end of Mesopotamian civilization.

Not much more than an inch or so tall, these seals were made from every conceivable material: from limestone, marble and haematite; from semi-precious materials like lapis lazuli, carnelian, garnet and agate; and even from fired clay and faience. Being practically indestructible, they are unearthed in quantity wherever archaeologists dig in the region.

In time, the engraving became so fine that historians guess the seal-cutters must have had optical aids, perhaps based on the pinhole-camera principle – under Mesopotamia's burning sun even the tiniest hole would have let enough light through. It has even been suggested that after the invention of transparent glass, some form of primitive lens was used, though an oval of rock crystal unearthed from the Assyrian city of Nimrud in 1850 is no longer accepted as a lens by scholars of ancient technology.

To the historian, cylinder-seals are of inestimable value, since the images they produce give us for the very first time a picture of life in ancient southern Mesopotamia and beyond. Many, to be sure, show religious scenes: often unidentifiable gods and goddesses disporting themselves in a landscape of rivers and mountains, palaces and temples, the sacred herd clustered around the Great Goddess's reed byre – astonishingly similar to the reed houses still built by the Marsh Arabs today – or worshippers travelling to a temple by boat. There are great moments from mythology showing presumably famous heroes battling with each other or grappling with animals. Other seals seem to present snapshots of everyday life: animals in the fields, workers in the dairy, weavers, potters and metal-smiths, and, as time went on, increasing numbers of battle-scenes and pictures of military mayhem.

While these seals may have first been used as brand logos, they quickly became personal identifiers, equivalent to signatures in a society where, even after the invention of written script, literacy remained a skill exercised only by the few. Cylinder-seal impressions were used on documents of every variety, and to identify all kinds of personal property. In fact, so ubiquitously did the ancients deploy them that one is reminded of children who have just learned to write and insist on inscribing their names on everything, including the walls and the furniture. Such use suggests that citizens of Uruk and their neighbours valued the cultivation of individual identity, perhaps as much as we do. Unlike in so many other cultures, ancient and later, anonymity had no attractions for them; each person strove to leave his or her personal mark on the world.

This was particularly so after writing spread into general use. We know more individuals by name from Mesopotamia than from anywhere else in the ancient world. Names were written on texts of all kinds: on receipts, delivery notes and bills of lading, on commercial contracts and legal judgements, on marriage agreements and divorce settlements. The very first personal autograph so far found is on a scribal exercise from Uruk, dated around 3100 BCE, and signed on the back: GAR.AMA.

Perhaps it was this eagerness to record their individual existence in permanent form that first prompted some of the residents of Uruk to elaborate a simple accounting device into a sophisticated system of marking clay tablets, to set down first agreements and contracts, then ideas and beliefs, songs and stories, poetry and prose. If so, ancient Mesopotamia's cult of identity changed the course of human development. The idea of writing was surely the city of Gilgamesh's greatest gift to the world.

The Mystery of Cuneiform

According to legend the Septuagint, the Greek translation of the Hebrew Bible, came about when Demetrius of Phalerium, head librarian at Alexandria in Egypt, urged the emperor, Ptolemy II Philadelphus to acquire a copy of the Jewish Torah. Responding to the emperor's command, the high priest of Jerusalem sent seventy-two scholars, six from each of the Twelve Tribes of Israel, to Alexandria, where they lived on the island of Pharos, ritually bathed in the sea every morning and, each working alone, miraculously created identical translations. (Actually, Septuagint means seventy, not seventy-two, but, as the old Jewish joke has it, who's counting?)

It was presumably in reference to this story that in 1857 the Royal Asiatic Society of London gave a newly discovered Mesopotamian document to four of the leading scholars of the day: Edward Hincks, Jules Oppert, Henry (later Sir Henry) Creswicke Rawlinson and William Henry Fox Talbot (of photographic fame). They were asked to attempt a translation without conferring. Their work was submitted under seal and, miraculously or not, the translations were sufficiently alike for the Society to pronounce the mystery of cuneiform solved: 'the Examiners certify that the coincidences between the translations, both as to the general sense and verbal rendering, were very remarkable. In most parts, there was a strong correspondence in the meaning assigned, and occasionally a curious identity of expression as to particular words.'

If written documents define the beginning of history, the four decipherers' achievement was to set back the date of that beginning, previously believed to have occurred at the time of the ancient Hebrews, to a date thousands of years earlier than had ever been imagined.

The story of the deciphering of Mesopotamian script had begun half a century previously, when Georg Grotefend, a German Latin teacher in his early twenties, made a bet with friends in a pub that he could explain the meaning of some texts *cuneatis quas dicunt*, 'said to be in cuneiform', gathered from the ancient Persian royal city of Persepolis. His report to the Royal Society of Göttingen established that, of the three different, though obviously related, kinds of script, one was in a known form of Old Persian, was alphabetic in nature, with each sign representing a spoken sound, and was read from left to right. Using a combination of undoubted genius, sheer good luck and dogged application, he managed to read some names – Darius, Xerxes, Hystaspes – and some of the royal titles.

The second step came when an intrepid British army officer named Henry Rawlinson, equally youthful, risked life and limb by clambering up a cliff-face at Behistun in north-western Persia to copy out a lengthy inscription left by the Persian Emperor Darius in around 500 BCE. This also proved to be trilingual.

Based on Grotefend's work, the Old Persian version of Darius's message yielded fairly quickly to translation, making it possible to attack the other languages carved into the rock. The second to be decrypted turned out to be a syllabic script, each character signifying a combination of sounds – like 'a', 'ba', 'ab', or 'bab' and so forth. Translation with the aid of the Persian text showed it to be in an unknown language which, when other documents using this writing were found in that part of Persia anciently called Elam, came to be known as Elamite.

The third variety of cuneiform found at Behistun, however, proved much harder to crack. It had a very large number of signs, an order of magnitude more than in the other two scripts. It was neither alphabetic nor fully syllabic. The same signs, combinations of wedge-shaped marks, were sometimes used as logographs – that is to say they were to be read as complete words, as for instance in modern Chinese – and at other times as phonetic symbols, indicating the sounds of speech. Some signs designated several different things, and were also to be read as several different sounds. Some sounds were represented by several different signs. There were symbols that seemed to have no meaning themselves but were just there to specify the general sense of the symbol that came after or before – what philologists now call determinatives or classifiers. Thus a vertical wedge always accompanied the names of people, a star shape the names of gods, and yet another cipher accompanied the names of places – but not always. Good reason led the great French Assyriologist Jean Bottéro to describe cuneiform as a 'devilish' script.

None the less researchers eventually established that this writing represented a Semitic language, thus related to ancient Phoenician, biblical Hebrew and modern Arabic. It was this understanding that enabled the three experts to deliver equivalent translations in response to the Royal Asiatic Society's 1857 challenge. (They called the writing Assyrian, after the bloodthirsty biblical empire. Today it is known as Akkadian, of which Babylonian and Assyrian are southern and northern dialects.)

That was not, however, the end of the story. As more of the texts were read, scholars slowly realized that underlying the Akkadian writing system there had to be another, older, language layer that nobody had previously suspected. This awareness dawned because of the many signs that were used equally as ideograms or as pronounced syllables. Sometimes the sign that usually meant 'ox' expressed the sound *gud*. Another, which designated 'to separate' had the value *tar*. 'Mouth' sometimes represented the syllable *ka*. But none of these sounds were to be found in Semitic, where ox was *alp*, 'separation' *paras* and mouth *pu*. The original creators of this writing system therefore had to be people in whose language 'ox' was *gud*, 'to separate' *tar*, and 'mouth' *ka*.

There was at first great resistance to the attempted supplanting of Semitic from its place as first language of the Middle East. Leading the opposition was a French Jewish Orientalist from Adrianople, Joseph Halévy, who had made his name exploring southern Arabia by posing as a rabbi from Jerusalem collecting alms for the poor.

European Jews had only recently gained respect by being associated with the Semitic originators of civilization. Halévy was appalled by the demotion of the ancestral Semites from that position and the elevation of some newly discovered upstart Sumerian nation. He refused to believe that there had ever been any such people, maintaining that Sumerian writing was no more than a secret cipher devised by Semitic priests to keep the common folk in ignorance. Publication of his book *Le Sumérisme et l'Histoire Babylonienne* in 1900 led to a famous fracas when two distinguished academicians attacked each other with umbrellas in the hallway of the École des Hautes Études in Paris.

The issue was settled in 1905, with the publication of a coherent and convincing translation of a group of Sumerian inscriptions which managed to reconstruct much of the grammar. Sumerian turned out to be a very strange language indeed, not part of any known linguistic group, with an unusual syntax and a lexicon consisting largely of words of one syllable. As a result it had a great number of homophones, words that sound the same – in some cases up to ten different words, all pronounced alike. So 'A' meant water, canal, flood, tears, semen, offspring or father; 'E' was house, temple or plot of land; 'U' translated as plant, vegetable, grass, food, bread, pasture, load, sleep, strong, powerful, to nourish or to support. These could then be joined together to make further words: 'e' (house), plus 'an' (sky or heaven), gave Eanna, House of Heaven, the Great Goddess's temple in Uruk; 'lu' (man), plus 'gal' (big), made 'lugal', big man, lord or king.

Scholars have continued to worry away at this issue. Some think that these apparently identical syllables were differentiated, as in Chinese, by variations in pitch or tones. In the late 1980s Jean Bottéro suggested that the monosyllabic vocabulary might be an illusion caused by the fact that the inventors of writing notated only each word's first syllable: he called this 'acrophony'. More recently a Danish scholar has proposed that Sumerian may have been a Creole, the result of children learning as their mother tongue a pidgin, a language cobbled together to enable speakers of different tongues, in this case the multi-ethnic founders of Eridu, Uruk and their neighbours, to communicate at a basic level. Hence it was afterwards revered as the language of the founders of civilization.

There is not even agreement over the origins of Sumerian writing. Currently the battle-lines are drawn between those who see its emergence as the culmination of a gradual process thousands of years in the making, an ancient system of keeping count of animals and commodities originally using pebbles, and then clay tokens, which came to be protectively sealed into clay containers. First the tokens were impressed on to the outside of the envelope to show what was contained. Later their images were drawn on the clay with a pointed stick. Eventually the tokens themselves were abandoned, leaving only the 'envelope', in the form of a clay tablet, as the permanent record.

Others believe that writing was one of those quantum leaps so characteristic of the innovative southern Mesopotamians, appearing suddenly towards the latter end of the fourth millennium BCE and evolving in a mere few centuries from a rudimentary shorthand to a sophisticated system capable of recording poetry and literary prose as well as contracts and business accounts.

There is general agreement, however, that in principle, ironically enough, Joseph Halévy's claim contained a tiny grain of truth. The earliest texts were not really writing at all but were indeed a kind of code. The first signs represent not language but things. They are records of transactions, notated by simplified drawings of items delivered or received: animals, people, commodities. A drawing of an ox's face meant an ox while an image of a bevelled-rim bowl referred to food. The image did not have to be of the object itself: a god was represented by a star, a temple by what might have been intended to represent a ground-plan.

In its first stages this system provided no more than a simplified personal memorandum, a rather ambiguous aide-memoire, such as 'Two | Sheep | Temple | God | Inanna'. Moreover officials or administrators who jotted down notes in this way doubtless had their own favourite choices of signs and preferred ways of drawing them. To make the symbols truly useful they had to be made recognisable to anyone who saw them, to be standardized by collective agreement. Hence the 'lexical lists', the long registers of titles, jobs, animals and commodities, the equivalent of dictionaries, that were to be the foundation of scribal education, ensuring that everyone employed exactly the same image for an ox, a bowl of food, a sheep, a temple or a goddess.

From this very simple foundation, over the centuries a large repertoire of symbols was eventually accumulated: several thousands. But there had to be a limit. The number of items that needed symbolizing was in principle infinite; no one could possibly have remembered all the signs if every single object in the world had its own. There was, however, a simple solution to this difficulty, one familiar to us from our own world and our own use of images.

Take the icon of an aircraft as an example. In an air terminal this can be used to indicate the arrivals and departures area; on a road sign it can mean 'to the airport', or warn of low-flying planes; in an advertisement it can refer to a package holiday or foreign travel in general. In other words, the meaning of the icon can easily be extended from 'airplane' to 'flying' to 'holiday' to 'travel' and, no doubt, to many other related ideas. In the same way, in the early Uruk system of signs, the drawing of a lower leg came to mean not only the limb itself, but also 'foot', 'walking', 'going', 'standing', 'kicking', and more. The context dictated which applied. And where extending the meaning was not enough, signs were combined to make little composite pictures. A food-bowl next to a head meant 'eating', and 'woman' plus 'mountain' (three little hills), at first signified 'foreign woman', and later 'female foreign slave'.

Some combinations were designed to distinguish between the various meanings of a sign. Thus the drawing of a plough was combined with the sign for a man to mean 'ploughman' or with the sign for 'wood' to refer to the implement itself (which was made of wood); names of gods were prefixed with the symbol for god, a star. These are the signs known as determinatives, and much use would be made of them in the later development of the script.

Typically, *Homo ludens* was at work here, for there is something playful about the way many of the signs were devised. For example several combinations that include the sign for head, with the symbol for 'fury' being particularly entertaining: a head with a great shock of hair standing on end. The concept 'woman' could have been illustrated in many different ways, but someone chose to represent her by her pubic triangle, while the sign for 'man' seems to be an ejaculating penis.

However, drawing freehand with a pointed tool requires some graphic ability and not every scribe could be expected to be a competent draftsman. In time the signs became less and less like images, and more and more like stylized symbols, and eventually they would lose all recognisable connection with the objects they originally depicted. Rather than drawing with a point, a stylus of triangular or square cross-section was impressed into the clay, creating the wedge-shaped marks that give us the name cuneiform. And in the process, the signs lost whatever light-hearted quality they may originally have possessed.

The next step, however, which was the truly revolutionary one, more than made up for the loss. And it must surely have first come about in jest.

However useful it may have been, all that had been devised thus far was a technique for noting down things, items and objects, not a writing system. A record of 'Two | Sheep | Temple | God | Inanna' tells us nothing about whether the sheep are being delivered to, or received from, the temple, whether they are carcases, beasts on the hoof, or anything else about them. Yet for administrative purposes this was apparently sufficient. Early Mesopotamia supported an oral society, in which memory was highly prized. All that was needed was a simple reminder, something as neutral as a sign of a left-pointing finger, which can be read as 'go left', 'à gauche', 'links gehen', 'a sinistra', 'влево', or 'يپ ـسد'. To be more precise would demand the use of real language, but for a long time the idea of representing actual speech in the form of marks on clay simply did not occur to anyone.

It seems to me most likely that the real leap that advanced writing from the recording of things to the recording of speech sounds, or at least the idea that inspired it, initially came about as a playful bit of fun. The Sumerian language, being full of homophones, different words pronounced either exactly, or only more-or-less, the same, must have made it a highly rewarding playground for punsters. The fact that, among hundreds of other examples, the word for 'arrow' and the word for 'life' sounded alike – *ti* – or that the word for 'reed' and 'restoring' were pronounced *gi*, must have given much opportunity for verbal buffoonery. It is easy to imagine some wit among the Sumerian temple bureaucrats applying the same sense of humour to the signs written on a clay tablet and extracting from the note a punning and comic meaning – an ancient equivalent, perhaps, to the 1970s TV comedy-sketch in which a hardware-store customer reads out 'fork handles' from his shopping-list, but the shopkeeper hears 'four candles'.

In jest or not, what had been stumbled on was a way of recording matters which either could not be drawn at all – how does one draw a picture of 'life'? – or for which no sign had been devised. There was in Sumer a kind of drum called tigi; it was rendered as an arrow, *ti*, plus a reed, *gi*. (A shame, really. As a result we have no idea of what a tigi drum looked like.)

Once the idea had been conceived, one might have thought that, the usefulness of writing signs not for things but for words, and so for representing sounds, would have quickly been recognized. But it seems to have taken several centuries for the new method to be put into regular use. None the less, over the course of time, the sounds-not-things principle did become firmly established, although phonograms (signs for sounds) never fully displaced logograms (signs for things) in the written texts for as long as cuneiform continued in use.

Where phonograms proved their true utility was not just to express words which couldn't be pictured, like 'life' or the tigi drum, but more importantly those parts of language which are essential but have no meaning in themselves: 'to', 'with', 'by', for example, and also what philologists call bound morphemes: the prefixes, suffixes and particles that every real language uses to shape its sentences, to distinguish singular from plural, present from past, active from passive, and also to extend meaning, as in adding 'ness' to 'happy' to get 'happiness'. Since Sumerian seems to have been a language largely of monosyllables, it was always possible to find a word for which a sign did exist and that sounded close enough to the particle to represent it in writing.

Thus, over time, an effective and elegant script was developed, able to express the Sumerian language in its entirety, though it was never to be a simple, easy to learn, system. It took many years of study and training for scribes to be able to master all its resources effectively – and even more to deploy them creatively. It is as if the difficulties were fondly cherished. When others – Elamites, Persians and the citizens of Ugarit – simplified the signs and reduced their number, eventually creating a short alphabet in which each character just represented a single sound, Mesopotamians insisted on retaining the full panoply of cuneiform's baroque complications during the entire three millennia of their civilization's existence. Alphabets must have seemed to them a very bare and impoverished form of script. The richness of the cuneiform signs, their ambiguity and multiple meanings, contributed as much to the overall effect of the text they encoded as does fine calligraphy to the literature of the Far East.

Cuneiform writing was not just used for high literary purposes, of course. It also set down the very first contemporary records of people and events. From now on whatever happened in the world need never be forgotten. And though much appreciated by archaeologists 5,000 years later, the real impact of this development was on its own world, which was radically transformed.

Here too is an eerie foreshadowing of our own times. Just as the technological and political revolution in Uruk seems most closely comparable to our recent industrial revolution, so did the development of a simple accounting technique into an effective medium of communication prefigure the post-modern era. An unassuming administrative device, the electro-mechanical punched card tabulator designed by mining engineer Herman Hollerith for the 1890 US census, began a process that has led, step by step, to the brave new world of today's Information Age. At the end of the fourth millennium BCE a simple accounting technique using clay tokens was elaborated in the City of Gilgamesh into a sophisticated, versatile and flexible writing system, the achievement that marks the moment when true history begins.

But for every new beginning there must be an ending of what came before. A division line is drawn. That was then; this is now.

4

The Flood:
A Caesura in History

The Chaldean Account of the Deluge

Between the era of myth and the time of legend falls the deluge; between the oral tradition and the written record lies the Flood. And between the Mesopotamian setting of the origins of the world in Genesis 1–9, and the Canaanite tales of nomad desert patriarchs that follow Genesis 12, the Hebrew Bible tells of Noah, his Ark and his descendants.

The story of God's extermination of all air-breathing creatures, sparing only one man, his family and what he could save aboard his giant lifeboat, is central to the Judaeo-Christian-Islamic concept of the human story. The Primate of All Ireland in the early seventeenth century, Archbishop James Ussher, deduced, in a virtuoso display of devotional mathematics, that the ark grounded on Mount Ararat on Wednesday, 5 May 1491 BCE. Since his time, more than two hundred expeditions have set out for Armenia in search of the ark's remains, the explorers somehow expecting vestiges of its perishable materials to have survived, by Ussher's reckoning, over 3,500 years of exposure to the elements. None the less, some forty parties have returned with eye-witness accounts of wooden structures looking like sections of a seagoing vessel frozen under glacier ice or embedded in the rocks.

Even some of those who do not take the biblical report at face value, and can no longer accept the notion of a universal divine punishment for mankind's irredeemable sin, still believe that the tale is at least based on a real disaster with a real historical setting. One proposal is that the story recalls the reflooding of the Persian Gulf, which had been a dry river valley until the rising Arabian Sea overtopped the rocky shelf across the Straits of Hormuz. This would have occurred around 10,000 BCE. Others have suggested that a more likely model was the breaching of the Bosporus by the Mediterranean Sea, which inundated the Black Sea basin – until some 7,500 years ago containing only a much smaller freshwater lake. 'It is possible that this flood affected the Late Palaeolithic people so deeply as to form the legend of the Great Flood,' according to a paper read to the Geological Society of America in 2003.

The conviction that the story of Noah's flood reflected history was reinforced by the public announcement in 1872 that the ancient Assyrians had also told a tale that had astonishing similarities to the one in the Book of Genesis. All the themes of the biblical story were there: the warning to the one man to be saved, the construction of a huge vessel, the storm, the flood, the abatement of the waters, the grounding on a mountain, the sending out of birds: a raven, a dove. And afterwards the offering of a sacrifice, of which God 'smelled the sweet savour'.

The discovery of this Assyrian precursor was even more piquant because the finder was one of those extraordinary self-taught amateurs almost unique to English scholarship. His name was George Smith. Born in 1840, he left school at fourteen to be apprenticed to a firm of banknote engravers near the British Museum. Perhaps the painstaking and meticulous manual work did not satisfy his lively mind, for he spent most of his mealtimes and many evening hours exploring and studying the Museum's Middle Eastern collections. Inspired by a chance meeting with the famous Sir Henry Rawlinson, one of the men to whom the decipherment of Mesopotamian script is credited, as well as by a museum attendant's offhand remark, regretting that nobody was attempting to decipher 'them bird tracks' on the thousands of clay tablets in the storeroom, he somehow taught himself to read cuneiform and the Assyrian language. The Museum's scholars were astonished that it apparently took this young workman with no higher education a mere few months. Smith, they noticed, seemed to base his translations not on familiarity with the vocabulary and syntax of the ancient language – which he did not have – but on a kind of intuitive and inspired second sight, lauded in his obituary, after his untimely death at the age of thirty-seven, as

'The marvellous instinct by which Mr. Smith ascertained the substantial sense of a passage in the Assyrian inscriptions without being always able to give a philological analysis of the words it contained, which gave him a good right to the title of "the intellectual picklock", by which he was sometimes called.'

Smith soon made several spectacular discoveries, and Rawlinson, greatly impressed, suggested to the trustees of the Museum that it was about time Smith was given an official job. They appointed the twenty-seven-year-old to a post of assistant in the Assyriology Department, and there he achieved international fame when he began to translate what turned out to be part of the eleventh tablet of the *Epic of Gilgamesh*, unearthed at Nineveh in northern Iraq. 'On looking down the third column,' he later wrote, 'my eye caught the statement that the ship rested on the mountains of Nizir, followed by the account of the sending forth of the dove, and its finding no resting-place and returning. I saw at once that I had here discovered a portion at least of the Chaldean account of the Deluge.'

Unfortunately the tablet from which Smith was working was broken, and several crucial lines had been lost. None-the-less, he presented his findings to the public in an 1872 lecture at the Society of Biblical Archaeology, with no less a person than Prime Minister Gladstone in the audience. Sensing good copy, the *Daily Telegraph* offered to fund an expedition to the site of Nineveh on what one might have thought a fool's errand: to locate the missing portion. So Smith set out for the Middle East and after many adventures arrived at the mound of Kouyunjik, where the North Palace of Assyrian Emperor Ashurbanipal had once stood.

He found a scene of complete devastation. As he wrote in his book, *Assyrian Discoveries*:

> Here was a large pit made by former excavators from which had come many tablets; this pit had been used since the close of the last excavations for a quarry, and stones for the building of the Mosul bridge had been regularly extracted from it. The bottom of the pit was now full of massive fragments of stone from the basement wall of the palace jammed in between heaps of small fragments of stone, cement, bricks, and clay, all in utter confusion.

He prised some of these stones up with a crowbar and generally did his best to collect every fragment of tablet that he could reach, though without much real hope of success. At the end of the day,

> [I] sat down to examine the store of fragments of cuneiform inscriptions from the day's digging, taking out and brushing off the earth from the fragments to read their contents. On cleaning one of them I found to my surprise and gratification that it contained the greater portion of seventeen lines of inscription belonging to the first column of the Chaldean account of the Deluge, and fitting into the only place where there was a serious blank in the story. When I had first published the account of this tablet I had conjectured that there were about fifteen lines wanting in this part of the story, and now with this portion I was enabled to make it nearly complete.

(That fragment of tablet is still to be found in the British Museum, duly labelled in black ink 'DT', for *Daily Telegraph*.)

Thus it was established that long before Genesis was committed to writing, the ancient Mesopotamians had themselves told the story of a universal flood sent by divine decree to destroy humanity. Soon other texts were discovered that gave similar accounts in several different languages – Sumerian, Old Akkadian, Babylonian – and in several different versions. In the oldest, found on a tablet from the city of Nippur, dated to around 1800 BCE and written in Sumerian, Noah's role is taken by a King of Shuruppak, called Ziudsura or Ziusudra, meaning 'He Saw Life', because he was awarded immortality by the gods. In another, written in the 1600s BCE in the Akkadian language, the protagonist is called Atrahasis, meaning 'Extremely Wise'.

The Mesopotamian accounts differed from the Hebrew Bible in one important respect, however: God's motive for sending the Flood. The reason given in Genesis is humanity's wickedness. The Atrahasis epic, on the other hand, explained that the supreme god Enlil decided to destroy mankind because of insomnia:

> ... the land extended and the peoples multiplied.
> The land was bellowing like a bull,
> The god was disturbed by their uproar.

Enlil heard their noise.
And addressed the great gods:
'The noise of mankind has become too intense for me,
With their uproar I am deprived of sleep.'

Whereupon he unsuccessfully tried several different ways of getting rid of humanity before settling on a worldwide deluge. Some have tried to read an ethical meaning into this passage, conjecturing that 'noise' related to iniquity or sin. But could it not perhaps be the reverse: that there was far too much prayer and sacrifice going on for Enlil's comfort? Recall the Lord's reaction to God-botherers in Isaiah 1:11–14:

To what purpose is the multitude of your sacrifices unto me? saith the Lord: I am full of the burnt offerings of rams, and the fat of fed beasts; and I delight not in the blood of bullocks, or of lambs, or of he-goats.

When ye come to appear before me, who hath required this at your hand, to tread my courts?

Bring no more vain oblations; incense is an abomination unto me; the new moons and sabbaths, the calling of assemblies, I cannot away with; it is iniquity, even the solemn meeting.

Your new moons and your appointed feasts my soul hateth: they are a trouble unto me; I am weary to bear them.

A single witness, the Bible, might be thought unreliable, but now that several supposedly independent narrators had been found to agree that there really had been a universal deluge, its historical truth seemed established. All that remained was to find physical confirmation, and this came on 16 March 1929, when the archaeologist Leonard Woolley announced in a letter to the *Times* that he had discovered evidence of Noah's Flood.

He was sinking a pit, he later wrote in his bestseller *Excavations at Ur*, when about three feet down, 'there were no more potsherds, no ashes, only clean water-laid mud, and the Arab workman at the bottom of the shaft told me that he had reached virgin soil.' This made no sense to Woolley who persuaded the workman, against his better judgement, to keep on digging. After eight feet of nothing but mud, the digger broke through into a lower stratum that again showed clear signs of human habitation.

I got into the pit once more, examined the sides, and by the time I had writ-
ten up my notes was quite convinced of what it all meant; but I wanted to
see whether others would come to the same conclusion. So I brought up two
of my staff and, after pointing out the facts, asked for their interpretation.
They did not know what to say. My wife came along and looked and I asked
the same question, and she turned away remarking casually, 'Well, of
course, it's the Flood.' That was the right answer.

It made a wonderful story and helped spread Woolley's fame – for which
he was competing with Egyptologist Howard Carter, whose discovery of
Tutankhamun's tomb in the Valley of the Kings in 1922 had made him
a household name. But Woolley's report wasn't quite true. A terrifyingly
brilliant essay by a fifteen-year-old schoolboy, Jacob Gifford Head, which
won Oxford's Wainwright Prize for Near Eastern Archaeology in 2004,
points out that it was actually Woolley's assistant, Max Mallowan (who
later became 'Mr Agatha Christie'), who supervised the excavation, and that
his meticulous site notes give a quite different, and much more sober,
account. The young essayist quotes a letter to the Iraqi High Commission
in 1928 from a Foreign Office official, emphasizing their desire to 'stimu-
late an interest in archaeology in Iraq, and assist in the raising of funds
for further excavation', and concludes that Woolley was a committed self-
publicist, that his version of the flood story was produced with the aim of
promoting 'himself and his subject in the public's eyes'.

Any academic faced with the need to attract funding for his or her spe-
ciality, and warned by superiors to 'publish or die', will surely understand
Woolley's embellishments. For who would have been remotely interested
had he announced that he had found evidence not of *the* Flood, but of
a flood, one of at least two which had overwhelmed Ur many centuries
apart? Or that similar flood layers, of varying thickness, but dated to different times were to be found in many, though by no means all, southern
cities? Some sites, like Eridu, only eleven kilometres from Ur, showed no
signs of inundation at all.

Then why, ask believers, would all the ancients of the Middle East agree,
even if precise details differ, that there was once a single overwhelming
flood that destroyed their entire world, leaving only a handful of survivors? An event like that, with all its terror and horror, would never be

forgotten whenever it happened; the tale would be passed along from generation to generation until finally written down in its various versions.

Whether based on a true disaster or not, there was another, more important reason for Mesopotamians to tell and retell the story of the Flood: it played a crucial structural role in the ancients' view of their history. To the Sumerians the Deluge was the boundary marker that separated the preliterate from the literate period, the age of folklore from the era of history. More to the point, it was the gulf that lay between the time when all Mesopotamia followed Uruk's cultural and ideological lead, and the following epoch when Sumer, the southernmost part of the Mesopotamian plain, was a land of separate city-states, each pursuing its own destiny.

Archaeology tells us of momentous changes around 3000 BCE. Suddenly, or so it seems, contact between the many centres of civilization distributed all over greater Mesopotamia ceased. Trade routes, like those to the Afghan lapis-lazuli mines, were cut. Uruk outposts disappeared from across the region: from Iran, Syria, Anatolia. In towns and villages outside the south the inhabitants went back to their former ways; older dietary preferences were re-established; accounting was abandoned; the art of writing forgotten. In the Uruk heartland, buried remains hint that less care was taken with agriculture: the grain was full of weeds, the soil contaminated by salt. Life expectancy was severely reduced. Rural settlements were abandoned, the people either fleeing to the city or taking up nomadism. In Uruk itself, the lands belonging to the temples were taken over by peasants. The monumental buildings of the Eanna quarter were demolished and replaced by terraces and light post-and-reed constructions.

All signs point to a collapse of the Uruk ideology: the quasi-egalitarian social system and the command temple economy that had successfully sustained the city's cultural dominance for centuries. The usual suspects have been indicted for causing the disaster. Climate change brought colder and drier weather: sufficient rain no longer fell to water the foothills directly or to keep river levels high enough for successful irrigation. Envious and hostile foreigners launched raids and invasions: massive fortifications were thrown up around outlying settlements. Typical were the ramparts, ten feet thick, topped with watchtowers and pierced by gates, doubled by a solid brick wall fifteen feet behind it, that protected Habuba

Kabira, a former Uruk colony on the banks of the Euphrates in northern Syria.

These are, as ever, merely the external factors linked to Uruk's decline. Yet there are indications that all was not well within, either. We recognize from our own times some of the strains that can beset supposedly egalitarian societies running managed economies; how what begins as willing acceptance of a utopian ideology can all too often end in resistance and revolt. The tyranny that ensues is almost always unstable, and increasing poverty is usually the result.

The dominance of the Urukian way of life had, in any case, not been achieved entirely by peaceful persuasion. A recent expedition by the University of Chicago and the Syrian Department of Antiquities to the site of Hamoukar, in today's Syria, found a devastated war zone. Clemens Reichel, the American co-director, called it 'no minor skirmish', but '"Shock and Awe" in the Fourth Millennium BCE'. The 3-metre-high city wall had been breached by a heavy bombardment of slingshot balls, the buildings set on fire and the inhabitants massacred. 'It is likely that the southerners played a role in the destruction of this city. Dug into the destruction debris that covered the buildings excavated this season were numerous large pits that contained a vast amount of Uruk pottery from the south. The picture is compelling. If the Uruk people weren't the ones firing the sling bullets they certainly benefited from it. They took over this place right after its destruction.' Later on, towards the end of the era, muscular methods seem to have been needed even in the southern heartland of Uruk's world, to enforce the authority of the system.

The clay tablet from Uruk that bears the earliest known personal autograph signature is a scribal-school exercise listing a series of official titles and professions. The first entry, presumably the most senior rank, reads NAM GIS SITA, meaning Lord of the Mace, the favoured close-quarter weapon of the period. It is a title that in later ages meant king. Images on cylinder-seals show severe discipline being administered. A typical example represents prisoners being beaten, their arms bound behind their backs, while one pleads with the official in charge who stands holding a spear and looking on. This is no battle scene; the prisoners do not seem to be fighters but workers. It is tempting to interpret the punishments as connected to the forced intensification of agriculture made necessary by a growing urban population. As in the twentieth century with the USSR's collectivization programme, the result was, paradoxically, a reduction rather than an increase in the productivity of the soil.

Salination, bringing up mineral salts from the subsoil to the surface soil, which ruins the land for agriculture, is always a hazard of irrigation, as modern development scientists have found to their cost. Salinity was a particularly severe problem in ancient Sumer because the great rivers, the Tigris and Euphrates, are unusually heavily laden with minerals. Over many centuries Mesopotamian farmers had learned how to cope with the problem, as their tribal descendants do to this day. They managed by leaving the fields fallow every other year. Professor McGuire Gibson of the University of Chicago explains how,

> As a result of irrigation the water table in a field approaching harvest lies about half a metre below the surface…Wild plants draw moisture from the water table and gradually dry out the subsoil until winter…In the spring, since the field is not being irrigated, the plants continue to dry out the subsoil to a depth of two metres…Since they are legumes, the plants also replenish the land with nitrogen, and retard wind erosion of the topsoil. In the autumn, when the field is once again to be cultivated, the dryness of the subsoil allows the irrigation water to leach salt from the surface and carry it below, where it is normally trapped and harmless.

It is not hard to imagine the temple authorities, faced with a rising number of mouths to feed, insisting on a Great Leap Forward in grain production and forbidding what may have seemed to them – temple administrators after all know little of farming – a practice that wasted half the available land every year. Force may well have been their means of getting their way. And the Atrahasis epic described the inevitable consequences:

> The black fields became white,
> The broad plain was choked with salt.
> For one year they ate grass;
> For the second year they suffered the itch.
> The third year came.
> Their features [were twisted] by hunger,
> [They were] on the verge of death.

Highly organized complex societies are delicate machines. It does not take much to bring them to ruin. 'For want of a nail... the kingdom was lost', as the old rhyme has it. Civilizations based on ideology are even more fragile than most. As we know from twentieth-century history, once people stop believing in the system, the end is near; no amount of coercion can keep it going indefinitely. The late Urukians, as they looked around them and saw their fields ruined, their fellow-workers coerced, their outposts unable to withstand attack, must have begun to question the convictions with which they had been indoctrinated so successfully and for so long. Their world probably collapsed as much because its citizens lost faith in the benefits of their beliefs, the ability of their ideology to assure them a happy and rewarding life, as from any external pressures.

The later Sumerians did not remember, or did not choose to remember, any of this. We find no explicit references in the myths, legends and epics that have come down to us. Perhaps it was because writing was still in its primitive stages, and used for bookkeeping rather than recording history. There seems to be just one shadowy hint of the great loss of faith, preserved from the ancient oral tradition. In the Atrahasis epic, the Flood is preceded by the god Enlil's attempts to reduce humanity's numbers with plague, followed by salination, drought and famine. The people rebel:

> *I have called the elders, the senior men.*
> *Start an uprising in your own house,*
> *Let the heralds proclaim...*
> *Let them make a loud noise in the land:*
> *Do not revere your gods,*
> *Do not pray to your goddesses.*

Official Sumerian history, as outlined in Utu-hegal's King List, ignored the whole issue. It simply declared that the old order had been utterly erased at a single stroke: 'and then the Flood swept over'. It was as if the recorders of the new dispensation wanted to draw a line under the past: that was then, this is now. The Flood symbolized the wholesale rejection of what had gone before. The era of Uruk's regional dominance was dead and best forgotten. It was time for a new beginning.

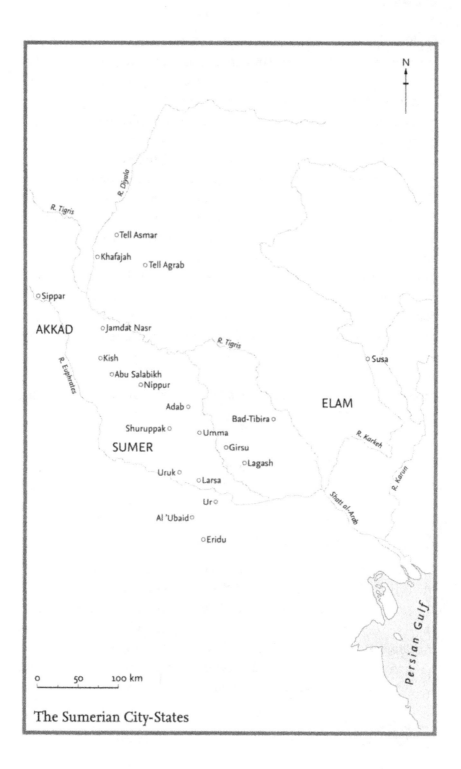

The Sumerian City-States

5

Big Men and Kings: The City-States

c.3000 to 2300 BCE

Still Visible after Five Thousand Years

In April 2003, an account appeared widely online, claiming that 'the Iraqi cities of Al-Kut and Nasiriyah launched attacks on each other immediately following the fall of Baghdad to establish dominance in the new country.' The allied western conquerors, it said, responded by ordering the cities to stop fighting, and by confirming that Baghdad would remain Iraq's capital. Nasiriyah supposedly backed down immediately. However, 'Al-Kut placed snipers on the main roadways into town, with orders that invading forces were not to enter the city.'

It is hard to establish whether this is part truth or total legend. The source of the information is nowhere given. Yet, whether true or false, the pattern is a familiar one. It goes back at least 5,000 years, to the very first appearance of cities in the ancient Middle East.

Around 3000 to 2900 BCE, as the fog of prehistory begins to lift and the details of history come slowly into view, we can start to make out the shape of things to come. We perceive a scene of almost incessant strife. The major population centres of the Tigris–Euphrates plain were born struggling against each other like Jacob and Esau emerging fighting from the womb.

In spite of repeated attempts to call an end to the destructive rivalry, during much of the third millennium BCE the conflicts all too often led to the ruin of entire cities and the massacre of their inhabitants. Yet the contenders for Sumerian superiority were well aware, even proud, of sharing a common culture and a common history. Some interpreters see evidence that suggests there was even at times a coalition or confederation, what the Greeks would later call an *Amphictyony*, a league of neighbours, focused on the temple of the supreme god Enlil at Nippur, which collected together supplies, material, and even armed men, for the common defence of a *Kengir* (Sumerian) League. Just so, in medieval Italy, were the nobles of cities like Ferrara, Florence, Genoa and many others, almost constantly at war with each other, in spite of recognizing and acknowledging their common culture and heritage, and yet at other times allying with each other against external enemies.

In the film *The Third Man* Orson Welles famously quipped: 'In Italy, for thirty years under the Borgias, they had warfare, terror, murder and bloodshed, but they produced Michelangelo, Leonardo da Vinci and the Renaissance. In Switzerland, they had brotherly love, they had five hundred years of democracy and peace – and what did that produce? The cuckoo clock.' In third-millennium Mesopotamia they had rivalry and conflict between independent cites, they had fratricidal strife, a struggle of all against all to achieve domination, they too had warfare, terror, murder and bloodshed. Yet meanwhile, brick by sun-baked brick, the foundation of our own civilization continued apace to be constructed.

It took no more than a few centuries for the city-state, familiar from classical Greece to modern Singapore, fully to take shape; for warlords and kings to replace temple priests as dominant powers, for the relatively egalitarian society of religious rule to fragment into classes of rich and poor, weak and strong. All this proceeded with a kind of inevitability as the side-effect of a remarkably well-organized, efficient, effective and productive agricultural system, the traces of which are still visible after 5,000 years.

From the early 1960s, the CIA switched their surveillance of the Soviet Union from using spy-planes towards observation from space, in particular to the CORONA series of satellites, which could distinguish any feature on the ground over two metres wide. Cold War politics aside, the greatest beneficiaries of late have been archaeologists, who have used the 3D images, declassified in 1995, to study in unprecedented detail aerial views of the whole of the Middle East, finding revealed in them the permanent traces left by the ancient inhabitants and their activities.

These images show a region dotted with long-gone villages, towns and cities – Eridu and Eshnunna, Girsu, Isin and Kish, Lagash and Larsa,

Nippur, Sippar and Shuruppak, Umma, Ur and Uruk and more, in total some thirty-five – evenly spread, with innumerable smaller settlements filling the spaces in between. Each comprised a walled urban area, plus its dependent villages, surrounded by a jealously guarded domain of intense cultivation and wild steppeland into which radiated tracks leading out from the city centre. Every morning for several thousand years, farmers and herdsmen trailed out at first light from their town-houses along these paths to their plots, and then returned as the day began to fade, leaving the surface of the soil where they walked flattened, hardened and sunk below the level of the plain by a foot or two. The impressions they left are still visible 5,000 years later in the satellite images.

Indeed they are still so clear that you can easily imagine yourself joining the daily exodus to the fields in the dawn light one morning in the third millennium BCE, some thousand years before the date usually ascribed to the Patriarch Abraham. You are walking alongside farmers dressed in their linen or wool sarongs, carrying their hoes, rakes, clod-mallets and ditch-spades over their shoulders, some leading panniered donkeys or dangling their legs over the sides of creaking ox-carts with four solid wooden wheels, each cleverly crafted from three sections – a simple slice of log would allow the soft outer sapwood to wear away too quickly.

Your companions will be conversing in one of the two most commonly used languages in this part of the world: one we call Sumerian, the other the Semitic language which will in later times be known as Akkadian (since the City of Akkad still waits to be founded we can hardly call it by that name yet). In the southernmost part of the Mesopotamian plain that abuts what we now call the Persian Gulf, you will probably be hearing Sumerian; further to the north where the Tigris and Euphrates most closely approach, Semitic; while in between both are in use. Earlier researchers claimed that there was a power-struggle between Sumerian-speakers and Semitic-speakers, which was eventually won through military conquest by the latter. That idea has now been discounted; we can be almost certain that both tongues were spoken here from early times, with no more antagonism between the two than between speakers of French, German, Italian and Romansch in today's Swiss cantons.

How can we know about something as evanescent as the everyday speech of a vanished people? Not by their documents, which at this stage were restricted to the Sumerian for which writing was invented, but by their names, which they proudly recorded on their seals and texts. In those early times, names were mostly pious phrases. We know of people named 'Enlil is my strength', 'My god has proved true', 'I seize the foot of Enki', and even 'In the midst of thy food is a slave', *Sag-gar-zu-erim* in Sumerian, which seems to be a line from a prayer. As the scholar George Barton wrote, 'Either the parent who gave this name had a sense of humour or he was a literalist as utterly lacking humour as some of the Puritans who gave their children names consisting of long sentences.'

Now you pass out through the high gateway that pierces the towering brick wall of your home city. Immediately beyond you find orchards and vegetable gardens, planted with apple trees and grapevines for fruit, as well as flax and sesame for fibre and oil, and a plentiful variety of vegetables and legumes – beans, chickpeas, cucumber, garlic, leeks, lentils, lettuce, mustard, onions, turnips, and watercress – plus diverse herbs and spices like coriander, cumin, mint and juniper berries. Ducks and geese raised for eggs and meat – eventually joined by chickens somewhat later in the millennium, when they arrived here from south-east Asia – forage around the vegetable patches. Here and there stand isolated groves, mostly of date palms, important to the local diet, although you would also see poplar, willow, tamarisk and dogwood, grown for timber, which is always in short supply.

The garden produce provides for a varied, rich and elaborate cuisine, detailed in several later cuneiform cookery collections. Investigated in 1987 by Jean Bottéro, the recipes make clear the sophistication of ancient Mesopotamian taste. There are even directions for preparing pastry, that acme of the chef's art – although the texts do suffer from what one might call grandmother's-instructions-syndrome, where no detailed quantities are given, but only 'enough' of this, 'not too much' of that, and 'the right amount' of the other:

After cleaning the flour, soften it with milk and, once it is puffy, knead it, adding siqqu [a fermented fish sauce] and include samidu [an onion-like herb], leeks and garlic, and enough milk and pot-oil to keep the dough soft. Carefully keep an eye on the dough while kneading it. Divide the dough into two portions: save one half in the pot, and shape the other into smallish

bread sepetu [perhaps a kind of crouton, which Bottéro calls 'fleurons']
which you should bake in the oven.'

The full recipe, for a poultry pie, which Bottéro was able to decipher in its entirety, was cooked and photographed for a magazine. The journalist claimed the result to be 'a real treat', although in a letter to his translator Professor Bottéro himself 'confessed that he would not wish such meals on any save his worst enemies'.

The basis of the diet was, of course, a cereal. Back in the third millennium BCE, as you leave the city behind, you pass field upon field of grain, stretching away as far as your eyes can see on either side of the trackway. By now your fellow citizens are growing more barley than wheat, for barley is more salt-tolerant, and the land has never recovered fully from the salination of the previous era. A network of broad and navigable canals, narrower flumes, tight and muddy ditches, finger their way among the fields to water the crop that is the staff of Sumerian life.

Perhaps – imagine yourself to be educated and literate – you carry in your pocket for ready consultation a copy of the late third millennium text called 'The Farmer's Instructions', a document typical of the ancient Mesopotamian proto-scientific passion for accurate observation and careful classification. (This is still the ancient world, though. To protect your produce from vermin, 'perform the rites against mice'.) 'The Farmer's Instructions' is a complete handbook, in the guise of a wise old father's advice to his son, containing all you need to know to grow grain successfully. It begins with the biennial return from fallow to production:

When you have to prepare a field, inspect the levees, canals and mounds
that have to be opened. When you let the flood water into the field, this
water should not rise too high in it. At the time that the field emerges from
the water, watch its area with standing water; it should be fenced. Do not
let cattle herds trample there.

After you cut the weeds and establish the limits of the field, level it re-
peatedly with a thin hoe weighing two-thirds of a mina [about 650g]. Let
a flat hoe erase the oxen tracks, let the field be swept clean. A maul should
flatten the furrow bottoms of the area. A hoe should go round the four
edges of the field. Until the field is dry it should be smoothed out.

There follow instructions on preparing tools, equipment and the plough oxen. Next,

> *After working one plough's area with a* bardili *plough [maybe what we would call an ard or scratch-plough], and after working the* bardili *plough's area with a tugsaga plough [perhaps a soled plough, to turn the sod], till it with the* tuggur *plough [probably a kind of harrow]. Harrow once, twice, three times. When you flatten the stubborn spots with a heavy maul, the handle of your maul should be securely attached, otherwise it will not perform as needed.*

A single ox-drawn plough was expected to work between 130 and 160 acres, or a field just under a kilometre long by a kilometre wide. This is exhausting, back-breaking labour. But don't let that deter you:

> *When your field work becomes excessive, you should not neglect your work; no one should have to tell anyone else: 'Do your field work!' When the constellations in the sky are right, do not be reluctant to take the oxen to the field many times. The hoe should work everything.*

If you followed the instructions to the letter, you could be assured of a plentiful barley harvest, crucial to your standing in the community, for barley was central to the entire Mesopotamian way of life. It was the basic staple, the 'bread and potatoes', of all classes. If the barley harvest failed, people starved. And they also thirsted, for barley was also the source of the main Mesopotamian beverage, beer, drunk as much for everyday thirst-quenching as for merry-making and for religious and ceremonial occasions.

For while those who lived on the far-off mountains and foothills had recourse to crystal-clear rills and sparkling springs, the only sources of drinking water here on the plain were rivers, canals and ditches, either badly contaminated or fruitfully fertilized, depending on the point of view. From early times, even back in the Uruk age before 3000 BCE, household sewage had been piped directly into the watercourses through an elaborate disposal system of baked-clay piping, with each house having pipes draining both waste and storm-water into a sewer under the street outside. These were connected to form a city-wide waste disposal system with its outfall sloping parallel to the natural fall of the ground, the eventual outlet being located well beyond the city walls. (Many houses in Britain did not have that convenience until halfway through the twentieth century.) A magnificent engineering achievement but a potential disaster for public health.

If the watercourses were unsafe, boreholes and wells were no more providers of drinking water, as the saline water-table was too close to the surface. Beer therefore, sterilized by its weak alcohol content, was the safest drink, just as in the western world, as late as Victorian times, it was served at every meal, even in hospitals and orphanages. In ancient Sumer beer also constituted a proportion of the wages paid to those who had to serve others for their living.

There seem to have been many varieties of Mesopotamian beer, brewed to different strengths and, in the absence of hops, flavoured with different ingredients. It has generally received a rather bad press in the academic literature. The fact that it was often drunk through straws from large containers suggests to many academics – who may, as a class, have special expertise in beer – that it was full of particles and grit that were excluded by the straw, rather like *umqombothi*, the thick maize-and-millet homebrew served in backstreet South African shebeens. This is surely unfair. That Sumerian beer was carefully filtered was clearly indicated in a hymn to Ninkasi, goddess of strong drink, dated to 1800 BCE but reflecting the techniques of a thousand years earlier:

> *The filtering vat,*
> *which makes a pleasant sound,*
> *you place appropriately on top of*
> *the large collector vat.*
> *When you pour out the filtered beer*
> *from the collector vat,*
> *it is like the onrush of*
> *the Tigris and Euphrates.*

In any case, the proof of a beer is in the drinking, and several attempts have recently been made to try out the methods detailed in the Ninkasi hymn. In 1988 the Anchor Brewing Company of San Francisco collaborated with an anthropologist, Dr Solomon Katz, to resurrect the Sumerian beverage, which turned out to be more like Russian kvass than beer, part of the malted barley being first baked into loaves, or even twice baked, into rusks, before being mashed and fermented. The resulting drink was quite palatable, with an alcohol concentration of 3.5 per cent by volume, like many modern lighter beers, and it was described as having 'a dry taste lacking in bitterness, similar to hard apple cider'.

In Sumerian times they would have celebrated with a drinking song. All together now:

The gakkul vat, the gakkul vat! The gakkul vat, the lamsare vat!
The gakkul vat, which puts us in a happy mood!
The lamsare vat, which makes the heart rejoice!
The ugurbal jar, glory of the house! The caggub jar, filled with beer!
The amam jar, which carries the beer from the lamsare vat!...
As I spin around the lake of beer, while feeling wonderful,
Feeling wonderful, while drinking beer, in a blissful mood,
While drinking alcohol and feeling exhilarated,
With a joyful heart and a contented liver,
My heart is a heart filled with joy!

Whatever I Propose Shall Remain Unaltered

In Sumer after the flood, the command temple-economy of the previous Uruk era was gone and forgotten – which is not, of course, to say that the temple priests had suddenly lost all their influence; far from it. But from now onwards private property would play an increasingly significant role in social and economic affairs. Midway through the third millennium documents begin to detail sales of land, of fields and palm groves, as well as contracts and agreements relating to the inheritance of plots from parent to child – both men and women. And where private property exists, with its implied right to buy and sell, there must be a mechanism for determining the price. It seems that, for the very first time in history, supply and demand played a role.

There has been much debate between scholars about the place of the market, in its widest sense, in early Mesopotamian life. Here, more than in other fields of study, political stance plays a major part in determining viewpoint. Marxists and conservatives interpret the past in very different ways, some of the former denying that market forces played any role in Sumerian economics at all, many of the latter convinced that these forces controlled the terms of trade from the start. There is not much to be found in the written record to support either position. Professor Morris Silver of the City College of New York has trawled the literature for evidence:

> *Texts dating from the third millennium... refer to the Sumerian lú-se-sa-sa (Akkadian* muqallû*) who roasted grain and sold it on the market.*
>
> *A literary document from about the same time speaks in proverbial terms of: 'The merchant – Oh how he has reduced prices!'*
>
> *An official reports in a letter to his king that he has purchased for shipment to the capital city a substantial quantity of grain (over 72,000 bushels) but now the price of grain has doubled.*

In answer to the observation that Sumerian cities had no market-places in which to trade, or at least no word for them, he noted evidence 'from as early as the third millennium, of food peddlers who sold imports such as salt and wine, and domestic beer, roasted grain, pots, and alkali (used for soap). The term for streets (Akkadian *sūqu*), often found in the documents, also connotes a marketplace. Texts from the second half of the third millennium speak of goods being "on the street".'

Where there is a market, a *sūqu*, suq or souk, there is competition. Where there is competition there must be winners and losers. And where there are winners and losers, there will be rich and poor, employers and workers, entrepreneurs and proletarians. Unlike during the previous apparently largely egalitarian era, social classes now began to separate out like coloured inks on blotting-paper. Looking around your companions on the morning trek to the fields, you won't see many members of the wealthier classes, who can now afford to pay others to do their agricultural work for them. On the road you will mostly meet smallholders, wage labourers and a few slaves, fallen into servitude in lieu of debt repayment, or by capture in war. The rich stay back at home, enjoying their new-found wealth and devising ways of increasing it still further, which might now include setting up private workshops, outside the control of the temple priests, where textiles, pottery, metalwork and other artisan-made goods can be produced for sale and export. These are history's first industrial factories, although judging by later records they might better be called sweatshops.

The consequences of such accumulation of assets will prove to be profound. 'By exchanging their reserves for land, which they may have distributed amongst their followers,' writes Czech scholar Petr Charvát of the Sumerian nouveaux riches, 'they became masters of social groups entirely independent of the traditional temple-centred communities and chiefs of the primeval states of Mesopotamia.' A new power structure was in the making.

You have walked no more than a few miles from the city walls when you come to the end of cultivated fields and the great steppe begins, stretching from the foothills of the Zagros Mountains all the way across to Arabia, the tract called in Sumerian *edin*, which some think gave us the name of Adam and Eve's garden in the Bible. Here is grazing for the flocks and herds, and ample game for the hunting: boar, deer, gazelle, oryx, ostrich, wild ass, wild ox. But here also lurks danger, for lions and cheetahs, jackals and wolves, prowl the wilderness. The lion-hunt, a familiar theme of Mesopotamian art, is a necessity, not an indulgence, if the city's sheep, goats and cattle are not regularly to be decimated. The popular cylinder-seal image of a lion attacking a bull or a stag is no flight of artistic fancy, but a regrettably common sight.

Human predators are a regular risk too: raiders from the eastern highlands, or from the western deserts. At times, particularly during the harvest, you need armed men close by for protection. The danger of attack is greatest in the Semitic-speaking north of the alluvial plain. The valley of the Diyala River, which flows 400 kilometres down from its source high in the Zagros Mountains to join the Tigris just below where Baghdad now stands, offers an easy route to marauders descending from the Iranian plateau. It is therefore no great surprise to learn that the most important political development of the third millennium, kingship, was first conceived in this area – in particular, in the city known to history as Kish. 'After the flood had swept over, and the kingship had again descended from heaven,' it says in the Sumerian King List, 'the kingship was in Kish.'

Apart from its strategic location, is there anything about Kish that marks it out as special, as different from the cities of the Sumerian-speaking south like Eridu and Uruk, where the past history of the area had been centred, and where we might have expected such a momentous development to take place? Today Kish (not to be confused with the resort island of the same name off the southern coast of Iran) is, like so many other famous Mesopotamian sites, no more than several thousands of acres of dusty, deserted hillocks. Yet there is one important difference between this and the ruins further south: it is nothing like as dry and desert-like. Indeed, the mound, or tell, is surrounded by scattered green fields, for the area is unusually well watered, lying not only near where the Diyala River empties into the Tigris, but also not far from where the Tigris and Euphrates approach each other most closely, only about 50 kilometres apart. If anywhere were in danger of flooding, it would be here, and excavation has revealed that Kish was indeed flooded several times over. However, the converse of the danger of deluge is easy irrigation, and Kish's environment made for heavy harvests and fat flocks. Perhaps that is what prompted the barbarians from the eastern mountains to mount frequent razzias, raids for loot and booty, to relieve the citizens of their produce, rather like the bandit attack on the peasant village in Akira Kurosawa's film *Seven Samurai*.

When news came that brigands were on their way, spotted perhaps by herdsmen tending their animals out in the wild far from the city walls, the call would go out for men to mount resistance. Farmers turned themselves into a citizen-militia, dropping their spades and hoes, and picking up clubs and spears. Yet while this may have been an adequate defensive response to small bands, it was insufficient to repulse a battalion-sized incursion. For that, a trained body of semi-professional fighters was needed, and eventually a fully professional army. The older power-centres of Sumerian society, the temple priesthood and assemblies of elders, would have been able neither to muster the appropriate number of men, nor to lead them into battle. That task would have fallen by default to the new economic elite described by Petr Charvát, the 'big men', Lugalene (Sumerian: 'lu', man; 'gal', big; 'ene', plural ending), with their great estates and retinues of followers, whose economies of scale meant that part of their workforce could be spared for regular training in the arts of war. But no military force can be commanded by several generals competing with each other. Inevitably one would rise to become principal Lugal, top Big Man of Kish, what the Romans, millennia later, would call Dux Bellorum or War Leader. The King List names the first Lugal of Kish as Ghushur, followed by twenty-two successive holders of the post, though their 'reigns', of marvellous length, adding up to '24,510 years, three months, and three and a half days', are hardly to be taken as truth.

Though no history of those times was ever written, a heavily disguised and coded account does occur in the very much later Babylonian creation myth called *Enuma Elish*. The gods are threatened with attack by monsters unleashed by the primeval salt-water goddess Tiamat, here a personification of chaos. Unable to withstand the assault they call on the young hero–god Marduk to be their champion and defender. He agrees, but only on one condition:

> *If I am to be your avenger, to conquer Tiamat and give you life,*
> *Establish an assembly, make my position pre-eminent, and proclaim it...*
> *With my word equal to yours, I will decree fate.*
> *Whatever I propose shall remain unaltered,*
> *The word of my lips shall never be changed or ignored.*

While the Lugal may have begun by defending his town against raiders, he must soon have found border skirmishing against other settlements in the neighbourhood a good way to consolidate his position. Surveys suggest that Kish allowed no other city in the northern part of the plain to challenge it in size or pre-eminence. In time its influence must have been exercised over the whole area, as the King List implies. Forever after in Sumerian history, the title Lugal of Kish was adopted by any leader claiming hegemony over the entire country.

However Kish would not get its own way for ever. The cities further south, with their long histories and, doubtless, their great civic pride, eventually learned the lesson of their northern neighbour. Every city needed an army at least to maintain, if not to extend, its sphere of power and influence. We do not know how long it took, but eventually Big Men came to the fore in most of the cities. Uruk assembled enough fighting manpower to rival, challenge, and eventually overthrow Kish. With that began the compulsive rivalry, the incessant game of devastatingly destructive military musical-chairs that is such a feature of the early third millennium BCE in southern Mesopotamia. In between enumerating the series of Lugalene in each city – by convention called dynasties, although successive war leaders were mostly unrelated – the Sumerian King List tells the story all too clearly. Modern political careers are said always to end in failure; in Sumer each city's temporary place in the sun ended in inevitable defeat:

> *Kish was defeated and the kingship was taken to Eanna* [i.e. Uruk]...
> *Then Unug* [Uruk] *was defeated and the kingship was taken to Ur...*
> *Then Ur was defeated and the kingship was taken to Awan...*
> *Then Awan was defeated and the kingship was taken to Kish...*
> *Then Kish was defeated and the kingship was taken to Hamazi...*
> *Then Hamazi was defeated and the kingship was taken to Unug...*
> *Then Unug was defeated and the kingship was taken to Urim...*
> *Then Urim was defeated and the kingship was taken to Adab...*
> *Then Adab was defeated and the kingship was taken to Mari...*
> *Then Mari was defeated and the kingship was taken to Kish...*
> *Then Kish was defeated and the kingship was taken to Akshak...*
> *Then Akshak was defeated and the kingship was taken to Kish...*
> *Then Kish was defeated and the kingship was taken to Unug.*

These bald statements of conquest tell us nothing about what really happened. But we do possess a detailed account of one important war, albeit from one side only – one that is not mentioned in the King List. This was a fight between the cities called Lagash and Umma, and it went on for well over a hundred years.

Of course the descriptions we have are expressed in a way that is consonant with ancient Mesopotamian culture and beliefs, so they require some interpretation. In medieval, early modern and even modern times, politics was and is conducted by people, even though all sides in any conflict usually proclaim the support of God – mostly the very same God. In the ancient Sumerian world, by contrast, politics, and its extension, war, were perceived to be the business of the gods; men acted only on the gods' behalf. Thus the Sumerian Hundred Years' War between Lagash and Umma was a conflict between the god Ningirsu of Lagash and the god Shara of Umma. Men fought and died and cities were destroyed, but the actual argument was between the gods.

The dispute was over a patch of land, described in inscriptions as a field, called *Gu-Edin*, the 'edge of the steppe'. Though the reference is to an irrigated tract of arable soil, it is actually more likely originally to have been, as its name suggests, an enclosed part of the steppe used for grazing. In ancient Mesopotamia grazing land for animals, a gift of Nature, was always in shorter supply and more bitterly contested than plots for raising crops, which were essentially human creations. With the land in the immediate vicinity of the city given over to the growing of grain, livestock had to be fed on the steppe beyond. But cattle and sheep, if contained within too small an area, quickly reduce it to uselessness. Cattle eat the green leaves of bushes and trees as well as occasionally the bark, while sheep nibble newly growing shoots and undergrowth and so prevent regeneration. Once the natural herbage of the steppe has been destroyed by the flocks, the only use for the land is to give it over to agriculture. Thus, two cities which may initially have been at a comfortable distance apart would find themselves in dispute, not over agricultural land, but for residual steppe used for grazing.

This, it seems, is what happened to Lagash and Umma, whose separation by a seemingly generous 30 kilometres none the less eventually led them into collision. Yet to see this conflict merely as a disagreement over borders and grazing rights is probably to give it less significance than it merits. For the two cities were really battling for supremacy over Sumer itself. The geo-strategic development of the entire alluvial plain was bound up with their fate. It may have seemed a fairly trivial spat, a tussle over a small patch of ground, but in retrospect, after advantage had continued to sway from one side to the other over the course of many decades, an entirely new political dispensation, labelled with the title of a new era, had come to pass.

The specific details of the long war is mainly of interest to specialists: an account of how originally a certain Mesilim, called King of Kish and therefore nominal overlord of all Sumer, had been commanded by his god Kadi to arbitrate and define the border between the cities. But then, 'at the command of his god, the Ensi [governor] Ush of Umma raided and devoured the *Gu-edin*, the irrigated land, the field beloved of Ningirsu... ripped out the boundary marker and entered the territory of Lagash.' Lagash responded by turning out to battle behind their leader, Eannatum, who, 'by the word of the god Enlil, hurled the great net upon them and heaped up their bodies in the plain... the survivors turned to Eannatum, they prostrated themselves for life, they wept.' Peace treaties were made and summarily broken. 'Eannatum, ruler of Lagash, battled with him in Ugiga, Ningirsu's beloved field. Enmetena, beloved son of Eannatum, defeated him. Urluma fled, but he killed him in Umma. His asses – numbering 60 teams – were abandoned on the banks of the Lumagirnunta canal. The bones of their attendants were strewn about the plain.'

Was there anything to show for all this bloodshed? It did bequeath us one of the great masterpieces of early Mesopotamian art: the Stele of the Vultures, so called because of the carrion-feeding birds shown devouring the corpses of the slain. A round-topped stone, just under 2 metres high, sculpted on one side with images of King Eannatum of Lagash arrayed in his fighting outfit, both on foot and riding in his chariot, leading a stern phalanx of men into battle. On the other face we find the god Ningirsu, who has captured the army of Umma in his great hunting-net and is cracking their heads open with his mace. An inscription comprising a detailed narrative of the dispute, with a full account of the wickedness and perfidy of the men of Umma, completes the work. It is little surprise that this stele, now in the Louvre, had to be restored from numerous fragments dug up at Girsu; the monument had been smashed to pieces in antiquity, presumably by the people of Umma who did not much like what it said about them.

Great quantities of time and energy, as well as social capital, must have been expended on such warfare. It is impossible to know how many men were fielded in conflicts like these but, according to the *Cambridge Ancient History*, 'one temple alone in the city of Lagash furnished 500 to 600 men from its tenants for the military levy'. And this was probably not one of the largest centres. When whole armies clashed in the field, as many as 10,000 warriors may well have been involved – a large number, even by today's standards.

The Stele of the Vultures – like the other great work of ancient art that presents Sumerian men of war, the so-called Standard of Ur, which was probably the decorated soundbox of a musical instrument – shows soldiers equipped for close-quarter conflict: spearmen protected by leather helmets, capes and shields, formed into a tight phalanx, their Big Man in the lead, wielding a spear, axe or a stone-headed mace. In their support what are usually called chariots trundle up behind, though that word gives a quite false impression of their speed and manoeuvrability, given that these were clumsy, four-wheeled, two-man vehicles drawn by asses: they cannot have moved very much faster than a man can walk. It may be better to think of them as mobile armouries, an interpretation supported by the large bucket at the front containing what look like spare javelins. If these are indeed throwing-spears, they are the only missiles represented in the illustrations, which has led scholars to conclude that Sumerian armies fought hand to hand; bows and arrows are not depicted in scenes of warfare from this era.

But absence of evidence is not evidence of absence, and may be no more than artistic convention. Archaeological remains, like that found at Hamoukar in today's Syria, attacked by Urukians in an earlier period, gives a very different and rather unexpected picture of ancient warfare.

The discoveries at Hamoukar tell us that ancient Mesopotamia's fighting forces had much more in common with modern armies that had previously been imagined, in particular in their use of missiles. Indeed, it turns out that the 'bullet', has a continuous history from ancient Mesopotamia to the modern battlefield, and was as important to the Sumerian warrior as it is to today's infantryman. The difference is that today bullets are propelled from assault rifles; in ancient times they were projected from slingshots. As described in one of the epic tales of those days:

> From the city it rained missiles as from the clouds;
> slingstones like the rain of a whole year
> whizzed loudly down from the walls of Aratta.

When I Samuel 17:50 describes the confrontation between David and Goliath, with David prevailing over the Philistine 'with a sling and with a stone, and smote the Philistine, and slew him; but there was no sword in the hand of David', it suggests that David was equipped with no more than a boy's toy. That is, however, a most disingenuous interpretation. In properly trained hands, the slingshot turns out to have been one of the deadliest weapons of all.

A sling works by increasing the effective length of a stone-thrower's arm. Modern cricket bowlers or baseball pitchers can achieve maximum ball velocities of over 150 kilometres per hour. A slingshot as long again as the thrower's arm will double the projectile's speed, making the velocity of the bullet when it leaves the sling nearly 100 metres per second. This is already considerably greater than that of a longbow arrow, at only about 60 mps. Intensively trained from childhood onward, there is no reason to believe that a professional slinger could not beat 100 mps fairly easily and perhaps even begin to approach the muzzle velocity of a .45 calibre pistol round: about 150 mps. What is more, a smooth slingshot projectile has a far greater range than an arrow, as much as half a kilometre, because an arrow's flight feathers produce so much drag. The modern world-record distance for a stone cast with a sling was achieved by Larry Bray in 1981, who managed 437 metres, and thought in retrospect that he could surpass the 600-metre mark with a better sling and lead projectiles.

It has always been thought that the weakness of the slingshot as a weapon was its inherent lack of accuracy as well as the inability of stones to pierce armour. But the discovery of the Hamoukar projectiles has contradicted both beliefs. Their pointed shape tells us two things: that they could be armour-piercing; and that the slingers must have had a technique for sending them off with a spin, like a rifle bullet, so as to keep them properly oriented during their flight to the target. The accuracy of the slingers must have easily matched the left-handed Benjamites referred to in Judges 20:16, of whom 'every one could sling stones at an hair breadth, and not miss'. Even later, Livy in his *History of Rome* reported that the slingers from Aegium, Patrae and Dymae, 'Having been trained to shoot through rings of moderate circumference from long distances, they would wound not merely the heads of their enemies but any part of the face at which they might have aimed'.

So we should see a Sumerian military unit as consisting of a central shock-force, a tightly packed phalanx of several hundred, perhaps thousand, spearmen. To control them, drill them and keep them in proper formation would have required many skilled and loud-voiced NCOs; to keep them in step, marching steadily forward or manoeuvring in close order, they would have needed music, perhaps a corps of drummers. And behind this central strike-force another thousand or so slingers, the equivalent of today's riflemen, fusiliers or even gunners, would have been drawn up in looser formation, buzzing around like angry wasps, sending lethal showers of both small and large projectiles into the heart of the enemy's formations, supported by the ass-drawn battle chariots carrying supplies of missiles.

A city Lugal, Big Man, capable of assembling such an army would have been a formidable figure indeed.

The Sumerian word Lugal is usually rendered in English as king, because later Akkadian glossaries translated it that way. It is not at all clear at exactly what point the Dux Bellorum became a monarch in the sense in which we use the word today. There is a profound difference between the two: a war leader is a human figure: wealthy, certainly; socially powerful, surely; with a charismatic and magnetic personality, undoubtedly; but still, just a man. Even the legendary Gilgamesh needed the approval of at least one of Uruk's citizen assemblies before embarking on his campaign against Aga of Kish.

A king or queen, on the other hand, is, officially at least, marked by the divine. Well into the 1820s the French monarch was still touching patients to miraculously cure the 'King's Evil' – scrofula or lymphatic tuberculosis of the neck. Only after World War II was the Emperor of Japan forced by the USA publicly to repudiate his incarnate divinity, though he never denied he was descended from Amaterasu, a sun goddess. To pass from one state to the other, to trade earthly humanity for heavenly semi-divinity, to go from whole man to part god, is no easy task. For your fellows to accept your new status, to have your co-citizens truly believe that you are now different in your very essence from them, demands that something quite extraordinary happen. In southern Mesopotamia, in the City of Ur, later credited as Abraham's home town, the transformation seems to have been achieved by mounting an outstanding dramatic spectacle, a stunning piece of religious theatre, and, as an unintended consequence, bequeathing to us not only the institution of divinely sanctioned monarchy, which has featured as an integral part of statehood ever since, but also one of the most glorious ancient collections of treasures yet discovered.

Theatre of Cruelty

On 4 January 1928, Leonard Woolley cabled back from Iraq to his sponsors at the University of Pennsylvania – in Latin to assure privacy – with exciting news: 'TUMULUS SAXIS EXSTRUCTUM LATERICIA ARCATUM INTEGRUM INVENI REGINAE SHUBAD VESTE GEMMATA CORONIS FLORIBUS

BELLUISQUE INTEXTIS DECORAE MONILIBUS POCULIS AURI SUMPTU-
OSAE WOOLLEY'.

On the faded telegram in the university museum, someone has scrawled a rough translation: 'I found the intact tomb, stone built, and vaulted over with bricks, of Queen Shubad, adorned with a dress in which gems, flower crowns and animal figures are woven. Tomb magnificent with jewels and golden cups. Woolley'

The Royal Graves of Ur vie with Tutankhamun's tomb in Egypt and the terracotta warriors of the First Emperor Shi Huang Di for the title of most spectacular archaeological discovery of the twentieth century. But while Howard Carter's find in 1922 demanded no more of him than to than make a 'tiny breach in the top left hand corner' of a doorway, peer through by light of a candle and see 'wonderful things', Leonard Woolley's achievement was the result of a very long period of extremely hard work, much of it done by Woolley, his wife, and a single assistant. In his own words: 'The clearing of the vast cemetery kept us busy for many months, and from beginning to end there was not a day which would not have been a red-letter day in an ordinary excavation; if one remembers specially the royal tombs it was not so much because others were unexciting as because of the extra labour involved.' (That heavy labour was performed by a large gang of locally recruited tribesmen, of whose supposed ignorance, recklessness and dishonesty Woolley often complained.)

Woolley uncovered two cemeteries at Ur, from slightly different periods. The earlier included the sixteen so-called Royal Graves. Two, identified as the final resting place of Meskalamdug 'Hero of the Good Land' and a lady whose name was formerly read in Sumerian as Shub-'ad, but now in Semitic as Pu-'abi, 'Word of my Father', yielded some of the most beautiful objects ever to emerge from the soil of Mesopotamia: deftly engraved cylinder-seals, finely wrought jewellery of lapis lazuli and carnelian. There were curiously fashioned musical instruments: harps and lyres, decorated with white shell inlay on a background of black bitumen and finished with bulls' heads marvellously modelled in precious metal, and oddly adorned with false beards of precious stone. There were weapons of copper and flint, and a profusion of silver and gold, including a golden helmet, in the form of a wig, delicately chased as if with waves, plaits, and locks of hair, which Woolley declared 'the most beautiful thing we have found in the cemetery'. (This is one of the objects looted from the Baghdad Museum in 2003 that has so far not been seen again.) The workmanship was so exquisite that 'Nothing at all resembling these things had ever yet been unearthed in Mesopotamia; so novel were they that a recognized expert took them to be Arab work of the thirteenth century AD, and no one could blame him for the error, for no one could have suspected such art in the third millennium before Christ.'

But the most astonishing thing found by the excavation was the evidence of large-scale human sacrifice. Whatever the rank of those buried here, and there is still controversy over the exact status of the interred, they were accompanied into the afterlife by large retinues of men, women and animals. Though a few scholars like Gwendolyn Leick point to a lack of evidence that the buried servants perished *in situ* and may instead have been long dead before being included in their masters' and mistresses' graves, most believe that they died in the tomb, apparently willingly. Woolley described one of the burial scenes as he believed it to have happened:

Down into the open pit, with its mat-covered door and mat-lined walls, empty and unfurnished, there comes a procession of people, the members of the dead ruler's court, solders, men-servants and women, the latter in all their finery of brightly coloured garments and head-dresses of carnelian and lapis lazuli, silver and gold, officers with the insignia of their rank, musicians bearing harps or lyres, and then, driven or backed down the slope, the chariots drawn by oxen or by asses, the drivers in the cars, the grooms holding the heads of the draught animals, and all take up their allotted places at the bottom of the shaft, and finally a guard of soldiers forms up at the entrance. Each man and woman brought a little cup of clay or stone or metal, the only equipment needed for the rite that was to follow. There would seem to have been some kind of service down there, at least it is certain that the musicians played up to the last; then each of them drank from their cups a poison which they had brought with them or found prepared for them on the spot – in one case we found in the middle of the pit a great copper pot into which they could have dipped – and they lay down and composed themselves for death.

Reading this account, you need constantly to remind yourself that this is all conjecture, that what Woolley actually found was no more than a huge pit filled with earth in which human remains were distributed. But the man had more than the eye of a superb archaeologist. He had a poet's or even film-maker's sensibility. If his description of the above scene was like the icing on the cake of his great discovery, the cherry on the top was surely his explanation for finding a silver ribbon, tightly coiled, close to a young girl's hand, rather than wound around her head as with the other attendants. She had been late, Woolley suggested, and had rushed to take her place in the pageant of death without having had time to put the silver filet in her hair as the final touch to her costume. As Agatha Christie, married to Woolley's one-time assistant Max Mallowan, wrote in her autobiography, 'Leonard Woolley saw with the eye of imagination: the place was as real to him as it had been in 1500 BC, or a few thousand years earlier. Wherever he happened to be, he could make it come alive... It was his reconstruction of the past and he believed in it, and anyone who listened to him believed in it also.'

A vivid illustration of this burial scene as its discoverer described it was published in the *Illustrated London News* and was included in Woolley's final report, as it has been in most accounts of the Royal Graves of Ur ever since. It has done much to establish the commonly held image of what took place there 5,000 years ago. We should remember, though, that the bones actually tell a much more ambiguous story, and that the precise details of the rites enacted at the Great Death Pit of Ur are beyond our means of discovery.

It is, however, clear that wholesale human sacrifice did not usually accompany funerary rituals in ancient Mesopotamia. In fact Woolley's cemetery at Ur, dated to the earlier part of the third millennium BCE – around 2600 BCE or before – provides the only known example. The rites that accompanied the burials of Lady Pu-'abi and of Lord Meskalamdug must have been very special occasions indeed. Could they mark the moment of transition when mortal Lugalene of Ur became semi-divine Kings?

Rituals are profound and mysterious events. They mimic the real world, but with a strongly intensified symbolic vocabulary. Performing rituals unites, and in some cases, as probably at Eridu, even creates communities.

While it is often assumed that rituals consist of the acting out of beliefs, a study of the religions most familiar to us demonstrates that the truth is usually the other way round: the rites come first and beliefs are later developed to explain and sustain them – teleology, it's called.

In Judaism, for example, the ancient, pre-Judaic, wheat-harvest festival Shavuot was interpreted as the anniversary of the handing down of God's Torah to Moses. In Christianity the immemorial commemoration of the winter solstice became Jesus' birthday celebration. In Islam an ancient pagan sanctuary, the Kaaba at Mecca, was explained as the creation of Adam, rebuilt by Abraham and Ishmael, and therefore worthy of the annual Muslim pilgrimage, the Hajj.

The less usual the components of a ritual or ceremony, the more memorable the event becomes. If the collective experience involves an awesome enactment of mass death, its impact, and the beliefs explaining and justifying it, become utterly unforgettable. Bruce Dickson of Texas A&M University calls such gruesome public events Theatres of Cruelty: 'State power united with supernatural authority can create extraordinarily powerful "sacred or divine kingdoms",' he writes. 'They are obliged to practise acts of public mystification, of which the Royal Graves appear to be examples... The graves themselves are part of the effort made by Ur's rulers to establish the legitimacy of their governance by demonstrating their sacred, holy, and non-ordinary status.'

Dickson gives many examples of disgustingly savage acts, like the horrific public punishment of William Wallace, the medieval Scottish leader who was dragged naked behind a horse through the City of London to the market at Smithfield, where he was hanged, cut down while he was still living, castrated, disembowelled, his innards burned before his eyes, before he was finally decapitated and his head displayed on a pike over London Bridge. The aim was to turn a commonplace offence – military resistance – into a crime of spiritual proportions: treason against a divinely appointed ruler.

Thus the purpose of mass human sacrifice in Ur might have been to provide evidence for, and a proof of, the godlike nature of the ruling house. On the other hand, it is likely that the sacrificial victims of Ur went willingly into the grave. Woolley certainly thought so. And, given what we know of Sumerian life expectancy – Lady Pu-'abi was about forty when she died – and of Mesopotamian ideas about the afterlife – the dead lived in a dark and gloomy underworld with poor accommodation and nothing decent to eat: 'the food of the netherworld is bitter, the water of the netherworld is brackish' says 'The Death of Ur-Nammu' – we would not be surprised to find middle-aged members of the lower orders of society happily exchanging that unwelcome outlook for a brighter future spent serving their betters in the realm of the gods.

However we interpret the precise meaning of these graves, if the aim of the gruesome obsequies celebrated at Ur was to underline the transition of the ruler from lugal to king, from mere mortal to semi-divine monarch, they seem to have been successful. From now on in Sumerian history, the title king applies better to their deeds and to their inscriptions than the simple designation Big Man. Indeed more than a few of the successors of those interred in the Royal Graves explicitly declared themselves to be gods.

Why was human sacrifice practised only at Ur? And why only during this brief historical period? Impossible to say. Perhaps the citizens of Ur were more resistant than others to the deification of their Big Men and needed a spectacular series of *autos-da-fé* to persuade them. Or maybe the fame of such extraordinary events spread rapidly throughout southern Mesopotamia and had its effect without need of replication.

Whatever the meaning of the ceremonies at the Great Death Pit of Ur to its participants and onlookers, to us they serve as a memorial of the moment when kingship came down from heaven, as the King List put it: a historical marker for the beginning of kingdoms in the full modern sense, ruled by monarchs whose spiritual heirs are still in power in many parts of the world today. The Divine Right of Kings was invented here.

The transition from a society directed in peacetime by a priesthood and only led into war by a Big Man, to a kingdom entirely dominated and ruled by a divinely sanctioned, or even semi-divine, monarch implies profound economic and social change. The lives of ordinary people would have been affected most, and largely for the worse. Yet this seems to have been a stage through which every society has needed to pass. No ancient polity managed to retain a totally theocratic government system into historical times. Indeed, no state has at any time in recorded history been governed by a theocracy for more than a few generations at a stretch, before succumbing to more pragmatic – and muscular – rulership.

It is tempting to propose that kingship emerged because powerful men built up and exaggerated the threat from supposed outside enemies to consolidate their domination of their own societies – the process is all too familiar from our own times. Yet in the ancient Middle East, although it is hard for us today to recognize what the attraction may have been, kingship seems to have exercised a huge appeal, even though its downsides were well understood.

So, for example, the Bible tells us that well over a thousand years after the change had taken place in Sumer, the Hebrew tribes in the Holy Land sought to move from theocratic to military government. They are described as complaining that unlike other nations they are still governed by religious judges and have no king to command them. They beg the prophet Samuel to intercede with God to allow them a royal ruler. In I Samuel 8:11–18, the prophet warns them of the consequences:

This will be the manner of the king that shall reign over you: He will take your sons, and appoint them for himself, for his chariots, and to be his horsemen; and some shall run before his chariots.

And he will appoint him captains over thousands, and captains over fifties; and will set them to plough his ground, and to reap his harvest, and to make his instruments of war, and instruments of his chariots.

And he will take your daughters to be confectionaries, and to be cooks, and to be bakers.

And he will take your fields, and your vineyards, and your oliveyards, even the best of them, and give them to his servants.

And he will take the tenth of your seed, and of your vineyards, and give to his officers, and to his servants.

And he will take your menservants, and your maidservants, and your goodliest young men, and your asses, and put them to his work.

He will take the tenth of your sheep: and ye shall be his servants.

And ye shall cry out in that day because of your king which ye shall have chosen you; and the Lord will not hear you in that day.

Because the Hebrews were coming to kingship relatively late in the day, Samuel did not need to be a prophet to predict how the Hebrews would fare under a monarchy. He had only to look back to the experience of the Sumerians.

In Lagash, for example, the squeezing of the citizenry and expropriation of temple property by the ruling families seems to have generated some kind of revolt by the priesthood during a pause in its interminable war with the city of Umma. After a short interregnum, during which the temple priests apparently tried to enlarge their control of the property of the gods, a new ruler, a usurper unrelated to the previous monarch, took the throne, perhaps assisted by a faction among the priestly class. His name was Urukagina, or Uruinimgina (the cuneiform symbol KA, mouth, can also be read as INIM, word), and he based the legitimacy of his rule on his claim to have ended the corrupt exploitation of the common people by both palace and temple. The account of his famous reforms was much copied and has been unearthed in several versions from the ruins of Lagash.

On his accession Urukagina found a dire situation. The bureaucracy was to blame for many excesses: The superintendent of the boatmen conducted his office purely in his own financial interest; the cattle inspector was seizing both large and small cattle; the fisheries regulator was concerned only to line his own pockets. The ruler and his family had expropriated most of the best city land. Most burdensome were the taxes imposed on everyone. A later proverb from ancient Lagash put the matter clearly: 'You can have a Lord, you can have a king, but the one to fear is the tax assessor.' Every time a citizen brought a white sheep to the palace for shearing he had to pay five shekels, about two ounces, of silver. If a man divorced his wife, he had to pay the ruler five shekels and his minister one shekel. If a perfumer created a new scent, the ruler took five shekels, the minister took one shekel, and the palace steward took another shekel, all in silver. The temple and its land were exploited by the ruler as if they were his personal property. 'The oxen of the gods ploughed the ruler's onion patches; the onion and cucumber plots of the ruler were sited in the god's best fields.' But the priesthood was not innocent of corruption either. A priest could enter a poor man's garden and cut down his trees or take away his fruit at will. Nothing was as certain as death and taxes. When a citizen died, the bereaved had to pay for the privilege of burying the body: seven jars of beer and 420 loaves of bread; the priest got one-half gur – over 60 litres – of barley, a garment, a bed and a stool; the assistant priest received 12 gallons of barley.

Urukagina claimed to have put an end to all this. He humbled the bureaucrats, he cut taxes and in some cases entirely abolished them; he restored the temple's property, but ensured that the priests no longer oppressed the lay public. He redressed the inequalities of power, the oppression of the poor by the wealthy: 'If the house of a rich man is next to the house of a poor man, and if the rich man says to the poor man, "I want to buy it," then if the poor man wishes to sell he may say "pay me in silver as much as I think just, or reimburse me with an equivalent amount of barley". But if the poor man does not wish to sell the house, the rich man may not force him.' He freed citizens who had fallen into irretrievable debt, or were falsely accused of theft or murder. 'He promised the god Ningirsu that he would not allow widows and orphans to be victimized by the powerful. He established freedom for the citizens of Lagash.'

Scholars are still debating what Urukagina's claims really meant to the people of Lagash. Were his reforms simply the actions of a good and just man, or were they rather a means to establish the bona fides of a ruler who had usurped the throne from its legitimate occupant? Was the return of property to the temple really an attempt to re-establish the role of the priesthood in Lagash society or was it that, by appointing himself and his family to positions within the temple hierarchy, as he did, Urukagina managed to feather his own nest while giving the appearance of altruism and generosity? We will never know. But the debate, while of interest to specialists, actually obscures something potentially more significant: the texts that describe Urakagina's acts introduce several entirely novel features into the history of government.

Though ancient chronology is still very much disputed, Urakagina's rule was almost certainly no later than about 2400 BCE. Elsewhere in the world, except in Egypt and perhaps the Indus Valley, at this period people were still living either in semi-nomadic kinship-related bands of hunter-gatherers or – the minority who had made the great leap forward to subsistence agriculture – gathered in small settlements under hereditary village chiefs, without writing and without metal technology. Yet in southern Mesopotamia, long before Plato and Aristotle, long before Confucius and Lao Tzu, long before the Buddha and Mahavira, long before the Hebrew prophets, long before Moses and Zarathustra, even long before Abraham, texts are already employing the great motifs of morality and justice: the concern for fairness, the responsibility to protect the widow and the orphan from the rich and powerful. Here too is the very first use of a word that can be translated as 'freedom': 'He established freedom, *amargi*, or the citizens of Lagash.'

A further implication of the reforms of Urukagina is that he was trying to elicit support for his rule on a principle very different from any that had gone before. Previous monarchs had bragged of their military success and the corpses they piled up on the battlefield; those buried in the Royal Graves of Ur had justified their control by their quasi-divine status; others had based their legitimacy on the sheer terror they inspired among their people. Now we find something entirely new: the texts suggest that Urukagina wanted to be approved of, even loved by, his people.

We often take it for granted that the lives of these ancient folk were so different from ours that we cannot hope to enter their mindset and see life as they saw it. Yet these documents contain evidence to the contrary. The story of Lagash, its long war with Umma and the reform of its social system by Urukagina, with protection for the widow and orphan and the concern for freedom for the citizens of his city, suggest that human attitudes have changed but little in the intervening 4,500 years.

Whatever Urukagina's true motives were in instituting his reforms, they did him little good in the end. His reign over Lagash lasted hardly more than eight years. While he was busily occupying himself with rolling back the state, advancing the interests of his citizenry, and cultivating the favour of his people, nearly 30 kilometres away, in the traditional enemy city Umma, a new, energetic and ambitious ruler called Lugalzagesi was quietly building up his strength and his forces, nurturing a passion for revenge after many decades of humiliation at the hands of Lagash. Then he launched a devastating attack. The lament composed after the consequent destruction of Lagash tells us:

> The ruler of Umma has set fire to the temple of Antasurra; he has carried away the silver and the lapis lazuli... He has shed blood in the temple of the goddess Nanshe; he has carried away the precious metal and the precious stones... The Man of Umma, by despoiling Lagash, has

commited a sin against the god Ningirsu... May the hand that he dared to raise against Ningirsu be cut off. There was no fault in Urukagina, King of Lagash. May Nisaba, the goddess of Lugalzagesi, ruler of Umma, make him bear his mortal sin upon his neck.

Prophetic words. But it took many years before that final curse was implemented. In the meantime, in addition to Lagash, Lugalzagesi also overcame Kish, Ur, Nippur, Larsa and Uruk, which he took as the capital city of his enlarged domains, and he inscribed on a vase dedicated to the high god Enlil in the temple city of Nippur his claim to have conquered the whole of Sumer as well as the surrounding countries:

When Enlil, the king of all countries, gave the kingship of the whole nation [i.e. Sumer] *to Lugalzagesi, he turned all eyes upon him; he threw all the foreign countries at his feet, and made everyone submit to him from the rising to the setting of the sun, from the Lower Sea* [the Persian Gulf] *along the Tigris and Euphrates Rivers to the Upper Sea* [the Mediterranean]. *Enlil took away every opponent from where the sun rises to where the sun sets. All the foreign lands lie under him in abundance, as at pasture. All nations are happy under his rule, all the rulers of Sumer and the chiefs of all the lands.*

Lugalzagesi's claim to control of the entire Fertile Crescent is dubious, to say the least. It may just possibly be the case that he achieved some kind of non-aggression pact with the surrounding powers, cities like Mari that may have exercised a degree of control over the tribes of Syria. But the hubris expressed in his grandiloquent vase inscription led inevitably to nemesis. Just as his destruction of Lagash was revenge for the long humiliation of Umma, so would his downfall be linked to one of his own first conquests.

When Lugalzagesi took the city of Kish, he deposed its ruler Ur-Zababa, and it would be the man who was once cup-bearer to that king who would bring down the goddess Nisaba's punishment on Lugalzagesi's neck. In doing so he would usher in a new era, a new ideology and a new principle of government: not fear, not love, but adulation and hero-worship. The new man of the age was Sargon, by-named the Great. He founded the very first true empire.

6

Rulers of the Four Quarters:
The Bronze Heroic Age

c.2300 to 2200 BCE

Imperial Ambition

In the course of the digging season of 1931, Reginald Thompson, assisted by Max Mallowan, the British team exploring the northern Mesopotamian city of Nineveh, onetime capital of Assyria, came upon a life-sized sculpted copper head. They saw at once that they had discovered a relic of an important turning point in ancient history. The figure was like nothing ever found before, a giant step from the familiar, rather stiff and formal, hieratic sculpture style of the Sumerians. The head must have represented the face of an earthly ruler, as it bears none of the signs or symbols that were always employed in ancient times to denote divinity, yet the quality of it indicated that the sculpture could only have been intended to represent a very august personage indeed.

The hair is carefully plaited, caught in a filet around the temples, and bound into an elegant chignon held in place by three rings at the back, from under which a series of charming ringlets fringe the neck. The strands are quite as finely delineated as on the golden helmet of Meskalamdug, one of the treasures found by Leonard Woolley in the death pit at Ur. An elaborately groomed full beard, layered in delicately represented rolls and curls, divides into two beneath the chin. Though Shelley's Ozymandias, awe-striking in his own day but forgotten by posterity, comes immediately to mind as the model for an ancient ruler, 'look on my works, ye mighty, and despair', here a faint beneficent smile, very human and quite different from the 'wrinkled lip and sneer of cold command', hovers on the figure's sensual lips, almost as

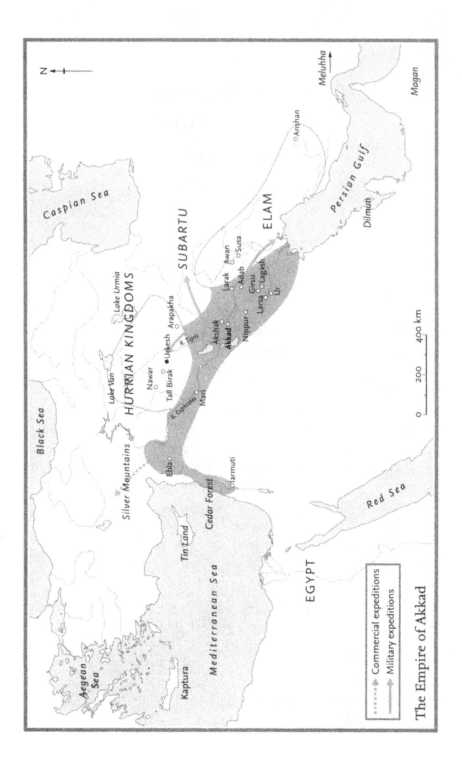

The Empire of Akkad

if the subject is amused by the very notion of distant posterity's close attention.

This magnificent object was found not far from the Ishtar Temple in Nineveh, at a destruction level dated to the seventh century BCE. The archaeological team determined that they had found the wreckage left by the razing and burning of the Assyrian city at the hands of a combined Median and Babylonian invasion force in 612 BCE, a blow from which the site would never recover. But reckoning by the material, the style and the sculptural technique, they deduced that the regal copper head had been created about 1,500 years before that. Presumably it was once part of a complete full-length statue, and must have been very carefully looked after, probably standing in a place of honour in the temple, regularly dusted, oiled, polished, burnished and maybe even the object of worship in regular rites.

Most scholars agree that the king most likely to be represented by this head is Sargon, the founder of the first true Mesopotamian Empire. Sargon, Sharru-kinu – not a name given at birth but a throne-name meaning 'Legitimate King' in Semitic – had risen from nowhere some time between 2300 and 2200 BCE to crush Lugalzagesi's combined kingdom of Kish, Lagash, Larsa, Nippur, Ur and Uruk, and to begin building a Semitic-speaking regional imperial state that at its height claimed to stretch all the way from what is now the Strait of Hormuz in the Gulf, through the highlands of Iran and the mountains of Anatolia, to the Mediterranean Sea from Cilicia to Lebanon.

I write 'from nowhere' more metaphorically than strictly accurately. In fact Sargon was probably a palace insider. Later legend says that he was brought up as a gardener, working for the ruler of Kish, Ur-Zababa. The Sumerian King List, written not so very long after the event, tells us that gardening was his father's profession and that he had reached the position of cup-bearer to the monarch, a royal office of some significance, before launching himself into history as the original empire-builder.

His master Ur-Zababa soon vanishes from the record, probably killed or deposed by Lugalzagesi of Umma, in his quest for hegemony over the whole Mesopotamian plain. Kish must immediately have been plunged into turmoil and confusion. Ancient autocracies seem to have had no settled mechanism for replacing an eliminated ruler – no deputy, vice-regent or official second-in-command. Even the monarch's offspring would often have had to fight, literally, for their right to succeed.

Sargon, who must surely have been nurturing an appetite for power for some time, long enough to have gathered a party of supporters sufficiently large to ensure success, grabbed his opportunity, and the throne. Then he swiftly pursued what look like long-cherished imperial ambitions. Beginning with the south, he marched on Uruk, demolished the famous walls built by King Gilgamesh, easily vanquished a massed defence by fifty Sumerian city governors and, according to an inscription on the pedestal of a statue preserved in a later copy, captured Lugalzagesi himself, dragging him back 'in a neck-stock to the Enlil gate' at Nippur. Having made a clean sweep of the southlands he symbolically washed his weapons in the 'lower sea', the Gulf.

That was merely the beginning. A late Babylonian document, 'The Chronicle of Early Kings', tells us that Sargon,

> had neither rival nor equal. His splendour was diffused over the lands. He crossed the sea in the east. In the eleventh year he conquered the western land to its farthest point. He brought it under one authority. He set up his statues there and ferried the west's booty across on barges. He stationed his court officials at intervals of five double hours and ruled in unity the tribes of the lands.

Sargon's aim seems to have been to accrue wealth by free trade and open markets, and ferry it back home to the heartland. When this met resistance, he did not hesitate to send the ancient equivalent of a gunboat, even though distances were great and travelling times long.

'The King of Battle', an epic written in later days, of which fragmentary and variant copies have been found in places as far apart as Egypt, Syria and Anatolia, tells of how a distant trading-post in Purush-khanda was persecuted by the local king. The merchants call for Sargon to come to relieve their plight. His military advisors, rather wimpishly, remind him how far off the place is, and how hazardous the route:

> When will we be able to sit? Will we rest even for a moment,
> When our arms have no more strength
> And our knees are exhausted from walking the trail?

If, as scholars now believe, Purush-khanda is today the mound called Acemhöyük in the mining region of central Anatolia near the great salt lake called Tuz, it lies over 1,100 kilometres from Akkad, even as the crow flies – more like 1,600 kilometres on foot. Xerxes's army covered 450 kilometres in nineteen days in the course of his invasion of Greece in 480 BCE. Alexander the Great's soldiers could manage 31 kilometres in a marching day, but regular rest days brought the average down to about 24. At those speeds even 1,100 kilometres would have taken Sargon's forces between forty and fifty days of forced marching. The riverside roads of the Mesopotamian plain, flat, regularly maintained, and well-patrolled, would have been safe enough. Climbing the rough tracks through the foothills and squeezing an army through the narrow passes of the Taurus Mountains would have been much more hazardous. Nevertheless, the epic tells us that Sargon sets out on the march, arrives and attacks the town, forcing the Lord of Purush-khanda, 'Enlil's Favourite', into submission. He stays long enough – three years – to ensure that the local ruler hence-forth recognizes his duties to his imperial overlord.

This tale being literature rather than history, the adventure is hardly likely to be true, if for no better reason than that Sargon's absence from his capital for three years would certainly have led to his loss of the throne. Yet it confirms that Akkadian emperors were not thought reluctant to support even their most distant trading colonies by military action.

The conquest of an empire is not merely another stage in the continuous saga of territorial aggrandizement, a natural progression from village chief, to town mayor, to city governor, to state king, to emperor. One can readily acknowledge, if not share, the desire of a man or woman to be the leader of his or her own people. No very great psychological step is needed to move from being first among equals, to Lugal, Big Man, and then to monarch. Nor is it hard to appreciate the attraction to any person subject to humanity's usual foibles, follies and weaknesses, of having the power of life and death over fellow-beings and of bathing in the respect, adoration and adulation inevitably directed towards the figure who represents and symbolizes the collective citizenry and at the same time acts as the earthbound agent of the real sovereign, the city god. It is another matter to want to move beyond your own kind and not just beat the inhabitants of foreign lands into submission, forcing them to pay generous tribute, as had been done so many times before, but rather to include them among your followers and put yourself at their head. Now you are no longer leader merely of your own people but of a mixed multitude. To take that step demands a new way of seeing yourself, one that underplays your particular origin and your service to your particular god, and that makes much more of your individual and personal qualities, irrespective of your original language or culture. To be an emperor, in other words, is to be out on your own, no longer among your own kind. That demands a certain kind of heroic self-sufficiency.

So it was that when Sargon established his empire, he recognized that he could never detach himself from all the encumbrances of traditional kingship and from deference to Zababa, god of Kish, without moving away and creating for himself a new centre, a new capital: a city associated neither with Semites nor Sumerians; a city founded, not by a god, like all others, but by the Emperor Sargon himself. The new capital was called Agade in Sumerian, and Akkad in Semitic. From the city Akkad was derived the name of the entire northern, Semitic-speaking, part of the alluvial plain, Akkad; its variety of the Semitic language, Akkadian; and the name of its people, Akkadians.

That is not to say that Sargon ignored the divine powers. He chose to put himself under the protection of Ishtar, descendant of the prehistoric Great Goddess, model for Greek Aphrodite and Latin Venus, who had, like other divinities of southern Mesopotamia, Enki and Ea of the sweet waters, Nanna and Sin of the moon, Utu and Shamash of the sun, fused with her Sumerian equivalent, in this case Inanna. Her composite powers over war and love, fighting and procreation, aggression and lust, made her the 'adrenaline goddess', deity of fight, flight and frolic, the perfect heavenly dominatrix and protectress for a Bronze Age warrior hero.

What luck that we may well have an image of the remarkable man who achieved all this. And since the sculpture found by Thompson and Mallowan could well have been modelled during Sargon's own lifetime – he reigned for more than fifty years – it might even be a good likeness, if a flattering one. (One would imagine that it had better have been, at least from the point of view of the health and safety of the sculptor.)

Yet the head was found seriously damaged, and that damage was not the result of excavation but had already been inflicted in ancient times. Nor was it accidental. Most apparent at first glance is what happened to the eyes. The inlay that once represented the pupil, perhaps with precious stone, is gone from both, but while the loss on the right side looks natural, associated with the corrosion blemishing the otherwise smooth copper surface, the eye on the left has obviously been purposefully extirpated in an attack with a sharp chisel. It may be significant that only one eye was mutilated in this way. In addition, the head's ears have been sheared off, also apparently with chisel blows, the tip of the nose and its bridge have been attacked and damaged, and the ends of the beard broken off. To be sure, all this could just possibly have occurred accidentally in the course of the sacking of the city and its temples. But, given that Nineveh was overcome in 612 BCE by Medes in alliance with Babylonians, these particular disfigurements cannot help but bring to mind the horrific mutilations imposed on Median rebels that Persian Emperor Darius the Great bragged about in his rock-inscribed autobiography at Behistun in Iran less than a hundred years later. For example, a certain Fravatish, who claimed the throne of Medea in 522 BCE, and whose insurrection took Darius several months to suppress: 'Fravatish was taken and brought unto me. I cut off his nose, his ears, and his tongue, and I put out one eye, and he was kept in fetters at my palace entrance, and all the people beheld him. Then I crucified him in Hagmataneh [Ecbatana].' Here too both ears were cut off, the nose and one eye. The strong implication is that the damage to the copper figure was purposeful and symbolic: the desecration of a revered national hero's sacred image, an attack on the pride of the defeated nation, an expression of contempt for the traditions and beliefs of the Assyrian Ninevites.

If such is the case, it tells us that for at least 1,500 years after his death, Sargon the Great, founder of the Akkadian Empire around 2230 BCE, was regarded as a semi-sacred figure, the patron saint of all subsequent empires in the Mesopotamian realm. Indeed, two much later kings, one who ruled Assyria around 1900 BCE and the other at the end of the eighth century BCE, adopted his official name, or rather title, Sargon, Legitimate King, as if to steal a bit of his thunder for themselves.

That the fame, honour and glory, of an individual ruler should remain unblemished and untarnished for a millennium and a half is already quite extraordinary. Even more that his legend should still have the power to impress, after 4,000 years.

She Set Me in a Basket of Rushes

During his rather absurd International Babylon Festival in 1990, Saddam Hussein celebrated his birthday. According to *Time* magazine, 'few birthday parties could match the spectacle staged by the Iraqi President Saddam Hussein for his 53rd last month. Saddam invited Cabinet members, prominent government officials and diplomats to his home village of Tikrit for lavish festivities that included a two-hour parade and banners proclaiming 'Your Candles, Saddam, Are Torches For All The Arabs'.

The festivities came to a climax when a wooden cabin was wheeled out and large crowds dressed in ancient Sumerian, Akkadian, Babylonian and Assyrian costume prostrated themselves in front of it. The doors opened to reveal a palm tree from which fifty-three white doves flew up into the sky. Beneath them a baby Saddam, reposing in a basket, came floating down a marsh-bordered stream.

Time magazine's reporter was particularly struck by the baby-in-a-basket theme, describing it as 'Moses redux'. But why on earth would Saddam Hussein wish to compare himself to a leader of the Jews? The journalist was missing the point. The motif was a Mesopotamian invention long before the Hebrews took it up and applied it to Moses. The Iraqi dictator was alluding to a much more ancient and, to him, far more glorious precedent. He was associating himself with Sargon, representing himself as a successor to the most famous ancient Semitic emperor of all.

An extraordinary hero needed an extraordinary story of origin. In the Sumerian 'Sargon Legend' – written down a thousand years after the time of which it tells, though still long before the era usually ascribed to Moses – the great man speaks with his own voice:

> *My mother was a priestess, I did not know my father.*
> *My father's kin live out on the steppeland.*
> *My city is Azupiranu, on the banks of the Euphrates.*
> *My priestess mother conceived me, in secret she bore me.*
> *She set me in a basket of rushes and sealed my lid with bitumen.*

She cast me into the river which rose over me.
The river bore me up and carried me to Akki, the drawer of water.
Akki, the drawer of water, took me as his son and reared me.
Akki, the drawer of water, appointed me as his gardener.
While I was a gardener, [the goddess] Ishtar granted me her love.

There had been Mesopotamian heroes before of course. The famous kings of early Uruk, like Gilgamesh and his father Lugalbanda, were the protagonists of a series of fantastical accounts and tales of outlandish deeds that became mainstays of the Sumerian literary canon and were copied and recopied in scribal schools and palace scriptoria for centuries, sometimes millennia. But they belong to the age of mythology rather than heroic legend; they told of intimate intercourse with the gods, battles with fearful monsters, the search for immortality and extraordinary other-worldly adventures. With the advent of Sargon, his sons and grandsons, the tales become, not necessarily more believable, but at least centred on the here-and-now of earthly life.

Unlike the Sumerian literature of myth, copied by scribes and students innumerable times, the Akkadian texts dealing with the lives of their rulers are few in number. Only pieces of six documents relating to Sargon have so far been unearthed, all late copies, and another six that tell of his grandson Naram-Sin. Most read like dictation taken down as a record of an oral performance. From these fragments, many inscribed at least a millennium after the events they relate, we may guess that bards and other popular entertainers went on performing epic tales about Sargon and his dynasty for centuries after his lifetime. These tell of their protagonists' heroic prowess at arms, of their religious piety, of their overriding concern for personal worth and honour; of their boldly doing what no man had done before, and boldly going where no man had gone before: 'Now any king who wants to call himself my equal,' Sargon challenges his successors, 'wherever I went, let him go too!'

Yet at the same time, the great kings can be shown in a very human light. In a composition known as Naram-Sin and the Enemy Hordes, after disobeying the will of the gods and consequently losing a long series of battles, the king sinks into Shakespearean introspection.

I became confused. I was bewildered.
I despaired. I groaned, I grieved. I grew faint.
Thus I thought: 'What has god brought upon my reign?
I am a king who has not kept his land prosperous,
And a shepherd who has not kept his people.
Upon myself and my reign, what have I brought?'

As one scholar, Joan Westenholz, has pointed out, this last line is tantamount to declaring 'The fault, dear Brutus, is not in our stars, but in ourselves,' a remarkable insight for a Bronze Age hero nearly 2,000 years before the birth of philosophy in ancient Greece.

The poet Hesiod, who may have lived around 700 BCE and shares with Homer the title of founder of Greek – and therefore European – literature, was the first to realize that the appearance of such heroes was related to the era we know as the Bronze Age. Not that he meant the same thing by that name as we do. For him the Bronze Age had nothing to do with technology but was merely the third stage in his story of the decline of humanity through its Golden, Silver, Bronze and Iron Ages. In *Works and Days*, he wrote that after the Gold and Silver Ages,

> ... *Zeus the Father made a third generation of mortal men, a brazen race, sprung from ash-trees; and it was in no way equal to the silver age, but was terrible and strong. They loved the lamentable works of Ares [god of savagery and bloodshed] and deeds of violence; they ate no bread, but were hard of heart like adamant, fearful men. Great was their strength and unconquerable the arms which grew from their shoulders on their strong limbs. Their armour was of bronze, and their houses of bronze, and of bronze were their implements: there was no black iron.*

However, as a kind of addendum, Hesiod here interpolated another contrasting time, which did not fit into the metallic pattern of the others, an age

> ... *which was nobler and more righteous, a god-like race of hero–men who are called demi-gods, the race before our own, throughout the boundless earth. Grim war and dread battle destroyed a part of them... but to the*

others father Zeus the son of Kronos gave a living and an abode apart from men, and made them dwell at the ends of earth. And they live untouched by sorrow in the islands of the blessed along the shore of deep swirling Ocean, happy heroes for whom the grain-giving earth bears honey-sweet fruit flourishing thrice a year, far from the deathless gods.

Honour and glory were the watchwords of this breed of men. They craved neither luxury nor fortune, but fame and adulation. They dominated their people by a new governing principle. Those led by heroes of such greatness followed them neither out of fear, nor out of love, and certainly not out of confidence in the excellence and efficiency of their administration, but in awe of their heroism and bedazzled by their splendour, craving to bathe, if but for a few moments, in whatever beams of reflected glory might chance to fall their way.

Of course Hesiod was not writing history but poetry, recording not fact but myth. Yet he did somehow hit upon a connection between the age of bronze and an age of heroes that stands up to closer scrutiny. Across most of the societies whose early times we have been able to study through archaeology and literature, in Mesopotamia, Europe and Asia, we do find that an age of heroes corresponds to the high tide of the Bronze Age, the age when the deployment of metal replaced the use of stone for tools and weapons. As elsewhere, Mesopotamia seems to prefigure the much later developments of further west.

The scholar Paul Treherne has pointed to a profound change in the masculine self-image in Europe during the Bronze Age. Grooming items like tweezers and razors appear among grave goods as never before. These are evidence, he suggests, for an increasing sense of the individual, and a new emphasis on masculine bodily ornament. This in turn he associates with the glorification of warfare and the hunt, with the ritual consumption of alcohol, and a cult of 'the warrior's beauty'. All point towards the establishment of a new male warrior class with high social status. In Greece, this was the age Homer wrote of in his account of the Trojan War and his descriptions of its heroes like Achilles. 'The Homeric, like the later Spartan, Celtic, or Frankish warrior,' writes Treherne, reminding us of the sculpted head of Sargon with its elaborate coiffure, 'grew his hair long and delighted in its grooming.'

This elite class could not appear in society while stone technology was still the mainstream. Stone is an egalitarian material. Even the special varieties needed for tool-making are found widely distributed, and by long tradition going right back to the beginning of the genus *Homo*, each household made its own tools. There were always, no doubt, specialists who excelled at the manufacture of particular items, but in the main, making stone tools was seen as a private, domestic activity.

The introduction of metal-working changed all that. The materials needed, copper ore and tinstone, are rare and may have to be brought – found, traded for and transported – great distances. Many years of training are needed to master the craft of the bronze-smith. Working with metal requires elaborate and expensive equipment. This is no household occupation but a professional specialism that only relatively few could undertake. The products of the bronze-smith would, at least at first, have been very costly, available only to the wealthiest. And if the original use for bronze was the manufacture of weapons, as it probably was, those who controlled the technology, organized the transport and paid the armourers, soon acquired monopoly power.

Moreover there is little glory or heroism to be gained in fighting with Stone Age arms. It is hard to display detached insouciance and effortless superiority while brawling with a spear, a mace or even a flint dagger. Victory in a Stone Age battle is often a collective achievement, dependent largely on numbers and momentum. But bronze technology makes possible the sword, the close-quarter weapon *par excellence*, which raises man-to-man combat above the level of crude, inelegant and brutish rough-and-tumble. Armed with swords, warriors no longer form an indistinguishable mass, but each stands out as an individual fighter, placing himself a pace or so from his opponent and, rather than grappling hand to hand, or laying about him like a wild beast with club or axe, he skilfully trades precisely aimed and calculated thrusts, parries, lunges and ripostes. Fighting like this can be, and long has been, treated as an art with its own aesthetic.

Add to bronze weapons another important addition to the warrior's equipment, which now also appears for the first time in the texts and the images: the horse, probably first tamed and domesticated some time early in the third millennium BCE by the nomads of the steppe that stretches like a sea of grass from the Ukraine right across to Mongolia. What look very much like horses with riders on their backs begin to appear on cylinder-seal images around the time Sargon was establishing his empire.

How useful a horse would have been to a Bronze Age fighter is a moot point. Without saddles or stirrups – the latter not to be invented for another 2,000 years – it is hard to retain a secure seat in the heat of battle. In any case, at this stage of history, a horse would have been an exotic and rare prize – expensive to acquire, costly of upkeep. What must have appealed most to the heroic warrior is what has been called the horse's 'arch-necked pride'. A slightly later Sumerian king, Shulgi of the Ur III dynasty, compared himself approvingly to 'a horse of the highway that swishes his tail'.

Naturally, the changes brought about by the introduction of bronze and horses took time to work their effects. The new ideas, however powerful their impact on society, would have taken many generations to be accepted as entirely respectable or even admissible. Swords do not figure on sculptures or cylinder-seal designs until long after they must have become commonplace on the battlefield. Centuries later, the King of Mari, the city-state on the upper Euphrates in today's Syria, was reproved for publicly riding a horse, a sweaty, smelly beast, an insult to the dignity of the monarchy and an unwelcome reminder of the monarch's barbarian, semi-nomadic origins: 'May my lord honour his kingship. You may be King of the Haneans, but you are also King of the Akkadians. May my Lord not ride horses; let him ride either in a chariot or on a *kudanu*-mule so as to bring honour upon his kingship.'

And just as those commemorative statues of nineteenth-century generals usually show them with swords hanging from their belts, although they actually fought in the era of battlefield firearms, so the work of ancient Mesopotamian art that most explicitly expresses the new heroic mood of the age represents its central figure bearing traditional Stone Age weaponry, with nary a horse or a sword in sight.

Around 1120 BCE King Shutruk-Nakh-khunte of Elam, the state in the south-west of Iran, invaded Babylonian territory and, like many another victorious leader since, ordered many priceless works of art to be shipped back to his capital city Susa. Among them was a stele of pink sandstone, about 2 metres high – now slightly broken at the top as well as frustratingly eroded, but probably still intact when looted from Sippar, city of the sun god. It had been commissioned more than a thousand years earlier, by Naram-Sin, Sargon's third successor and almost certainly his grandson. To many Assyriologists, this was the noblest Akkadian of them all, presiding over the empire during the decades when it reached its greatest geographical extent and could claim, from its own point of view, to have included 'the four quarters' of the world.

The stele commemorated Naram-Sin's victory over the Lullubi, a mountain people of the Zagros. Apart from the fact that this is an outstandingly successful work of art, with a claim to an honourable place in the list of humanity's greatest creations, even a brief glance shows how far we have come in the two centuries or so since the days of Sumerian kingship depicted on Eannatum's Stele of the Vultures.

Formal organization of the carved figures has been abandoned. On the Stele of the Vultures, as on other Sumerian sculptures like the Warka Vase, the surface is banded with horizontal registers, perhaps derived from the lines into which writing is divided, like a strip cartoon telling a story when viewed in the correct order. Here, by contrast, the entire surface carries a unified composition intended to express, as in a snapshot, Naram-Sin's moment of triumph. This is not a design but a picture.

The scene is of a wooded mountain region. Naram-Sin and his men are moving up a slope towards the peak. The king, armed with spear, bow and battle-axe, leads the way, followed by two standard-bearers and four or five other warriors. The Lullubi have been utterly defeated. Naram-Sin holds a heroic pose – he is larger than the other figures – while trampling two foemen under his feet. Two more of the fallen, one totally disarmed, the other with a broken spear, plead for their lives, while another, on the ground, struggles to pull an arrow from his neck, and two further tumble headlong over the edge of a precipice. Every fighter, whether among the victors or the vanquished, is portrayed as a separate individual rather than one of an indistinguishable collective.

On Eannatum's Stele of the Vultures, the largest, most important figure is that of the god Ningirsu, who is shown on one side of the monument holding the captured enemy forces in his great net. The text makes plain that the triumph is the god's; Eannatum is just his dutiful agent. On Naram-Sin's stele, victory belongs to the king. To be sure, the gods

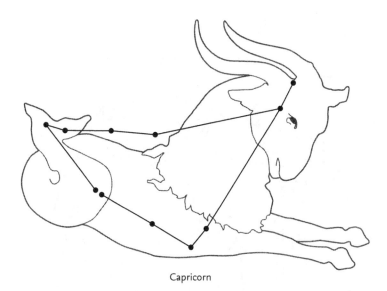

Capricorn

Capricornus, the Sea-Goat, one of the very earliest named signs of the zodiac. It was anciently associated with Enki, also known as Ea, the god of civilization. The constellation is best seen on a northern autumn evening, when it lies above the southern horizon.

two	temple
sheep	
god	
Inanna	

The emergence of writing: a simple *aide mémoire* from about 3100 BCE, one of the texts found in the archaic levels of the Eanna temple district of ancient Uruk. The clay tablet is shown on the left and its translation on the right.

Akkadian seal impression showing horse rider, from Kish, 2350–2200 BCE.

Cylinder seal impression showing horse rider, 2100–1800 BCE.

The Tower of Babel (Great Ziggurat of Babylon),
plan and elevation, from the eroded stele.

As the Great Ziggurat of Babylon may have originally looked.

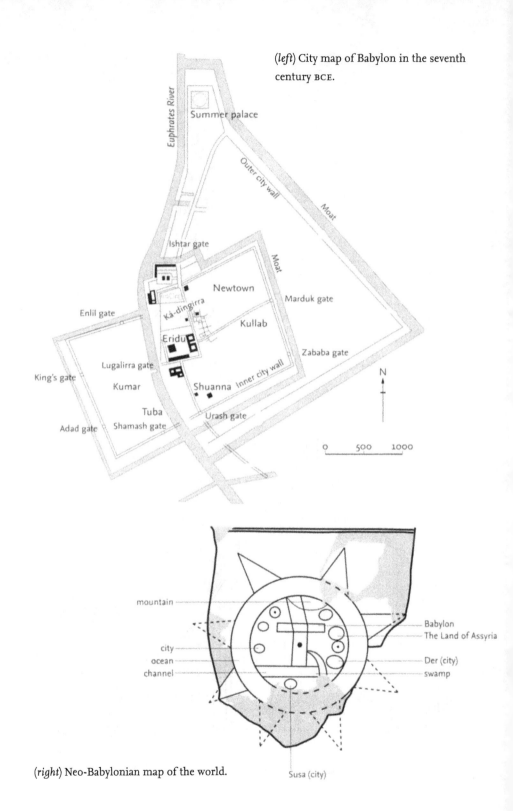

(left) City map of Babylon in the seventh century BCE.

Euphrates River

Summer palace

Outer city wall

Moat

Ishtar gate

Newtown

Marduk gate

Ka-dingirra

Enlil gate

Kullab

Moat

Eridu

Zababa gate

Lugalirra gate

King's gate

Shuanna

Inner city wall

Kumar

N

Tuba

Urash gate

Adad gate

Shamash gate

0   500   1000

mountain

Babylon
The Land of Assyria

city

ocean

Der (city)

channel

swamp

Susa (city)

(right) Neo-Babylonian map of the world.

Early Cuneiform Signs

At the earliest stage of the development of writing, the signs were simple drawings:

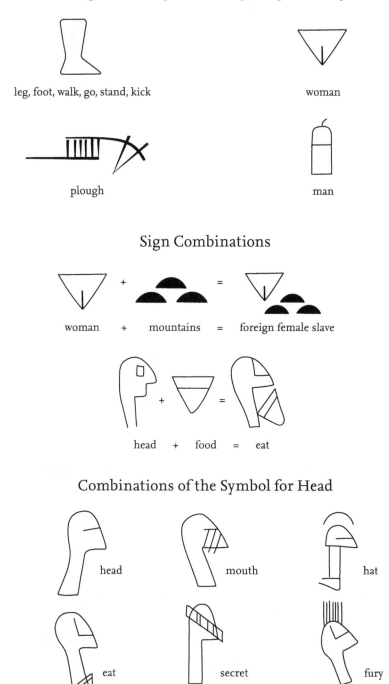

leg, foot, walk, go, stand, kick

woman

plough

man

Sign Combinations

woman + mountains = foreign female slave

head + food = eat

Combinations of the Symbol for Head

head

mouth

hat

eat

secret

fury

(*right*) As writing developed further and a pointed drawing stylus was replaced by a reed of triangular cross section, the signs became more schematic:

head · tongue · whistle
food · silence · beard
mouth · drink · pray
secret · thirst · mirror
hat · chew · above

Over the centuries the signs were further simplified until it was no longer easily possible to recognize what they originally represented:

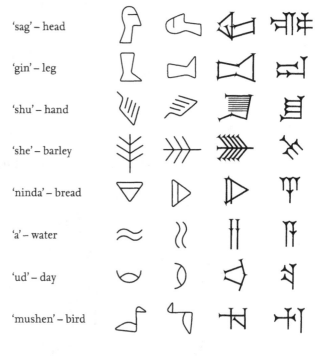

'sag' – head
'gin' – leg
'shu' – hand
'she' – barley
'ninda' – bread
'a' – water
'ud' – day
'mushen' – bird

3200 BCE   3000 BCE   2400 BCE   1000 BCE

'The beautiful cow to whom the moon god in the form of a strong bull sent healing oil': A late Assyrian hymn to Ishtar still expresses adoration of the Great Goddess's sacred herd, as shown on a temple frieze from Al 'Ubaid, built before 4000 BCE.

Homo Ludens: Sumerian pull-along toy from the fourth millennium BCE, dug up from the sands of the ancient city of Eshnunna, now Tell al-Asmar.

The first form of printing: Uruk era stamp seal and its impression, dating from the fourth millennium BCE.

Gods and goddesses disporting themselves in a landscape of rivers and mountains: Enki, Inanna and other deities depicted on a Sumerian cylinder seal from around 3000 BCE.

are still there; but represented as no more than two stars in the sky. Now, Naram-Sin is himself wearing the horned helmet that represents divinity. This is no aberration. At some point during his reign, the king's name came always to be preceded in written documents by the determinative DINGIR, the cuneiform sign that looks like a star and indicates that the following word refers to a god. It would seem that Naram-Sin had himself deified in the course of his rule. 'Naram-Sin the strong, King of Akkad', explains a text of unknown date,

> when the four quarters were all hostile to him, remained victorious in nine battles in a single year, because of the love Ishtar bore for him, and took captive those kings who had risen against him.
>
> Because he had been able to preserve his city in a time of crisis, his city asked from Ishtar in Eanna [here follows a long list of other city deities]... that he be the god of their city Akkad. And they built a temple for him in the centre of Akkad.

Of course this tells us nothing of what the deification of their ruler could possibly have meant to the inhabitants of his empire, but at the very least, we must recognize that a momentous change has taken place in the relationship between heaven and earth, between gods and people.

Up until now, civilization based itself upon the belief that humanity was created by gods for their own purposes. The cities, the repositories of civilization, were divine foundations, having started, we guess, as sacred pilgrimage centres. Each city was the creation and home of a particular god. It is as if 'real life' was the one lived by the gods in the divine realm while what went on down here on earth was a largely irrelevant sideshow.

The age of Sargon and Naram-Sin altered all that, switched the focus to the human world, and introduced a new conception of the meaning of the universe: one that made people rather than gods the principal subjects of the Mesopotamian story. Humanity was now in control. Men – and women – became rulers of their own destiny. To be sure, people were still pious, still presented sacrifices to the temples, offered the libations, performed the rites, invoked the gods' names at every opportunity. But the piety of the age now had a quite different flavour. When Sargon appointed his own daughter to the position of En-Priestess, perhaps the equivalent of managing director or CEO, of the temple of the moon god Nanna at Ur, mother-house of all moon temples, she brought an element of Bronze Age heroic style into the practice of religion itself. Even here the focus shifted from heaven to earth, from the gods to their worshippers. Sargon's daughter made herself the first identifiable author in history, and the first to express a personal relationship between herself and her god.

Zirru Priestess of the god Nanna

While the language of Sargon's court in the northern part of the alluvial plain was Semitic, and his daughter surely would have had a Semitic birthname, on moving to Ur, the very heartland of Sumerian culture, she took a Sumerian official title: Enheduana – 'En' (Chief Priest or Priestess); 'hedu' (ornament); 'Ana' (of heaven.). She moved into the Giparu at Ur, an extensive and labyrinthine religious complex, containing temple, quarters for the clergy, dining and kitchen and bathroom areas, as well as a cemetery where En-priestesses were buried – though some were interred under the floors of their houses. Records suggest that offerings continued to be made to these dead priestesses. That one of the most striking artefacts, physical proof of Enheduana's existence, was found in a layer dateable to many centuries after her lifetime, makes it likely that she in particular was remembered and honoured long after the fall of the dynasty that had appointed her to the management of the temple.

The evidence is an alabaster disc, unearthed broken by Leonard Woolley in 1926. On the back is inscribed: 'Enheduana, Zirru Priestess of the god Nanna, wife of the god Nanna, child of Sargon, King of Kish… made an altar and named it "Dais, Table of Heaven".' On the front, as restored from the separate pieces found by the excavators, a low relief strip mimicking the impression of a cylinder-seal shows the great lady herself, dressed in a pleated woollen gown and engaged in her religious duties, standing behind a naked, shaven-headed priest who is pouring a libation. To her right stand two further figures, one bearing a wand and another carrying a handled jug or ritual basket. She raises her right hand in a devotional gesture. The expression on her face, shown in profile, is stern. Her nose is fleshy.

Also found in the rubble were seals and seal impressions otherwise confirming her time at the temple, identifying among others 'Adda, Estate Manager of Enheduana', 'O Enheduanna, child of Sargon, Sagadu the scribe is your servant', and, charmingly, 'Ilum Palilis, hairdresser to Enheduana, child of Sargon' – though ownership of a hugely expensive item like a lapis-lazuli cylinder-seal means that this was probably the supervisor of the palace wig and make-up department.

Sitting in her chamber, or perhaps her office, for the director of an enterprise as large and prestigious as the Nanna temple of Ur must surely have been afforded the very best working arrangements, her hair beautifully coiffed by Ilum Palilis and staff, dictating to her scribe, perhaps the very Sagadu whose seal Woolley found, Enheduanna proceeded to make her permanent mark on history by composing, in her own name, a series of more than forty extraordinary liturgical works, which were copied and recopied for nearly 2,000 years.

Her compositions, though only rediscovered in modern times, remained models of petitionary prayer for even longer. Through the Babylonians, they influenced and inspired the prayers and psalms of the Hebrew Bible and the Homeric hymns of Greece. Through them, faint echoes of Enheduana, the first named literary author in history, can even be heard in the hymnody of the early Christian church.

Her most all-embracing composition, known as the Sumerian Temple Hymns, is a sequence of forty-two relatively short verses apostrophizing each of the temples of the land of Sumer in sequence:

> O Isin, city founded by the god An [god of the sky]
> which he has built on an empty plain!
> Your exterior is mighty, your interior artfully built,
> your divine powers are those which An has decreed.
> O low dais which Enlil loves,
> O place where An and Enlil determine all destinies,
> where the great gods dine, filled with great awesomeness and terror...
> Your lady, the great healer of the Land,
> Nininsina, the daughter of An,
> has erected a house in your precinct, O house of Isin,
> and taken her seat upon your dais.

City by city is addressed in this way, each described in turn with appropriate details. Only at the end of the series do we receive what may be a faint hint of the purpose of the entire exercise: that the task of writing these hymns may well have been undertaken as part of Sargon's imperial policy, to help unify his lands, with their multitudes of different gods, into a single confessional community. In a line that carries more than an echo of her father Sargon's self-presentation as ground-breaking hero, the High Priestess announces to him: 'The compiler of the tablets was Enheduana. My King, something has been created here that no one has ever created before.'

It is in Enheduana's greatest masterpiece that the new religious spirit of the heroic age is most clearly expressed: a long prayer to Inanna, known from its first words as 'Nin-me-sara', 'Lady of all the *Me*' – 'Nin' signifying Lady; '*Me*' being those principles of civilization that Inanna famously extorted from their guardian Enki; and 'sara' here meaning 'all'. Sargon's daughter chooses not to address her own lord and official husband, the moon god Nanna, but her father's patron and supporter Inanna, the resplendent warrior goddess whom he called Ishtar.

If only we could translate adequately into modern language the ancient Sumerian, with all the richness of multiple meanings and readings that cuneiform writing makes both possible and inevitable, this passionate address by a priestess to the goddess Inanna would be prized among the jewels of word literature. Unfortunately we can only know it by its content rather than its artistry. For example, the astonishing barrage of praise and adulation with which the prayer begins, some forty lines in which every conceivable aspect of the goddess's appearance, powers and acts are described and lauded, starts with 'Lady of all the *Me*, rising in resplendent light...' Dr Annette Zgoll, its most recent translator, points out that the cuneiform also has the sense of 'Queen of countless battles, rising as a raging storm...' Yet even if the beauty of the writing is beyond our grasp, what it expresses is quite clear: an entirely new relationship between priestess and goddess.

Sumerian worshippers had always humbled and abased themselves before the gods, as slaves grovel before their owners. Enheduana wishes to be taken seriously and demands recognition. She may be no more than a human being but she expects Inanna to listen to her. She argues with the goddess and tries to persuade her to act, reminding her of the usual fate of those who refuse to recognize Inanna's authority.

> *Lady supreme over the foreign lands,*
> *who can take anything from your territory?*
> *... Their great gateways are set afire.*
> *Blood pours into their rivers because of you...*
> *They lead their troops all together captive before you,...*
> *Tempests have filled the dancing-places of their cities.*

And contrasts her own continuing devoted service.

> *Wise and sage lady of all the foreign lands,*
> *life-force of the teeming people:*
> *I will recite your holy song!...*
> *Deep-hearted, good woman with a radiant heart,*
> *I will enumerate your divine powers.*
> *I, En-hedu-ana the En-Priestess,*
> *entered my holy Giparu in your service.*

But something seems to have gone badly wrong with Enheduana's incumbency at Ur. A rebellious city leader of Uruk called Lugal-Ane, whom we know from other sources to have led a revolt against Sargon's grandson Naram-Sin, has, for good measure, expelled the King's aunt from the Giparu.

> *... Funeral offerings were brought,*
> *as if I had never lived there.*
> *I approached the light, but the light scorched me.*
> *I approached the shade, but I was covered with a storm.*
> *My honeyed mouth became scummed.*

Enheduana insists that her fate be reported to An, god of the sky.

> *Tell An about Lugal-Ane and my fate!*
> *May An undo it for me!*
> *As soon as you tell An about it, An will release me.*

For Lugal-Ane has shown himself to be impious and unworthy of the gods' support.

Lugal-Ane has altered everything.
He has removed An from the E-Ana temple.
He has not stood in awe of the greatest deity.
He has turned that temple,
whose attractions were inexhaustible,
whose beauty was endless,
into a scene of destruction.

As for Enheduana herself, her fate is lamentable:

He stood there in triumph and drove me out of the temple.
He made me fly like a swallow from the window;
my life-strength is exhausted.
He made me walk through the thorn bushes of the mountains.
He stripped me of the rightful crown of the En-Priestess.
He gave me a knife and dagger,
saying 'These are now the appropriate ornaments for you.'

In the end, it seems that Lugal-Ane was indeed brought to heel and Enheduana was restored to her rightful place in the Giparu. The goddess's reward for her assistance is unstinting praise:

My lady beloved of An,
may your heart be calmed towards me,
the brilliant En-Priestess of Nanna!
It must be known! It must be known!...
Be it known that you are lofty as the heavens!
Be it known that you are broad as the earth!
Be it known that you destroy the rebel lands!
Be it known that you roar at the foreign lands!
Be it known that you crush heads!
Be it known that you devour corpses like a dog!
Be it known that your gaze is terrible!
Be it known that you lift your terrible gaze!
Be it known that you have flashing eyes!
Be it known that you are unshakeable and unyielding!
Be it known that you always stand triumphant!

Broadened Horizons

History usually records only the personalities and the acts of the great and the good – or of the very bad. It is much harder to discover how the ordinary middling citizens of one of the Akkadian Empire's flourishing cities may have experienced this brave and heroic new Bronze Age world.

We can make some reasonable guesses. This must have been a highly militarized society, with armed warriors often seen patrolling the streets, particularly in provincial cities, on whose loyalty the centre could not always depend. Sargon wrote that every day 5,400 men, perhaps the nucleus of a standing army, took their meal before him in Akkad. More terrifying to the inhabitants would have been the insurrections and rebellions that frequently broke out, with patriotic city leaders attempting to shake off imperial rule, as when Sargon's son Rimush faced revolts by a King of Ur and four other cities. In every case, the uprisings were ruthlessly put down. Naram-Sin 'was victorious in nine battles in a single year': what these insurgencies cost the innocent urban population is not recorded; loss of life and property must often have been grievous.

But no empire can survive without the support or at least the silent assent of a large proportion of the population. There were compensations for the burdens of imperial rule. Citizens of the core territories of Sumer and Akkad would certainly have recognized that their horizons had been immeasurably broadened. Valuables, goods and materials from the entire wider region poured in. Ships from as far afield as Bahrain (in Akkadian, Dilmun), Oman (Magan), and even the Indus (Meluhha) docked at Akkad's quaysides and unloaded their treasures; foreign mariners speaking in strange accents thronged the streets near the harbours. Barges laden to the gunwales with grain from distant rain-watered farms far beyond the alluvial plain daily arrived in the harbour, unshipped their cargoes, and were promptly dismantled, the wood destined for recycling in expansive local building projects. Sargon even claimed to have crossed 'the western sea', the Mediterranean – a boast one easily dismisses until reminded that a seal inscribed with the name 'Apil-Ishtar, son of Ilu-bani, servant of the Divine Naram-Sin' was found on Cyprus in the 1870s.

The economic system had probably changed little from the mixed market practice of earlier times. The emperors may have held supreme power, but they chose to follow established custom and law. When they sought land to distribute to their followers and supporters, the sales may well have been forced and the sellers put under duress, but the palace did pay. An inscribed black diorite pillar from the reign of Sargon's son Manishtushu records the purchase of several large estates, totalling a little less than one and a half square miles, which apparently cost the monarch the going rate in silver, plus an additional sum for the buildings, and a gift of jewellery and clothing for the goodwill. To keep everyone onside the king also apparently entertained – 'caused to eat' – 190 workmen, five officials of a district called Moon God City, Dur-Sin, and forty-nine officials of the capital Akkad, including governors, a chief minister, a divination priest, a temple soothsayer, three scribes, a barber, a cup-bearer, as well as the king's nephew, and two sons of Surushkin, governor of Umma.

Taxes were levied, of course, to pay for all this and an expanding bureaucracy and a burgeoning artisan class. Akkadian hero culture valued civilization as highly as war, recognizing that the softer arts were essential for maintaining peace and order across their domains. Bronze Age warriors loved poetry. We can be sure that bards, balladeers, musicians and entertainers were welcome at court, particularly if they sang of the ruler's heroic deeds. Such productions were evanescent, but we know that other arts and crafts were encouraged, judging by the heights reached in architectural design, stone sculpture and metalwork. Alas, precious metals are always fated to be recycled, so hardly any Akkadian jewellery has been recovered. But the lack is partly compensated for by the profusion of cylinder-seals unearthed by archaeologists, which show Akkadian seal-cutters to have reached standards of almost unrivalled perfection in both design and execution. As Marc van de Mieroop, Professor of Ancient Near Eastern Studies at Columbia University, has put it: 'The impression one obtains from the material remains of this period is one of skill, attention to detail and artistic talent.'

At the same time, the first steps were taken to put in order the chaotic Sumerian mensuration system. Until Akkadian times each city had fiercely defended its own systems of weights and measures, as well as ways of recording them – and to add to the confusion, different numbering systems, using different bases, were used for different items and commodities. Now universal measures of length, area, dry and liquid capacity, and weight were introduced, units which would remain standard for over a thousand years. Official year names were prescribed:

The year when Sargon went to Simurrum.
The year when Naram-Sin conquered...
and felled cedars on Mount Lebanon.
The year after the year when
Shar-kali-shari went down to Sumer for the first time.

Perhaps the most important and historically significant change imposed by Akkadian rulers was the use in official documents of their Semitic language, which we can now properly call Akkadian, although Sumerian continued to be used to the very end of Mesopotamian history as a scholarly and religious language. Sargon and his descendants had no intention of replacing southern Mesopotamian culture, but rather of gaining glory by enhancing it.

Cuneiform script had for some time been extending its range to record Semitic as well as Sumerian speech. To the untutored eye the cuneiform looks much the same. But the new official status of written Akkadian brings into focus an additional layer of complexity added to an already difficult system. The Sumerian meanings of the signs were not replaced but ran in parallel with their Akkadian equivalents. So each could be read as a Sumerian word or words, or alternatively their phonetic values; it could equally well be read as the equivalent Akkadian word or words, or alternatively their phonetic values. The sign that looks like a star could remain silent, only signifying that the next word referred to a divinity, or it could be read as God or Heaven, in Sumerian DINGIR or AN, *shamum* or *ilum* in Akkadian; it could also be used to represent just the sounds of those words.

This makes deciphering cuneiform something of a headache for today's scholars, but was presumably much clearer to those whose native languages these were. In any case there seems to have been in ancient times a hierarchy among scribes, and those who specialized in practical tasks did not need to know or understand the more arcane complexities of the system. To ensure uniformity, a standardized style of writing the signs, an economical and elegant 'old Akkadian hand', was taught in scribal schools across the region, from the highlands of Iran to the headwaters of the Tigris and Euphrates in Anatolia to the shores of the Mediterranean. And through the spread of this formalized script the Akkadian language became the lingua franca of the entire Near East, remaining so until the rise of Aramaic a thousand or more years later.

Thus did the Akkadian Empire, anticipating Shakespeare's Julius Caesar, bestride the narrow world of the Fertile Crescent like a colossus: militarily, economically, culturally and linguistically. In spite of regular uprisings, insurrections and insurgencies, Sargon and his descendants, Bronze Age heroes all, maintained a tight hold for more than a century, spreading Sumerian–Akkadian civilization over the entire Mesopotamian plain, over the headwater valleys of the Tigris and Euphrates, as well as over the surrounding lands to the east, west, north and south. Or, as they themselves called the cardinal compass points: the directions of 'the wind from the mountains, the wind from the Amorites, the storm wind, and the wind of a ship sailing upstream'.

And yet this world of extraordinary promise was to disappear in the blink of an eye – or so it seems in the *longue durée* of historical perspective. Barbarians struggled for many centuries to drive Caesar's Roman Empire out of western Europe into its final redoubt in Constantinople. The Roman state's successor in Asia Minor, the Ottoman Empire, declined over two hundred years or so. Modern European empires collapsed in fewer than fifty. Sargon's empire seems to have utterly vanished in a fraction of that time.

Since 1979 a team from Yale University has been excavating at Tell Leilan in Syria, once called Shekhna. In Akkadian days this was a great provincial centre, commanding the Khabur River Valley between the upper Euphrates and Tigris Rivers. Even today the ancient walls rise in places to 15 metres above ground level. The archaeologists have been able to trace in considerable detail the rise of the ancient settlement and its incorporation into the Akkadian Empire when, provincial though it may have been, it became an imperial showpiece. A group of magnificent buildings stood on the acropolis, equipped with all facilities: grain silos, religious cult platform, school, bath-house, a huge fortified administrative office block, and in between, large areas of garden.

Right on the main street, opposite the schoolhouse, a massive building project was underway, which must have aimed at outshining all previous constructions. For in addition to the usual sun-dried and kiln-baked brick, the walls and foundations of this showpiece of Akkadian imperial power were to be of stone, 2 metres thick, dressed from great basalt boulders brought to the site from at least 40 kilometres away.

Construction was seemingly going well when, apparently overnight, all work suddenly stopped. The Yale excavators found that the foundations had been laid, the walls partially erected and rendered, when the workers abruptly downed tools and left. Dr Harvey Weiss, the leader of Yale group, reported that 'Several basalt boulders were situated to the south-east of the building near a partially built wall, abandoned several meters from its corner wall. These basalt boulders were in various stages of preparation, some already worked into usable blocks, some with visible chisel marks but not yet a usable shape, and some still unworked.' What is more, this sudden break in activity was matched by evidence that urban life had completely ceased everywhere else in the city too; Shekhna seems to have been totally abandoned, not to be reoccupied for several centuries.

Archaeologists working among the mounds and ruins of other parts of northern Mesopotamia also come upon a sudden end to the relics of civilization. Just above the level associated with the last incumbents of Sargon's dynasty was – nothing. Artefacts, potsherds, seals, written tablets – all absent. Signs of human occupation – all either vanished completely or severely reduced. At Tell Brak, another ancient foundation nearby, the urbanites had withdrawn to huddle in a quarter of the former area.

Something devastating had happened. But what? The Sumerian King List throws up its hands in despair. '157 are the years of the dynasty of Sargon. Then who was king? Who was not king? Irgigi was king, Imi was king, Nanum was king, Ilulu was king. The four of them ruled for only 3 years.' After that it seems the empire shrank to the area immediately around Akkad city, where independent sovereignty limped on for a while before being finally extinguished by a wave of barbarians from the hills.

The guilty party was named by the ancients as the Gutians, who swept down from the upper Diyala Valley leaving devastation in their wake. 'Kingship was taken to the hosts of Gutium who had no king,' says the King List. A later poetic lament, The Cursing of Agade, explains that the god 'Enlil brought out of the mountains those who do not resemble other people, who are not considered part of the Land, the Gutians, an unbridled people, with human intelligence but with the instincts of dogs and the appearance of monkeys.'

The catastrophe they visited on Akkad was merciless.

> *Nothing escaped their clutches, no one avoided their grasp. Messengers no longer travelled the highways, the courier's boat no longer passed along the rivers.... Prisoners manned the watch. Brigands occupied the highways. The doors of the city gates of the Land lay dislodged in mud, and all the foreign lands uttered bitter cries from the walls of their cities.*

Earlier historians, who habitually ascribed all cultural change to invasion and conquest, took this for history, and accepted as a matter of course that Sargon and Naram-Sin's empire had simply succumbed to overwhelming barbarian attack. But while there is good reason to believe that Akkadian imperial times were indeed followed by a decades-long or even century-long dark age, when uncivilized tribesmen ruled the roost in much of Mesopotamia, it seems very unlikely that the Gutians alone were able to overwhelm the empire by force of arms. Akkad had previously had little difficulty in resisting assault by much better organized enemies.

In line with their own world-view, the Mesopotamians themselves blamed the disaster on the gods' anger at the hubris of the emperors and their blasphemous practices. Nemesis had necessarily followed, and the gods had punished arrogance by altering the course of nature and causing starvation.

> *For the first time since cities were built and founded,*
> *Fields produced no grain,*
> *Water meadows produced no fish,*
> *Irrigated orchards produced neither syrup nor wine,*
> *The gathered clouds did not rain, the masgurum tree did not grow.*
> *At that time, one shekel's worth of oil was only a half-quart,*
> *One shekel's worth of grain was only a half-quart.... .*
> *Who slept on the roof, died on the roof,*
> *Who slept in the house, had no burial,*
> *People flailed themselves from hunger.*

Scholars regularly warn us that documents always say much more about the times when they were written than they do about the times they claim to describe. Since 'The Cursing of Agade' was set down long after the event, its account of widespread famine was never taken very seriously. But the Yale excavations at Tell Leilan suggest that there may have been rather more truth in the epic lament's details than was previously thought.

Analysis of a layer of soil nearly two feet thick, lying above the last vestiges of human occupation, showed nothing but fine wind-blown sand and dust, without even earthworm holes and insect tracks. This is the immediately recognisable signature of extreme drought – desertification. The same deathly blanket was found over an extended area around Tell Leilan and elsewhere. Researchers were able to detect similar change in undersea cores and land soundings right across the Middle East; what happened to Shekhna was no mere local event. The whole of northern Mesopotamia had simply dried up for about 300 years, 'the first time an abrupt climate change has been directly linked to the collapse of a thriving civilization,' noted Dr Weiss. 'Some time after 2200 BCE seasonal rains became scarce, and withering storms replaced them. They emptied out towns and villages, sending people stumbling south with pastoral nomads, to seek forage along rivers and streams. For more than a hundred years the desertification continued, disrupting societies from south-west Europe to Central Asia.' Crops and animals perished. People became destitute, starved and died. The transport of rain-watered grain to Akkad and the cities of the south ceased, putting Sumer itself under pressure to feed its masses. Thousands left their homes in the north and flooded the roads leading towards the ancient cities, compounding the problem. But with so much less rain making the great rivers themselves flow more slowly and more shallowly, irrigation became more difficult, and it proved impossible to produce enough food to make up for the losses in the north.

Climate change next unsettled the surrounding barbarian peoples, sending Hurrians, Gutians and Amorites pouring from all directions on to the plains, to grab what they could for survival's sake. Amid such turmoil, things fell apart, the centre could not hold. Mere anarchy was loosed upon the world. Who was king; who was not king?

It is far from difficult to imagine the suffering of the inhabitants of Shekhna and the other northern imperial possessions as their fields withered and their skeletal livestock died. We have seen enough similar disasters happen even in the twentieth century.

As might be expected, some scholars strongly disagree with the Yale University account of the fall of the Akkadian Empire, accusing Dr Weiss of exaggerating the significance of his findings, over-interpreting his results and taking ancient texts far too literally. But whether Akkad was destroyed by climate change, barbarian attack, population pressure, bureaucratic ossification, or any of the other reasons put forward to account for its remarkably sudden disappearance – or, indeed whether it was destroyed by a combination of some or all of these things – the fact is, it did collapse.

The political entity that Sargon and his descendants had created, the empire of Sumer and Akkad, was simply not robust enough to withstand all the pressures put upon it. The empire had extended its boundaries and stretched its resources to the ultimate possible limit. Though it had developed a bureaucracy and an improved accounting system far in advance of anything seen before, this was still an agrarian economy, a world where the fastest transport of goods was by donkey caravan and supplies could be carried no more than perhaps 25 kilometres a day. Without the necessary infrastructure, Akkad's ambitions had well exceeded its capacity to fulfil them.

If cities and civilizations are like machines, then it is tempting to see the Akkadian imperium like one of those fighter aircraft of mid-twentieth-century warfare, the Spitfire or the Messerschmitt 109, which owed their success and their dominance of the skies to the fact that they were designed to fly on the very borderlines of stability. When all was going well they were magnificent. When damaged in a vulnerable part, they would spin and crash to the ground. Other, more conservatively fashioned – and duller – planes could limp home even with wings and tail assemblies shot full of flak holes.

Once again, as it had been with the expansion of Uruk in the fourth millennium BCE, the most progressive society proved itself the most fragile. Once again, the more cautious and traditional way of life of the Sumerian cities in the southernmost areas of the Mesopotamian plain showed itself as more stable and more able to withstand the shocks that history brought its way.

The best known city ruler of this post-Akkadian interregnum, Gudea of

Lagash, was careful not to call himself Lugal, king, but merely Ensi, governor, as if, reverting to ancient tradition, the true monarch was the city god Ningirsu, lord of the mace and the battle-axe. More than two dozen votive statues representing Gudea have been recovered, probably good likenesses, for they all represent recognisably the same man. All emphasize his deep piety and his many good works: mainly temple-building and restoration. The craftsmanship is superb, the skills of the sculptors masterly, but above all the Gudea statues express a return to Sumerian values: dignity and formality and serenity, a strong reaction against the humanistic, energetic, style of the Akkadian emperors seen in the copper head of Sargon, the victory stele of Naram-Sin.

Mesopotamia would not again step confidently into the future until the hold of the Guti could somehow be dislodged and the land had regained a measure of its former self-respect.

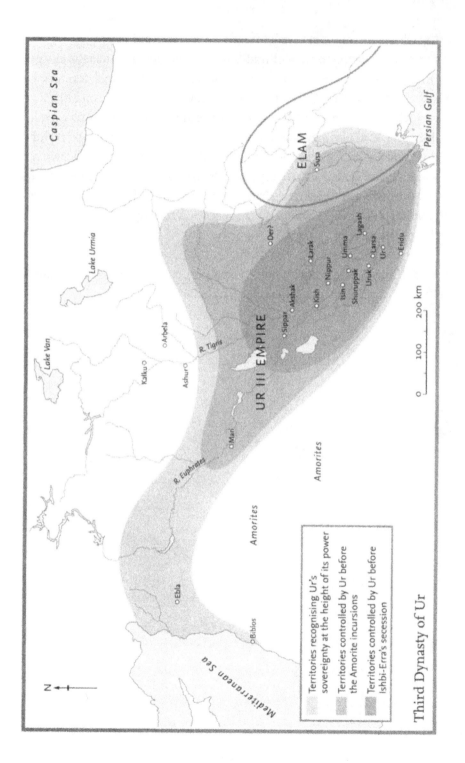

Third Dynasty of Ur

Caspian Sea

Lake Urmia

Lake Van

Mediterranean Sea

Persian Gulf

ELAM

UR III EMPIRE

Amorites

Amorites

R. Euphrates

R. Tigris

Biblos
Ebla
Mari
Ashur
Kalku
Arbela

Sippar
Akshak
Kish
Isin
Nippur
Shuruppak
Uruk
Umma
Larsa
Lagash
Ur
Eridu
Der
Susa

N

0   100   200 km

Territories recognising Ur's
sovereignty at the height of its power

Territories controlled by Ur before
the Amorite incursions

Territories controlled by Ur before
Ishbi-Erra's secession

7

Sumer Resurgent:
The Dirigiste *State*

c.2100 to 2000 BCE

Bringing the Kingship Back to Sumer

It was Utu-hegal ('the Sun God brings abundance') who claimed to have rid Mesopotamia of the Guti. He must have been preparing his revolt a long time before he made his move. He would have spent many months, perhaps years, assembling a large enough band of supporters, men prepared to risk their all for a share in the glory of freeing the land from 'the fanged snake of the mountains'. He would certainly have had agents reporting back to his fiefdom in Uruk, bringing him insider information about conditions in the areas over which these foreigners, 'people who are not considered part of the Land', exercised direct control.

He was well aware that the barbarians had disdained to re-establish the elaborate state machinery of their Akkadian predecessors, or had simply been inadequate to that task – because of them, says a chronicle, 'grass grew high on the highways of the land'. Instead, they depended for their dominance on the weakness of the ancient Sumerian foundations clustered near the head of the Gulf, which took many decades to recover from the disasters that had brought down Sargon the Great's dynasty. Indeed the Guti were never to be forgiven for being unlike other pretenders to the control of Mesopotamia in having no interest in picking up the baton of civilization and carrying it forward. The chroniclers keep reminding us that these were 'unhappy people unaware of how to revere the gods, ignorant of the right religious practices'. It could only be a matter of time before the reviving confidence of the southern cities led to a concerted effort to drive them off.

Utu-hegal wanted to be sure that he was the one credited with that achievement. On the other hand, maintaining the traditions of earlier times, before the pre-Akkadian heroic age, he would not claim sole credit. In fact, rebellion was not even his own idea: Enlil, the king of the gods, had decided that the Guti should be kicked out of Mesopotamia and had chosen him for the task. An inscription known from three later copies tells us about his famous victory, the first detailed account we have of a military campaign in ancient times.

His first stop was the temple, to keep his patron goddess Inanna informed: 'My lady, lioness in battle, who head-butts the foreign lands, Enlil has entrusted me with bringing back the kingship to Sumer. May you be my help!' The second was to get the support of the citizen population. 'Utu-hegal, the mighty man, went forth from Uruk and set up camp at the temple of [the storm god] Ishkur. He called out to the citizens of his city, saying: "The god Enlil has given Gutium to me. My lady, the goddess Inanna, is my ally". The citizens of Uruk and Kulaba rejoiced and followed him as of one accord.'

Having gained the approval of both his heavenly and earthly supporters, Utu-hegal set off with his élite troops, marching northwards along the course of the Euphrates, and then branching north-east along the Iturungal canal. His expeditionary force progressed at about 12–15 kilometres a day, camping on the fourth night at the city of Nagsu. The next day he halted his men by the Ilitappe shrine, where two emissaries from Tirigan, King of the Guti, came to parley with him, only to find themselves arrested and put into chains. The following evening the Uruk army pitched camp at Karkar but moved on secretly in the middle of the night to a point behind enemy lines upstream from Adab, some 80 kilometres from Uruk, where they set a trap for the enemy. In the ensuing battle the Gutian army was routed.

Tirigan abandoned his war-chariot and fled on foot, seeking refuge, together with his wife and children, in a place called Dabrum. But the citizens of that town, recognizing that the Gutian cause was lost, 'that Utu-hegal was a king endowed with power by Enlil', arrested the defeated king together with his family and handed them over to Utu-hegal's representative. 'He put handcuffs and a blindfold on him. Before Utu [the sun god], Utu-hegal made him lie at his feet and placed his foot on his neck...

He brought back the kingship to Sumer.' (The Guti, however, would get their revenge some 1,500 years later, when Cyrus the Great, in the course of his conquest of Babylon, sent in Gutian shock-troops before he himself arrived, after several days, to play the role of magnanimous liberator.)

In bringing 'the kingship back to Sumer', Utu-hegal laid the foundations for the most remarkable social system that ancient Mesopotamia ever devised, though he himself would not live to witness its full development.

The details in 'The Victory of Utu-hegal', the name given by Assyriologists to the text from which the above description comes, suggest that its account may be fairly accurate. But documents like these were no more written by disinterested and unbiased historians than are today's tabloid newspaper reports. Some were works of overt, even crude, propaganda; others had a more subtle agenda. When states first gain their independence, or regain it after a long period, they commonly try to establish a national story, justifying their existence and asserting their roots and origins.

In the years after the Judaeans exiled in Babylon were permitted by the Persian emperor to return to Jerusalem and start rebuilding their cult site, the Bible was assembled from its many sources, to develop into a great saga of Hebrew conquest, settlement and rule of the Holy Land. The Venerable Bede wrote his *Ecclesiastical History of the English People* when the Kings of Northumbria, the region in which he lived, began the centuries'-long process of unifying all England. In a similar way, the first version of the Sumerian King List was almost certainly compiled not very long after the expulsion of the Guti, aiming to show that Utu-hegal, a man presumably not of royal birth, was nevertheless inheritor of the mantle of legitimate monarchy, the latest descendant of a long line of rulers that went all the way back to the days before the flood.

For some narratives, accuracy and truth are not an issue. When, in this period of Sumerian resurgence, scribes wrote down the tales of the Great Flood, of divinities like Inanna and Enki, of semi-divine heroes like Lugalbanda and Gilgamesh, of earthly kings like Enmerkar and the Lord of Aratta, indeed when they wrote down most of the ancient myths and legends that had presumably been in the repertoire of bards and public reciters for centuries, the primary motive was not political persuasion, but preservation. It is as if the Gutian interregnum had delivered a great shock to the guardians of Mesopotamian culture, emphasizing the fragility of the oral tradition, the danger of losing the ancient wisdom, underlining the importance of setting down as much as possible in permanent written form. For just such reasons was the Holy Qur'an first written down after many of those who had memorized and recited it, the *Hufaz*, were killed in the civil wars that followed the death of the Prophet of Islam. We should be glad that the Sumerians learned the same lesson. Had the scribes not diligently encoded the stories onto clay tablets, to be unearthed thousands of years later, we would know nothing of them today.

Yet where documents are intended to establish a national story, readers should beware. A Babylonian chronicle, probably written some 300 years after Gutian times, which is mostly concerned with the proper provisioning of offerings for a new god, Marduk, tutelary deity of a new city, Babylon – both Marduk and Babylon being either quite unknown or at least of no importance in Utu-hegal's day – blames the clash between civilization and barbarism, between Sumerian and Gutian, on a simple matter of boiled fish: 'Utu-hegal the fisherman caught a fish at the edge of the sea for an offering. That fish should not have been offered to another god until it had been offered to Marduk. But the Guti took the boiled fish from his hand before it was offered. So by his august command, Marduk removed the Gutian force from the rule of his land and gave it to Utu-hegal.'

When the same text tells us that 'Utu-hegal, the fisherman, carried out criminal acts against Marduk's city, so the river carried off his corpse,' referring to a legend that the King of Uruk was swept to his death while supervising the construction of a dam, it is hard to know what to believe. In the several versions of the King List, as updated after Utu-hegal's time, the length of his reign is variously given as 427 years, or 26 years 2 months and 15 days, or 7 years 6 months and 5 days. After which, 'Uruk was defeated and the kingship was taken to Ur.' It seems that the governor of Ur, Ur-Nammu (or Ur-Namma) by name, who had been appointed by Uruk's king, took the opportunity of the unexpected power vacuum to fight, defeat and annexe Uruk. The details of exactly how this came about are, unfortunately, lost to us.

All we can be sure of is that at some time around 2100 BCE the land of Sumer began to reconstruct itself, and a resurgent Ur City, under its third dynasty – therefore known in the Assyriology trade as Ur III – built up a large regional imperial state. At its apogee this neo-Sumerian Empire included much of Mesopotamia, where the formerly independent cities became provinces, and a surrounding penumbra of vassal territories under military government paid taxes to the centre.

Sumerian was once again the language of administration – although Akkadian was spoken on the streets – and the military–clerical complex was back in power. The arts, too, reflected a return to the old Sumerian formalities. But if the outward style of neo-Sumerian culture was conservative, even backward-looking, there was no abandoning the advances in the science of governance achieved by Sargon's Akkadian dynasty: the improvements in management, organization, economics, politics, law and scribal culture, along with the mathematical, astronomical, calendrical and proto-scientific techniques needed to make them work. On the contrary, they were rigorously applied and developed yet further, creating a more centralized, *dirigiste* state apparatus than any ever attempted before.

Or so it is believed, on the evidence of the one class of text that we can put some trust in: the administrative document.

The neo-Sumerian state left us a vast number of bureaucratic records inscribed on clay tablets. Unfortunately many were dug up illegally, and their provenance never recorded. Approximately 50,000 have been transcribed and translated; as many as three times that number await study; and at least a hundred times more probably lie under the sands waiting to be discovered. It would take centuries to transcribe and translate them all.

With no political axe to grind, no purpose other than to record the facts of economic or social transactions, the administrative tablets make it possible to fill in details about ancient society that were never otherwise overtly described. We do not, however, receive a complete picture from them. Studying tablets from this period is like opening up an inspection hatch on to the interior arrangements of some intricate mechanism, whose overall purpose and plan yet remains vague. Or, to change the metaphor, we see plenty of trees, but the shape of the wood mostly eludes us. And we should also beware of gaining a distorted impression. The neo-Sumerians have been deemed utterly obsessed by bureaucracy. That is surely unfair. If, in our own day, every shopping list, railway ticket, till receipt, car-rental agreement and credit-card invoice were somehow miraculously preserved, the savants of the far distant future might well conclude the same about us. What is more, the attention of earlier excavators, always on the look-out for spectacular finds, was concentrated on the great institutions of state: the temples and the palaces. Thus the written records extracted from under the ground were always going to be biased against the small-scale, the domestic and the private. So much so that scholars used to write of the third dynasty of Ur as if it ruled over a totalitarian enterprise so tightly controlled and all-embracing that it made Leonid Brezhnev's Soviet Union look like a laissez-faire free-market economy.

That view has now been abandoned, superseded by the recognition that the everyday life of the ordinary citizen is ill-reflected in the documents so far retrieved. For example, while there are ample records of the grain, bread and sometimes meat and oil that were distributed by the state to feed the populace, there is no hint of where people obtained their clothes, their furniture, their kitchen utensils, neither the vegetables that went into the pot nor the fruits that garnished the table. Trade of some kind there must have been, but since it took place outside the state system it went unrecorded.

All that said, however, by standing back and squinting through half-closed eyes, as one does at an ultra-Impressionist painting, it is nevertheless possible to gain some idea of what kind of society this was. And the form that takes shape before our gaze comes, to me at least, as a surprise, as so often in Mesopotamian antiquity. The neo-Sumerians flourished a very, very long time ago, at the end of the third millennium BCE, rather more than a thousand years before the beginnings of our own civilization's history, rooted as it is in the ancient Greece of c.600 BCE. They lived before the earliest age of even our religious traditions as described in the legends of the tent-dwelling patriarchs in the Hebrew Bible. Yet this Sumerian state appears to have been so elaborate, so complex, so sophisticated and so highly developed, that – apart from the obvious and crucial lack of fossil-fuelled technology – one would hardly be surprised to find a similar political entity surviving somewhere in the world in the twenty-first century.

Indeed, the economic and social arrangements are more than a little reminiscent of some communist states of our recent past: the USSR, perhaps, or Mao's China, or at least communism as it was supposed to be, the centralized people's state. Specialists will be quick to point out that there is no real comparison here. The ideological underpinnings of the systems are too vastly different: the communists were militant atheists, the Sumerians passionately devoted, at least in public, to the service of their gods; the communist system arose through revolution and, at least in theory, by democracy; the Sumerian by evolution and autocracy. On the other hand there are only so many ways to organize a centrally controlled state and similarities are bound to occur. Both modern communist states as well as ancient Sumer were supported by totalitarian ideologies which were used to explain and justify their social and economic arrangements. Both ran centralized economies that in theory took from each according to his ability, and gave to each according to his needs – though in the socialist republics, as it surely was also in Ur III, some were always more equal than others. In Sumer, as in the Soviet Union, the individual had no voice. 'In the ancient Mesopotamian city individuals did not count as citizens,' writes Marc van de Mieroop. 'Cities were made up of various groups, which could be familial, ethnic, residential, or professional in nature. An individual outside any of these groups did not have a means to participate in the social and political life of the town.'

In both political systems, the state owned all land and productive resources, although fierce argument still rages about the relative importance of the public vis-à-vis the private sectors of the neo-Sumerian economy. Most persuasive is the view that in the empire every member of the populace was under obligation to serve the state for at least part of the year. What time was left, if any, could be deployed to the citizen's personal advantage. A concept known as *Bala*, meaning something like 'crossover' or 'exchange', a kind of tax-and-redistribute policy, required that every province pay grain and livestock into a central resource – by some estimates amounting to nearly half their production. From there each could draw supplies as and when needed. An entire urban centre, Puzrish-dagan, also known as Drehem was established, about 11 kilometres south of Nippur, dedicated to the collection and distribution of *Bala* commodities. Surviving records show more than a score of animals delivered to or dispatched from there every day. A state sheep-run near Lagash maintained more than 22,000 sheep, nearly 1,000 cows and 1,500 oxen.

Piotr Steinkeller, professor of Assyriology at Harvard, is 'reminded here of the system of compulsory deliveries which operated, at different times and in various forms, in the former Soviet bloc, especially in agriculture. Very much like in Ur III Babylonia, in communist Poland the independent farmer was required to deliver to the state a portion of his produce, for which he was paid a nominal price. The remainder he could theoretically sell freely, though not in a real free-market environment, since the state reserved the right of pre-emption, and since it regulated prices.'

But the Sumerians went much further than even the communists ever dared, keeping account of each citizen's obligations and rewards, for which the Ur III bureaucrats used a sophisticated, and remorseless, running balanced-account system. The lowest social layers, unskilled workers and slaves, were regarded simply as property of the state and seem to have had no duties other than to provide labour by the day. It was very different for their supervisors. No question here of Soviet-style 'We pretend to work and you pretend to pay us'. The performance of a work-unit foreman was carefully measured and weighed in the balance. In one column were itemized all the debits: the goods, materials and labour – grain, wool, leather, metals and numbers of workers – provided to the foreman by the state. These were then converted, according to a set convention, into standard worker-days. The sum total of these was added together. In the second column appeared the credits, the unit's production output: for example the quantity of flour ground in the case of millers, textiles woven in the case of a weaving team and so on. The number of worker-days equivalent to this amount was calculated, making allowance for time spent diverted to other projects (work gangs were often requisitioned for urgent labour elsewhere, such as harvesting, unloading ships or canal maintenance), and for the time off to which the workers were entitled: one day in ten for men and one in five or six for women. At the end of each accounting year, the difference between credits and debits was calculated and any surplus or deficit carried over as the first entry for the following period.

The conversions were so calculated as to make a surplus a very rare occurrence indeed. The expected daily output seems to have been well beyond the normal worker's ability, and many, or most, supervisors ended up carrying over an increasingly large debt owing to the state. This might not have mattered if the system had been a mere accounting device, not to be taken too seriously. But that was far from the case; the state could call in the debt at any time. In one, quite typical, document the foreman of a gang of thirty-seven female cereal workers, who would mainly have been engaged in grinding grain with hand-querns, began the year with a deficit of 6,760 worker-days and ended it owing 7,420. His debt, converted to shekels of silver, would have wiped out two years' wages. When he died, the debt would fall upon his heirs, who may have had no other way of discharging it than the drastic recourse of selling themselves into slavery.

The Industrial Park

To experience the vaguely Soviet flavour of neo-Sumerian life, join me at what has been called the 'industrial park' of Girsu, a major urban centre in the province of Lagash, in the year 2042 BCE, taking as our guide the analysis made by Wolfgang Heimpel of the University of California, Berkeley, of one particular collection of administrative records.

We are at the door of the office of the kitchens, whence are dispensed the supplies which are apparently the entitlement of many, most, or even all citizens of the Ur empire when engaged on state affairs. The quantities vary according to rank and station in life. As befits the well-organized arrangements of this institution, a resident auditor, an accounting scribe with both literacy and arithmetical skills, keeps a record of everything that enters or leaves the storehouse. He may well be assisted by a group of apprentices, for not only is their food accounted for, but some of the records are shoddily composed in a rather less than perfect hand, suggesting inexperience.

Today is the 16th of Harvest month; the auditor is itemizing the day's disbursements to travellers on the road:

> 5 litres good beer, 5 litres beer, 10 litres bread
> to Ur-Ninsun, son of the king;
> 5 litres good beer, 5 litres beer, 10 litres bread
> to Lala'a, brother of Lugal-magure;
> 5 litres beer, 5 litres bread, 2 shekels oil
> to Kub-Sin, en route for sickles.

Both Prince Ur-Ninsun and Lala'a have large retinues to feed; Kub-Sin is perhaps accompanied by several porters. And, naturally enough, the high-born, the Sumerian *nomenklatura*, are given 'good beer', rather than the 'beer' drunk by common folk. Others are provided with more standard rations:

> 2 *litres beer, 2 litres bread, 2 shekels oil*
> *to Sua-zi, en route for great linen;*
> 2 *litres beer, 2 litres bread, 2 shekels oil*
> *to Usgina, en route with cloth;*
> 2 *litres beer, 2 litres bread, 2 shekels oil*
> *to Kala, en route for reed boxes.*
> 2 *litres beer, 2 litres bread, 2 shekels oil*
> *to Adda the Elamite.*

These wayfarers, or their representatives, turn up at the kitchen office to apply for and collect their supplies. We assume that they are all travelling on government business. How do they prove who they are and identify themselves as entitled to support? They doubtless carry official seals of some kind, or perhaps clay tablets inscribed with a laissez-passer and the seal-impression of some higher official.

A stream of other applicants passes as we wait at the kitchen office door. We meet Lugal-ezen, 'keeper of the bird-house', a dovecote perhaps; several 'Amorite women', possibly prisoners of war; and a number of dog-handlers with their animals – then as now in the Middle East, everyone moves to avoid them: dogs are unclean and their handlers are socially the lowest of the low. Contemporary images show large mastiff-like creatures; the food they consumed suggests that they were nearly as heavy as the men who looked after them. They were most likely used as watchdogs and guard-dogs; their regular comings and goings suggest that they also accompanied caravans on the road.

Not everyone comes to the kitchen counter to collect their rations. The auditor notes deliveries of bread and meat to a number of other institutions in Girsu. Food is supplied to shipbuilders constructing vessels for trade with Oman, suggesting local access to the open sea, probably via the Tigris River; to the workers of the woodshed, a large timber storage-facility which also houses supplies of building materials like bitumen, reed and straw; to the guards and workers of the sheep-house and bull-house, stock-fattening institutions that provide animals for offerings; to the guards and inmates of the local prisons, of which there appear to be two of different sizes, with up to five prisoners in the larger, as well as to the prison boat used to transport them to and from their captivity.

Next to the prison is a *danna* house, a government rest-house, one of seven in the province. Such hostelries, sited at about two hours' walking-distance apart along the great trunk routes of southern Mesopotamia, that is, every 15 or 16 kilometres, precursors of the dak bungalows of the British Indian Empire, are places where travellers of all kinds can rest, eat, sleep and exchange their mules and donkeys for fresh beasts of burden. The *sikkum*, the state animal service for official couriers, has its home stables in rest houses like these.

Occupying several rooms of the *danna* house is the large entourage of a senior royal functionary called *zabar-dab*, bronze-holder, whatever that title may have implied. Several soldiers accompany him, perhaps his security guard, as well as an armourer, an outrider, a personal scribe, three cup-bearers and a cook. Commander Ur-Shulgi, 'en route to the fields', stayed here for a week. He works as estate manager for a distant temple household that holds lands in the local vicinity. 'As we can see,' writes Dr Heimpel, with an unusual and welcome lightness of touch, 'he spent considerable time in the field in execution of his office. He obviously believed in hands-on management and did not likely sit in his office sipping beer.'

Weaker members of the community are provided for too. The kitchen feeds four 'children of the nose-rope holders of the governor' (I suppose the nose ropes are attached to the governor's animals rather than to the governor) as well as two 'sons of the mule-keeper' who live in the rest house with their families. Rations are also distributed to a surprisingly large number of invalids. Ur-Damu and Urebadu, designated as 'work impaired', are 'sitting by' a building called the Depot, as watchmen no doubt, somewhat like the ubiquitous chowkidars of modern India. Invalids are also recorded as working in several households as cultivators, troopers and ox-drivers, while others work in the sheep-house and the woodshed. Their rations are smaller than those of able-bodied workers, but the Ur III state does concern itself with their survival. Maybe the intention is to ensure exploitation of even the most marginal economic resources; but it also has the effect of giving a secure place and status in society to those who, for whatever reason, are unable fully to compete.

Who devised these elaborate systems? There must have been many long meetings between bureaucrats with a mastery of state economics, those who knew about agronomy, experts in livestock-raising and irrigation engineers – all members of the senior scribal class. It was no small thing to have devised a national plan that kept account of, deployed, paid, and fed possibly as many as a million workers, spread over the whole of Greater Mesopotamia, all while using Bronze Age technology and donkey transport. That it seems to have worked so well for so many decades is a tribute to the thinking, planning and organizing skills of the committees responsible. No similarly complex controlled economy was attempted until modern times. Would that we could find some of the notes taken, the memorandums set down during their planning sessions.

We can be reasonably sure that the standard issue of rations detailed in the records from the Industrial Park of Girsu would have been applied in all the cities and dependent territories of Sumer and Akkad. Little offends people's sense of fairness and justice more than a situation where what you receive depends on where you apply. In any case, all empires like to impose uniformity within their territories, and Ur III was no exception. The ostensible reason is efficient administration, though commanding standard ways of doing things is often as much an expression of power as it is of practical policy.

To this end, a national curriculum for scribal training was introduced. Large state-run academies were established in major cities like Ur and Nippur. A uniform chancellery style of writing and a stock of phrases for use in official documents were prescribed. Weights and measures were regularized: an inscription tells us that the king 'fashioned the bronze sila-measure, standardized the one-mina weight, and standardized the stone weight of a shekel of silver in relation to one mina'. These measures remained the standard for the rest of Mesopotamian civilization's history. An imperial calendar was devised: all provinces had to follow it when recording state business, although some continued with their older local traditions when handling purely local affairs. Such reforms had been started in the days of Sargon's Akkadian dynasty, but the neo-Sumerians took the process very much further.

Where uniformity was of greatest importance however, was in the matter of law. In ancient Sumer and Akkad, criminals were arraigned before the ruler and then sent for judgement by one or other city assembly. In the murder trial mentioned earlier – famous among Mesopotamians as the account of it was used for centuries to educate scribes in the art of court reporting, and famous among modern archaeologists as it shows the difficulty of translating ancient texts – three men were found guilty of murdering a priest's son. 'Nanna-sig, son of Lu-Sin, Ku-Enlila, son of Ku-Nanna the barber, and Enlil-ennam, slave of Adda-kalla the gardener, killed Lu-Inanna, son of Lugal-urudu, the priest.' The king sent them for sentencing to the assembly at Nippur. As far as the killers were concerned, their fate was clear: execution awaited them. But the case was complicated by the fact that they had told the victim's wife what they had done, and she had failed to inform the authorities. 'When Lu-Inanna, son of Lugal-urudu had been killed, they told his wife Nin-dada daughter of Lu-Ninurta, that her husband had been killed. Nin-dada daughter of Lu-Ninurta opened not her mouth and covered it up.' Nine speakers took it in turn to demand the death penalty for the woman too: 'Ur-Gula son of Lugal-ibila, Dudu the bird-catcher, Ali-ellati the commoner, Puzu son of Lu-Sin, Eluti son of Tizkar-Ea, Sheshkalla the potter, Lugalkarn the gardener, Lugal-azida son of Sin-andul, and Sheshkalla son of Sharahar, addressed the assembly: "They have killed a man, they are thus not live men. The three men and the woman are to be killed before the chair of Lu-Inanna, son of Lugal-urudu, the priest."' But two assembly members spoke up in the woman's favour: 'Shuqalilum, the soldier of Ninurta, and Ubar-Sin the gardener spoke up: "Did Nin-dada, daughter of Lu-Ninurta, kill her husband? What did the woman do that she should be put to death?"'

After deliberation, the assembly delivered its judgement.

A man's enemy may know that a woman does not value her husband and may kill her husband. She heard that her husband had been killed, so why did she keep silent about him? It is she who killed her husband; her guilt is greater than that of the men who killed him.

In the assembly of Nippur, after the case had been resolved, Nanna-sig son of Lu-Sin, Ku-Enlila son of Ku-Nanna the barber, Enlil-ennam slave of Adda-kalla the gardener, and Nin-dada daughter of Lu-Ninurta and wife of Lu-Inanna, were given up to be executed.

Verdict of the assembly of Nippur.

The difficulty of reading cuneiform documents is demonstrated by the fact that in an earlier translation of the very same text, by Samuel Noah Kramer, the woman was acquitted and freed.

Whatever the verdict, it is clear that this trial assembly at Nippur was no gathering of oligarchs, restricted to the great and the good. Ordinary workers took part in the proceedings to plead for or against the accused: a bird-catcher, a potter, a gardener, a soldier attached to the temple of Ninurta, a man described as a commoner, the lowest rung of the social scale. Justice in the Ur III Empire was, as it is supposed to be with us, a matter of trial before one's peers. But unlike in our courts, punishment too was determined by these same common folk, rather than by professionals – rather like the People's Assessors in the courts of the former Soviet Union, who not only had the power to return a verdict, but also to call witnesses, examine evidence, determine punishment and award damages.

But therein lies a difficulty. Each city no doubt had its own legal traditions, and the outcome of a trial, the punishment imposed, might depend more on where the judgement was handed down than on the nature of the crime. To avoid such an unwelcome result, laws were now promulgated by the state, specifying punishments for a wide variety of criminal offences, to be applied throughout the neo-Sumerian Empire.

The first known of these legal compendiums is the Code of Ur-Nammu, as it is usually called – although it is neither a true law code, being far from comprehensive; nor, some say, even introduced by Ur-Nammu but by his son. (Ur-Nammu was the founder of the Ur III dynasty; his son Shulgi was the greatest of all neo-Sumerian monarchs.) Code or no, although we only have fragments, they are enough to show that the laws covered both civil and criminal matters. Among criminal provisions it specifies which should be capital offences: murder, robbery, deflowering another man's virgin wife, and adultery when committed by a woman. For other misdemeanours the penalty was a fine in silver.

> If a man committed a kidnapping, he is to be imprisoned and pay fifteen shekels of silver.
>
> If a man proceeded by force, and deflowered the virgin slave-woman of another man, that man must pay five shekels of silver.

If a man appeared as a witness, and was shown to be a perjurer, he must pay fifteen shekels of silver.

In contrast to the more famous laws of Hammurabi, drafted some three centuries later, with its savage provisions of 'an eye for an eye, a tooth for a tooth', mutilations too are to be financially compensated.

If a man knocked out the eye of another man, he shall weigh out half a mina of silver.

If a man knocked out a tooth of another man, he shall pay two shekels of silver.

If a man, in the course of a scuffle, smashed the limb of another man with a club, he shall pay one mina of silver.

May Your Might be Respectfully Praised

Ur-Nammu's universal legal pronouncements present a good example of the unifying drive of Ur's kings: the compulsion to regulate every aspect of life. It says something significant about the Ur III state that the ruler could override local tradition and insist on conformity to his diktat. Keeping such a tight grip on the many centrally controlled legal, economic, social and educational systems and institutions, demanded a particular kind of governing principle.

The Third Dynasty of Ur has been described as what the great German thinker Max Weber, one of the founders of modern sociology, called a Patrimonial State, meaning one constructed on the pattern of the patriarchal family, ruled – as often as not with a rod of iron – by a father-figure at its head, the population arranged as if in a pyramid shape below, with a complicated network of duties and rewards binding all parties together.

For a patrimonial state to be stable over time, it is best ruled with consent, at least with consent from the largest minority, if not from the majority. Instinctive obedience must be the norm, otherwise too much effort needs to be put into suppressing disaffection for the regime's wider aims to be achievable. Consent is, however, not always easy to obtain. The collective view of most societies is rather conservative: in the main people prefer to see the social arrangements of their youth perpetuated into their old age; they prefer that things be done in the time-honoured way; they are suspicious of novelty and resistant to change. Thus when radical action must be taken, for whatever reason, a great burden falls on the ruler, the father-figure, who has to overcome this social inertia and persuade his subjects to follow his lead. In order that his will shall prevail, he needs to generate huge respect, preferably adulation, and if at all possible sheer awe, among his people.

Like Naram-Sin, his Akkadian predecessor, the second and greatest king of the Third Dynasty of Ur, Shulgi, was, during his lifetime, declared a god, as were later kings in his line. Though no doubt very nice for the self-esteem of the men themselves, it is far from clear what being declared a god actually meant in practice. Was it merely a polite fiction, as mocked by the Roman Emperor Vespasian when he lay on his deathbed, sighing, 'Oh dear, I think I am becoming a god'? Or did King Shulgi's subjects really believe that he had supernatural powers? Surely not those close to him, who would daily have witnessed his physical humanity. But if it were only a matter of attracting success and good fortune to his city and his empire, then being pronounced a god would have meant little more than being appointed a kind of national or city mascot – a role mostly played for us by pet animals these days. Yet there is another way to understand the phenomenon. By applying the conceit that the neo-Sumerian Empire had something in common with the communist states of the twentieth century, deification of the king can be seen to be an ancient version of a political device all too familiar to us: the cult of personality.

A hugely complicated, centrally planned, social and economic system can only be kept on the rails for as long as people believe in it. When Vladimir Ilyich Ulyanov – known as Lenin – died, embarrassingly, in January 1924, after two years of increasingly severe strokes that were carefully kept from the public, Russian Party officials recognized that demanding the populace believe in Marxism, dialectical materialism or any other such abstract concept, was a lost cause. What had actually engaged the public's loyalty was the leader's personality. As Trotsky said, 'We asked ourselves with genuine alarm how those outside the party would receive the news – the peasant, the Red Army man. For in our government apparatus, the peasant believes above all in Lenin.' The cadres' response was therefore to institute the Cult of Lenin, and later of Stalin. Both serving to keep the Soviet Empire together for many decades.

To be sure, the Soviets never declared their leaders to be literally immortal. But their treatment of their founder Lenin, and, for a time, Stalin, came as close to that as they could manage, with their mummified bodies preserved for public viewing in the mausoleum on Red Square, where queues assembled to file reverently past on high days and holidays. Little children in school were taught to sing 'Lenin is alive, he will always be alive'. In fact, the combination of cult and ritual, faith and adoration accorded to the dead leaders of the USSR amounted almost to a kind of Soviet religion. Though neither Stalin nor Lenin were ever declared to be gods as Shulgi was, it is not easy to say which of the following lines were composed in honour of the General Secretary of the Central Committee of the Communist Party of the Soviet Union, and which for the ancient Sumerian king. Here is the first:

Who is as mighty as you, and who rivals you?
Who is there who from birth was as richly endowed with understanding
as you?
May your heroism shine forth, and may your might be respectfully praised!

And here the second:

Thou who broughtest man to birth.
Thou who fructifiest the earth,
Thou who restorest the centuries,
Thou who makest bloom the spring,
Thou who makest vibrate the musical chords…
Thou, splendour of my spring, O thou,
Sun reflected by millions of hearts.

In fact the first, relatively sober, example is the repeated refrain from one of more than twenty hymns written in glowing praise of King Shulgi of Sumer and Akkad, presumably composed to be sung or chanted in temples, the ancient equivalent of a PR campaign. The second, more absurd selection was addressed to 'Great Stalin, O leader of the peoples'. The poem was published in *Pravda* on 1 February 1935.

There is an interesting contrast between the adulation accorded to the two leaders separated by 4,000 years. While the praise for Stalin was sheer nonsense, indeed grotesque given Stalin's murderous inclinations, the composers of the hymns to Shulgi – often presented in the first person, as if he himself were boasting of his achievements – were careful to show their king in one particular light. He was not just a great ruler and warrior, defeater of all enemies, crusher of all opponents, bringer of prosperity and happiness to his land and his people, but even more he was the very embodiment, indeed the culmination, of Sumerian history and Sumerian civilization. Combining in his person the diplomat, the judge, the scholar, the musician, the diviner of omens, the skilled scribe, the patron of learning and the arts, the Shulgi of the praise-hymns brought Sumerian civilization to its highest peak yet.

> *I am no fool as regards the knowledge acquired since the time that mankind was, from heaven above, set on its path: when I have discovered* tigi *and* zamzam *hymns from past days, old ones from ancient times, I have never declared them to be false, and have never contradicted their contents. I have conserved these antiquities, never abandoning them to oblivion. Wherever the* tigi *and the* zamzam *sounded, I have recovered all that knowledge, and I have had those* šir-gida *songs brilliantly performed in my own good house. So that they should never fall into disuse, I have added them to the singers' repertoire, and thereby I have set the heart of the Land on fire and aflame.*

But it is not enough for a leader to receive paeans of praise from sycophantic palace poets, for such are fleeting and evanescent, and in any case they cost nothing. To attract the devotion of his people the great leader must also act in an appropriate way, which begins with creating what modern politics calls 'facts on the ground': physical evidence of his superiority, which will every day bring him immediately to the mind of the public.

In the years after his victory over Hitler, Stalin called into being the so-called Seven Sisters. Russians call them 'Stalin's wedding-cakes': monumental skyscrapers dotted around Moscow, designed to dominate the city's skyline. Stalin said, 'We won the war... foreigners will come to Moscow, walk around, and there are no skyscrapers. If they compare Moscow to capitalist cities, it's a moral blow to us.' They were built in a terraced, tiered, pattern, with each level slightly smaller than the previous one – hence the description 'wedding-cake' – to give the buildings a sense of upwards thrust toward a central tower. The original template for this style was the winning 1930s design for a Palace of Soviets, which looks at first sight like a crazily grandiose modernist version of Pieter Brueghel's painting of the Tower of Babel. At well over 450 metres including the statue of Lenin at the top, it would have been at the time the tallest building in Europe – Stalin demanded that it rise higher than the Eiffel Tower.

The Palace of Soviets was never completed. The Seven Sisters, however, the buildings based on that abandoned design, have served their purpose well: they still remind Muscovites of Stalin every day.

There are many accounts of the design sources for this Stalinist style of architecture, citing gothic, neoclassical and Russian Orthodox influences. Or maybe this is how all buildings designed to memorialize their creators in perpetuity need to look. It must be mere chance that the name for such a construction in Russian is *vysotnoe zdaniye*, 'high building', and that, when translated into Akkadian, the closest equivalent would be the word we pronounce Ziggurat. But perhaps we should not be surprised that the shape of Stalin's architectural monuments is oddly reminiscent of the memorial that best commemorates Ur-Nammu's rule in Sumer in around 2100 BCE: the Great Ziggurat of Ur. Ur-Nammu's architects created a design that would, after it was uncovered by Woolley in 1923, serve as a model for all further construction designed to remind the people of its builder's greatness.

Like Stalin's Seven Sisters, the Great Ziggurat of Ur too has fulfilled its promise well. After its abandonment sometime around the beginning of the Christian era, the site of the city of Ur continued to announce itself from miles away, by the tall brown hillock that Arabs called the Tell el-Mukayyar, or the Mound of Pitch, to any traveller approaching across the flat desert waste. The remains of Ur-Nammu's great construction still stand after 4,000 years, its top levels weathered away, its lower courses masked by the accumulated rubble of the millennia – thousands of tons of it, according to its excavator Leonard Woolley, who had it all carted off on a specially installed light railway. (It looks slightly odd today, like a new but only half-completed building, since the lowest part of the ruin was 'restored' in mid-twentieth century by the Iraqi Directorate of Antiquities.)

In ancient times the scene would have appeared very different. What is now a dusty wilderness trembling with mirages under a merciless sun, would have been a green and gold vista as far as the eye can see: fields of grain criss-crossed by glittering threads of waterway, fringed by date palms, willows and alders, the fallow fields cropped by flocks of fleecy sheep and herds of fat cattle. In the distance, the ziggurat rises above the horizon, as if keeping a watchful eye over its lands, the exterior surface rendered with lime plaster, either left a dazzling white, or more probably coloured, each level painted a different hue. Had you been permitted to mount to the top – which no ordinary mortals were – you would have seen another similar ziggurat rising, twelve miles way, over the first Sumerian city Eridu. In the course of time ziggurats would be built in the centres of many other Mesopotamian cities, all following the pattern originally set in Ur by the architects of Ur-Nammu's court.

Their works may be neither as large nor as old as the Great Pyramid of Giza in Egypt nor even, come to that, the conical earthwork in England called Silbury Hill, both of which are a few centuries older, but the ziggurats bow to no challenger as great works of art. Where those other monuments impress by their size and the extreme simplicity of their form, it is the design of the Ziggurats that expresses genius. They were planned by their Sumerian creators to allow the human scale and the divine scale momentarily to touch.

Here in Ur the building's footprint occupies a little over 600 metres by 45. It is built with a solid core of sun-dried bricks, encased in a 2.5-metre-thick skin of kiln-baked bricks set in bitumen. The sheer wall of the first stage is about 15 metres high, not blank but given subtle visual interest by alternating shallow buttresses and recesses, a feature of the local building style right down to the twentieth century.

Above the first stage rises the next level, somewhat smaller than the first, leaving a wide walkway along the front and rear and a terrace at either end. At the very top, level three, stood the sacred shrine of Nannar, God of the Moon. Three monumental one-hundred-step staircases climb from ground level to the first stage, one perpendicular to the front wall, the other two built flat against it. They converge in the great gateway that gives on to another stair leading up to the shrine. Ever on the lookout for biblical parallels, Leonard Woolley was reminded of a story about Abraham's grandson Jacob:

> When Jacob at Bethel dreamed of ladders (or staircases, the word is the same) set up to Heaven with angels going up and down, surely he subconsciously recalled what his grandfather had told of the great building at Ur whose stairs went up to Heaven – such was indeed the name of Nannar's shrine – and how on feast-days the priests carrying the god's statue went up and down those stairs in a rite meant to assure a bounteous harvest and the increase of cattle and of human kind.

What particularly impressed Woolley was the discovery that all the apparently straight lines of the construction were actually slight curves, designed to accentuate perspective and give the whole edifice an impression of strength combined with lightness, as if the colossal building could barely be restrained from lifting itself off the ground. Before the excavation of Ur-Nammu's ziggurat, architectural historians believed that such application of curves had been invented by the Greeks a millennium and a half later – *entasis*, they called it. 'The whole design of the building is a masterpiece,' Woolley wrote.

> It would have been so easy to pile rectangle of brickwork above rectangle, and the effect would have been soulless and ugly; as it is, the heights of the different stages are skilfully calculated, the slope of the walls leads the eye upward and inwards to the centre, the sharper slope of the triple staircase accentuates that of the walls and fixes the attention on the shrine above, which was the religious focus of the whole structure, while across these converging lines cut the horizontal planes of the terraces.

Since the unearthing of the Mesopotamian ziggurats, scholars have debated their exact purpose: maybe to represent the sacred mountain of the Sumerians' supposed original homeland; perhaps to raise the god's shrine high above the flooding that regularly afflicts southern Mesopotamia; possibly to keep the common people as far away as possible from the holy of holies. However true any or all of these explanations may be, what needs emphasis is that above all else ziggurats are artistic creations. As works of architectural art, their principal function, like that of all buildings, is to make a mark upon the landscape. In this they succeed wonderfully, forever bringing to mind the supreme ruler who originally commanded their construction: Ur-Nammu.

Great building projects, however, take a long time to complete; often longer than the lifetime of their initiators. They therefore mainly confer posthumous fame. Construction work on Ur-Nammu's ziggurats continued well into his son's reign, which left Shulgi with the problem of how to establish his own superhuman persona in his people's awareness.

He chose to run. From Nippur, the religious centre of Sumer, to the state capital Ur. About 100 miles. And back again. On a single day. His purpose was quite clear, as expressed in one of his praise-hymns: 'So that my name should be established for distant days and never fall into oblivion, so that my praise should be spread throughout the Land and my glory should be proclaimed in the foreign lands, I, the fast runner, summoned my strength and, to prove my speed, my heart prompted me to make a return journey from Nippur to brick-built Ur as if it were only the distance of a double-hour.' He was aiming to officiate in a religious festival in both cities on the same day.

Though the hymn is couched in the formal language of royal self-glorification, behind it one can still make out the faint outlines of a real event. The king prepares himself for the run by donning the Sumerian equivalent of running shorts: 'I, the lion, never failing in his vigour, standing firm in his strength, fastened the small *nijlam* garment firmly to my hips.' He sets off at a sprint, 'Like a pigeon anxiously fleeing from a snake, I spread my wings; like the Anzud bird lifting its gaze to the mountains, I stretched forward my legs.' All along the route spectators assemble, many rows deep, all agog to see their king – their king! – running like one of his own couriers, but so much faster, and for so very much further, that nobody would have believed the feat humanly possible. 'The inhabitants of the cities which I had founded in the land, lined up for me; the black-headed people, as numerous as ewes, looked on at me with sweet admiration.' He arrives at the temple in Ur 'like a mountain kid hurrying to its habitation'. There he participates in the rites. 'I had oxen slaughtered there; I had sheep offered there lavishly. I had *cem* and *ala* drums resound there and caused *tigi* instruments to play there sweetly.' Then comes the time for the return journey, 'like a falcon to return to

Nippur in my vigour.' But nature turns against him and puts him to the test. 'A storm shrieked, and the west wind whirled around. The north wind and the south wind howled at each other. Lightning together with the seven winds vied with each other in the heavens. Thundering storms made the earth quake... Small and large hailstones drummed on my back.' Yet he continues to run on, unafraid; he 'rushed forth like a fierce lion'; he 'galloped like an ass in the desert', and reaches Nippur before sunset. 'I traversed a distance of fifteen double-hours by the time [the sun god] Utu was to set his face toward his house. My priests looked on at me with admiration. I had celebrated the *Eshesh* festival in both Nippur and Ur on the same day!'

Could he really have done it? An earlier generation of Assyriologists thought the achievement impossible, dismissing it as fiction. More recent consideration, however, suggests otherwise. An article in the *Journal of Sport History* quotes two relevant records: 'During the first forty-eight hours of the 1985 Sydney to Melbourne footrace, Greek ultra-marathoner Yannis Kouros completed 287 miles. This impressive distance was accomplished without pausing for sleep.' In the 1970s a British athlete running on a track completed 100 miles in a time of eleven hours and thirty-one minutes.

There is no reason to believe that the Sumerians were any less athletically able. Theirs was, after all, a far more physical world than is ours: speed, strength and stamina would have been much more important to them than they are to us, with our mechanized transport and heavy-lifting machinery. Excavated documents and seal images indicate the enthusiastic pursuit of sports of many different kinds: wrestling, boxing, sprinting, even a game in which a wooden ball was hit with a stick, a variety of what we would call hockey. Running competitions were popular. Texts refer to regular city races, and plant-oil was set aside for the anointing of athletes. A little later, the Babylonians named one four-week period 'Footrace Month'.

But even if Shulgi could have run from Nippur to Ur and back in one day, why did he? After all, no other monarch was known to have done such a thing. Several explanations have been offered, from the religious to the practical: maybe the king wanted to demonstrate how well he had refurbished the road system with its rest-houses and way-stations. But the run, with its attendant and subsequent publicity, was clearly a political act, and political motive there must have been. There are times when a ruler in a hurry, seeking to push a difficult or painful policy against potential public opposition, decides that only a spectacular demonstration of physical superiority will invest him with the authority to carry it through.

Mao Zedong, supreme leader and Chairman of the Communist Party of China, was in his seventies when in 1966 he launched the Great Proletarian Cultural Revolution. He had been out of the public eye for over a year, at war with members of his own party, in danger of losing influence and power in the hidden but lethal chess game that Chinese politics had become. His solution was to throw the chessboard over, using groups of disaffected high-school students, the Red Guards, youngsters mostly without college places or the prospect of decent jobs, as his weapons.

He needed a symbolic act to launch his assault. On 16 July 1966 he joined 5,000 young swimmers in the annual race across the Yangtze River at Wuhan. The Chinese press reported in awe that he swam 15 kilometres in just over an hour (about twice the 2008 Olympic speed record), an apparent miracle explained by the fact that the river runs fast at Wuhan and Mao mostly floated. Cinema newsreels were distributed across the world, showing the small round head bobbing up and down among the young swimmers, great banners waving around him in celebration of his achievement. Combining the image of Mao's own physical prowess, even at well over seventy, together with the youth, spirit and energy of the youngsters was a masterstroke. It was enough to give Mao the authority to launch the frightful decade of Cultural Revolution that brought China so much misery, chaos and copious bloodshed.

Was there something in Shulgi's political strategy that might have demanded his well-publicized run? The details of his life, and the individual events of his time, lie well beyond our knowledge and probably always will. But we do know that he was the second king of the Third House of Ur, the son of the first king. We know that the famous run took place early on, in his seventh regnal year. We know that great efforts were made to publicize the king's feat and ensure that it was never forgotten: the praise-hymn telling the story of the run was written shortly after the event and was, presumably, chanted or sung in temples all over Sumer and Akkad; while Shulgi's seventh year was officially named The Year when the King Made the Round Trip Between Ur and Nippur in One Day. We also know that the full-blown Ur III economic and social system, with its tax-and-redistribute policies which made every citizen a servant of the state, with its remorselessly audited balance of every person's consumption and contribution, was not fully introduced until well into the great king's long, forty-eight-year, reign. It does seem possible, even likely, that Shulgi's run was a carefully calculated performance aimed at investing his persona with the moral authority, the charismatic power, to drive through the new political dispensation against the opposition of those with interests vested in the ways of the past.

If that was indeed the intention, it must be said to have worked, and worked well. The momentum of Shulgi's economic and social policy was maintained through his reign, and – according to the King List – through those of his son, his grandson and his great grandson.

The People Groaned

But belief in a system cannot be sustained for ever. Empires based solely on power and domination, while allowing their subjects to do as they will, can last for centuries. Those that try to control the everyday lives of their people are much harder to sustain. In early days, the inevitable difficulties, failures and, as Karl Marx called them, internal contradictions of any elaborate social and economic machine can be dismissed as teething problems. Later they are blamed on the failure of individuals or the enmity of malign foreigners. But in the end, they lead irrevocably to a loss of faith and a loss of nerve. When that happens, it can happen surprisingly quickly. (From the election of Mikhail Gorbachev as General Secretary of the Communist Party of the Soviet Union to the complete dissolution of the Soviet Imperium took a mere six years.)

It took hardly any longer for the Ur III Empire to collapse. Surviving records allow us to follow the process as if in awful slow motion. Early on in the rule of the last king, Ibbi-Sin ('Sin, the moon god, has called him'), taxes from outlying provinces stopped coming in. At the end of his second year, scribes at Puzrish-Dagan stopped dating tablets with the official imperial year-names; this spread in year four to Umma, in year five to Girsu, and in year eight to Nippur. By year nine the *Bala* system had evaporated as if it had never been. Outlying provinces declared their independence. Vultures gathered around the weakened empire, waiting for the first opportunity to grab a piece of its dying carcase.

In the east, traditional enemies from the foothills of the Zagros Mountains and further across the Iranian plateau, against whom the Ur III kings boasted of having sent incessant punitive expeditions, were poised to wreak their revenge. But the greater problem lay in the west, where Semitic-speaking barbarians, people Mesopotamians called 'westerners', Amurru in Akkadian and Martu, or occasionally Tidnum, in Sumerian – the tribes the Bible calls Amorites – took on a similar role to the one the Germanic peoples played 2,500 years later in the downfall of the western Roman Empire. In good times, they infiltrated by peaceful immigration, seeking protection and prosperity; when the empire weakened, they arrived in armed companies, sometimes of considerable size, and, like a dog turning on its master, fought for control of patches of Sumerian territory.

In the reign of Shulgi a wall had been built across the country, more than 250 kilometres long, to keep them out. It was called 'a wall to keep out the Martu'. Shulgi's second successor ordered it to be rebuilt and strengthened, calling it *Muriq-Tidnum*, 'It Fends Off Tidnum.' But walls must end somewhere and enemies can often outflank them: in 1940 Hitler made the impregnable French Maginot Line irrelevant by sending his tanks through the forest of the Ardennes. And so it was with *Muriq-Tidnum*. Sharrumbani, the commissioner responsible for the building work, explained to the king:

> You presented the matter to me as follows: 'The Martu have repeatedly raided the territory.' You instructed me to build the fortifications so as to cut off their route; to prevent them from swooping down on the fields through a breach in the defences between the Tigris and the Euphrates....
>
> When I had constructing the wall to a length of 26 danna [about 260 kilometres], and had reached the area between the two mountain ranges, I was informed that the Martu were camping within the mountain ranges because of my building work... So I set off to the area between the mountain ranges of Ebih in order to confront them in battle... If my Lord is agreeable, he will reinforce my labourers and my fighting forces... I now have enough labourers but not enough fighting men. Once my king gives

the order to release workers for military duty when the enemy raids, I shall be able to fight him.

In spite of all efforts to strengthen it, the wall was not enough to keep the western barbarians at bay. They continued their raids, adding to the travails of the failing empire. Without the subventions of the provinces, the cost of grain in Ur rose fifteen-fold; too expensive to be fed to livestock. When Ur seemed on the brink of starvation, its last king wrote desperately to General Ishbi-Erra, who was in the north of the country, imploring him to send grain to the capital, no matter at what cost. Ishbi-Erra replied:

I was ordered to make a journey to Isin and Kazallu in order to buy barley. The barley has a value of 1 shekel of silver per kor of barley. 20 talents of silver have been provided for the barley purchase. Reports were received that hostile Martu entered your territory, so I have brought 72,000 kor of barley, the entire barley, into Isin. Now the Martu have completely penetrated into the land of Sumer and have captured all the fortresses there. Because of the Martu I cannot give the barley to be threshed. They are stronger than I am.

How true this was is debatable. Having decided, so it seems, that the Ur III Empire was beyond saving, the general's real purpose was secession. In the eleventh year of Ibbi-Sin's kingship, Ishbi-Erra abandoned his master and set up his own kingdom in the city of Isin. Even closer to Ur, a mere 40 kilometres away, an Amurru tribal leader took the city of Larsa and declared himself its king. The future of Ur looked bleak indeed, its empire reduced to no more than a few square miles.

But while all eyes in Ur were fixed, like a rabbit's frozen in a car's headlights, on rebellion in Isin and the depredations of the approaching western barbarians, the actual *coup de grâce* came from the opposite direction. A new ruler had taken over Elam, had shaken off Sumerian suzerainty, and was now leading an expeditionary army into southern Mesopotamia, to appear with irresistible force outside Ur's walls.

The gates were breached, the city fell. King Ibbi-Sin was dragged off to Elam and was never heard of again; he had occupied the throne for twenty-four years. The days of Ur's hegemony were for ever over.

People littered the outskirts like broken potsherds. The walls were breached.
The people groaned.

On its lofty city-gates where people once promenaded, dead bodies lay
about. On the boulevards where festivals had been held, heads lay scattered.
In all the streets where people had once promenaded, corpses were piled. In
the places where the festivities of the Land had taken place, people were
stacked in heaps.

The city suffered further under the occupation of an Elamite garrison for
seven long years, until Ishbi-Erra managed to drive it out. Whereupon he
claimed his city Isin to be heir to the kingship of Sumer. But though he
founded a local dynasty that would survive, one way or another, through
fifteen successive rulers, the claim that Isin exercised any kind of control
over all southern Mesopotamia was a fiction. The territory had once again
quickly fragmented into fiercely independent city-states. What is more,
most of them were now ruled by Amurru chieftains.

The Mesopotamians were stunned by the sudden change in Ur's fortunes. Why, they asked themselves, had the gods so utterly abandoned
their own city? Their answer was reminiscent of what Voltaire said, when
asked why the Roman Empire came to an end: 'Because all things must
end'. Nearly 4,000 years before him a Mesopotamian author had come
to much the same conclusion: 'Ur was indeed given kingship, but it was
not given an eternal reign. From time immemorial, since the land was
founded, until the people multiplied, who has ever seen a reign of kingship that would take precedence for ever? The reign of kingship has been
long indeed but had to exhaust itself.'

Thus, in near-contemporary opinion, the neo-Sumerian state died of
old age. But the direct instruments of its fate were considered to be the
western barbarians, of whom, like the Guti before them, nothing good
could be said.

The Martu who know no grain;
The Martu who know no house nor town, the boors of the mountains…
The Martu who digs up truffles…
The Martu who eats raw meat.

Their god, also named Amurru, did not even have a house to call his own, says the *Cambridge Ancient History*, and had to be provided with a decent establishment and a wife before he could be admitted to divine society.

Was this a fair assessment? As it happens, we can get a faint glimpse of these Amurru incomers, and their way of life, from their own side of the cultural divide. For we have at last arrived at a point in history that intersects with stories we ourselves still tell about our own religious ancestry.

In Genesis 11:31, '... Terah took Abram his son, and Lot the son of Haran his son's son, and Sarai his daughter in law, his son Abram's wife; and they went forth with them from Ur of the Chaldees, to go into the land of Canaan; and they came unto Haran, and dwelt there.'

Those who believe in the Hebrew Bible as history have long sought the background to the tale of Abraham and his family, their trek around the arc of the Fertile Crescent, from Ur of the Chaldees in Sumer to Haran in the north, and from there westward to the land of Cana'an, in the years following the collapse of Ur's empire. Perhaps, they suggest, Terah took his family from Ur because of the Elamite onslaught and the consequent move of the moon cult from the conquered southern city to safer Haran in the north. Terah's family have names that coincide with nearby places known to have flourished in this era: Serug, Terah's grandfather, corresponds with Sarugi – Seruj today; Nahor, Terah's father and also the name of his second son, with Nahur on the Habur River; Terah himself has been identified with Til Turahi on the Balikh River; his third son, Haran, matches the name of the city itself, some 50 kilometres south-east of today's Şanlıurfa (formerly Edessa), in Turkey. Believers propose that the names of these towns record settlements founded by the figures mentioned in the Bible. Moreover, contemporary letters refer to Haran as the locus of a tribe known as Benjamites, meaning 'sons of the south'.

Terah's family were not Sumerian. They have long been identified with the very people, the Amurru or Amorites, whom Mesopotamian tradition blamed for Ur's downfall. William Hallo, Professor of Assyriology at Yale University, confirms that 'growing linguistic evidence based chiefly on the recorded personal names of persons identified as Amorites... shows that the new group spoke a variety of Semitic ancestral to later Hebrew, Aramaic, and Phoenician.' What is more, as depicted in the Bible, the details of the patriarchs' tribal organization, naming conventions, family structure, customs of inheritance and land tenure, genealogical schemes, and other vestiges of nomadic life 'are too close to the more laconic evidence of the cuneiform records to be dismissed out of hand as late fabrications.'

The Hebrew patriarchs of which the Bible tells are very different from the utterly uncouth savages of the Sumerian texts, as they travel the steppe with their 'flocks and herds and tents'. (Abraham's camels are an anachronism; camels would not be domesticated for several centuries yet.) Their customs may have been different from those of the city folk, but no less respectable and honourable.

Amazingly, we may actually know what some of Abraham's distant relatives looked like. The Amorites took over the town of Mari, on the banks of the Euphrates in today's Syria, in ancient times the most distant outpost of Sumerian civilization and a place that was believed to have once, around the twenty-fifth century BCE, exercised hegemony over all Mesopotamia. Here the nomadic newcomers established the centre of an important kingdom, where the king resided in a palace of extraordinary size and beauty. Some 300 rooms on each of two storeys covered an area of six acres.

Even after the ravages of 4,000 years the geometrical compositions that decorated the royal quarters are still astonishingly fresh. But even more remarkable are the brightly painted tableaux of Mari life that once adorned the administration block: religious ceremonies and battle scenes in the main. Most affecting are the details in the snapshots of humbler characters, Amorites of Abraham's era. A soldier in a tight round white helmet with attached chin-piece, wearing a cloak with gaily knotted ties around his neck, in a way not unfashionable today, rushes bravely forward into the fray in spite of the arrows that seem have pierced his body. A fisherman with short black hair and beard walks home glumly, though a large fish dangles from the stick over his shoulder. A sober-faced man in a black cap and formal robe leads forward a sacrificial ox, the tips of whose horns are sheathed in silver. Sadly the heads have flaked away from the two women shinning up a date palm, one wearing what looks remarkably like a bikini, the other a mini-dress of revealing shortness. Perched in the tree fronds, to quote André Parrot, who conducted excavations here for forty years on behalf of the French National Museums, is 'a magnificent blue bird, with outspread wings, ready to take flight. We had always regarded the bird as a creation of the painter's imagination, but while walking in the palace one day in April 1950, we noticed a great bird of prey almost exactly like it, which, at our approach, flew off in a panic from the ruins where it had its nest.'

If Terah and his family were indeed of Amorite stock and lived at this time, why would he choose to leave Sumer, where their ancestors had presumably arrived not so very long before, leaving most of his kinsmen behind, and just at the time when his fellow tribesmen were taking over the seats of Mesopotamian power? Why would he have given up life in the most advanced city on earth and go back to a tent on the steppe? And why would this detail be remembered for so long afterwards?

Perhaps it was to remind us that only by leaving Ur, would Terah and his little family keep their Amorite identity and their Amorite way of life which was so important to subsequent Hebrew history. Had Terah stayed in Sumer, Abram would have shared in a very different destiny. For the Amorite conquerors proved to be quite unlike the Guti, who had brought down the Akkadians' empire and who had taken so much effort and so long to dislodge. The Amorites would never leave. They would eventually merge into the general population so thoroughly that after a few decades it would be impossible to distinguish them from their predecessors. It probably helped that they spoke languages from the same broad family as the Akkadian *lingua franca* of Mesopotamia. Most likely they were simply dazzled by the extraordinary cultural wealth and richness of history they had stumbled upon and wanted to become part of it. And, crucially, they recognized that the traditions of Sumerian civilization could be success-fully continued whatever the origins of the man on the throne in the city palace. Their task was to take up the baton and carry it forward.

In doing so, Amorite rulers would move the civilized and civilizing arts and sciences to new heights. Their time could be said to be the veritable golden age of Mesopotamian civilization. They would forge all the differ-ent ethnic groups into a new people: the Babylonians. Their state would be centred on a new city: Babylon.

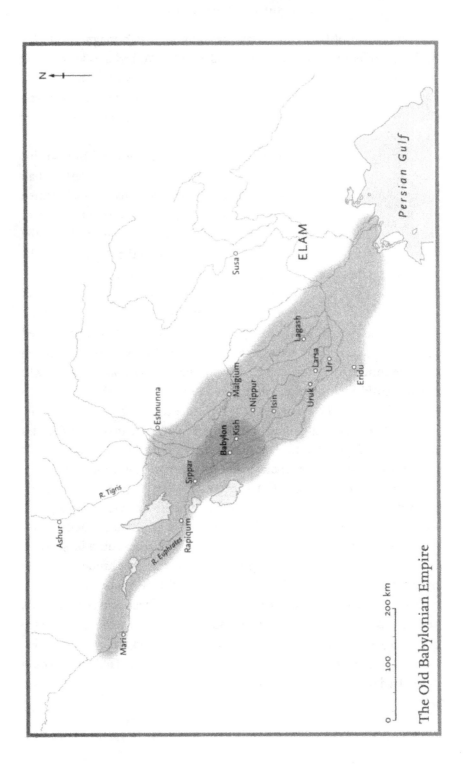

The Old Babylonian Empire

8

Old Babylon:
The Culmination

c.1900 to 1600 BCE

Wonderful, Mystical, Assyrian Babylon

And so, finally, we arrive at Babylon, the most famous, the most notorious, the most splendid, the most excoriated, the most admired, the most vilified city of antiquity. And the most persistent in European memory.

She derives her name from a Greek version of an Akkadian version of some earlier original designation. Akkadians rationalized it by taking it to mean Bab-Ilu, the Gate of God. Genesis claims it derives from a Hebrew root, *Balal*, meaning to mix up, referring to the confusion of tongues by which the hubris of Babel's tower builders was punished.

She owes her location to its strong strategic position: close to the centre of the Mesopotamian plain, near to where Euphrates and Tigris approach each other most closely, today some 500 kilometres from the head of the Gulf.

She can blame her evil repute squarely on the Bible, with its account of the Judaeans' Babylonian exile, 'By the rivers of Babylon, there we sat down, yea, we wept, when we remembered Zion', and of St John's vision, in the Book of Revelation, of the woman 'arrayed in purple and scarlet colour, and decked with gold and precious stones and pearls, having a golden cup in her hand full of abominations and filthiness of her fornication. And upon her forehead was a name written, Mystery: Babylon the Great, mother of harlots and abominations of the earth.'

Yet at the same time, the ancient city's name has borne far more positive associations, among both adults and children, who even in our own times still used sometimes to sing:

How many miles to Babylon?
Three score and ten.
Will I get there by candle-light?
Yes, and back again.
If your heels be nimble and light,
You'll get there by candle-light.

Nobody seems to know the origin or meaning of that children's rhyme, once associated with a street game of some kind, and appearing to refer to the average human lifespan, three score years and ten, as well as to the spirit of life itself, represented as a flickering candle lighting the way. Nobody is even sure that the verse always named Babylon – once upon a time it may have specified Bethlehem, or some other similar sounding place. Yet by our own day the version with Babylon has long overcome all competition, and still regularly appears in the titles of novels, plays, films and even songs. The English-speaking world's greatest experts on children's songs and games, Iona and Peter Opie, concluded that most nursery rhymes were not first sung by children, but are the vestigial remains of once popular ballads and folksongs, of forgotten street cries and passion plays, of long outdated prayers and proverbs. Somehow Babylon, the name of the ancient world's greatest city, though vanished from the surface of the earth these two millennia, has stuck in the popular imagination long enough to be still invoked by children playing in twentieth century streets.

The imperial centres of ancient Egypt or Assyria are familiar only to those tutored in their history. Most places known to Jews and Christians from the Bible – Jerusalem, Shechem, Bethlehem, Nazareth – derive their fame from far later times. Jericho may be one of the oldest inhabited urban centres of all, but is associated in popular culture only with Joshua's sonic demolition of its walls: 'Joshua fit the battle of Jericho, and the walls came tumbling down.' Babylon, on the other hand, is still readily remembered for its pagan greatness. Particularly in England. And even more particularly in London.

Already in the twelfth century, Peter Ackroyd tells us in *London: The Biography*, there was a part of the city wall called Babylon; 'the reasons for that name are unclear; it may be that in the medieval city the inhabitants recognized a pagan or mystical significance within that part of the stone fabric.' As London grew in size and importance over the centuries, the ancient name was increasingly deployed as a metaphor to represent the entire imperial capital. One might think that when the modern metropolis was referred to as Babylon, it would have a pejorative sense. But no. Ackroyd relates that eighteenth-century London was described as '*cette Babylone*' because she provided a safe asylum for the dispossessed: '*le seul refuge des infortunés*'. The poet William Cowper found this 'increasing London', with its multifarious population, to be 'more diverse than Babylon of old', and he meant that as praise; while to Arthur Machen, a Welsh author of the *belle époque*, 'London loomed up before me, wonderful, mystical as Assyrian Babylon, as full of unheard-of things and great unveilings.'

If, to modernizing Britain, the name Babylon symbolized a mysterious but vibrant multicultural megalopolis, other traditions recalled Babylon each in its own way.

To classical authors she was a city of this world, without mystical overtones. Greek and Latin writers from Herodotus in the fifth century BCE to Dio Cassius who lived on into third century Rome, left us prosaic, though sometimes fanciful, accounts of her history, topography, later fortunes and final decay. According to Dio, when Roman Emperor Trajan visited the place in the first century, he found no more than a heap of ruins. On the other hand Theodoret, Bishop of Cyprus in the fifth century, claimed that Babylon was still inhabited (by Jews) during his lifetime.

To devout Christians, Babylon would always be the whore of the Book of Revelation, representing everything that is sinful and wicked about urban living. To Rastafarians, following the teachings of Marcus Garvey, she is the ultimate symbol of everything that oppresses and crushes black people, playing a central role in reggae music's expression of suffering and call to resistance.

To the world of Islam, in whose territory the site lay after the Arab conquests of the seventh century, the name Babylon meant almost nothing. True, several important Arab geographers noted her former location, though sometimes wrongly. But the general attitude of Islam towards the time of *jahilliyah*, 'ignorance' (of the true faith), being so scathing, there was never any great interest in recalling the days when the ancient city flourished. The Qur'an refers to Babylon by name once only, in an entirely neutral sense, when recounting the story of two angels sent to earth by God to tempt humans to sin: 'It was not Solomon who misbelieved, but the devils who misbelieved, teaching men sorcery, and what had been revealed to the two angels at Babylon, Harut and Marut – though these taught no one until they said, "We are but a temptation, so do not misbelieve"' (Sura 2, The Cow, Verse 14).

Round about Al-Hillah, where Babylon's deserted mounds silently slept through the centuries, visible for miles across the otherwise level plain, Muslim villagers populated them imaginatively with demons, jinn and evil spirits, or their physical embodiments, snakes and scorpions; and with the angels Harut and Marut, hanging by their feet and howling loudly in an eternity of punishment. Good reason to keep well away.

Thus it was left to Jews to keep the multi-faceted reality of the ancient centre of civilization alive in western cultural consciousness, waiting for the time when a new spirit of enquiry would lead European explorers to investigate the remains properly, when a new discipline, archaeology, would begin to build a picture of Babylon as she once was, and when the name Babylon would be applied allegorically to the new centre of a world empire.

Ever since King Nebuchadnezzar II, after burning the Temple, exiled the Jerusalem ruling class to Babylon in 586 BCE, southern Mesopotamia had supported the largest and most important communities of Jews. It was there, during the fifth, sixth and seventh centuries of our era, in the Babylonian towns Nehardea, Sura and Pumbedita (this last was probably today's Fallujah), that the more influential of the two recensions of the Talmud was assembled: the compilation of legal precepts, national history and folklore which still lies at the root of all Jewish belief and observance. There, too, was to be found the seat of the *Resh Galuta*, the Exilarch or Head of the Exile, supposedly descended from the royal line of King David and the *de jure* ruler of all Jewry until the eleventh century.

It was unsurprising therefore that the earliest European traveller to write an account of a visit to the ruins of Babylon city should be a Jew: Benjamin, born at Tudela in Iberia, who journeyed around the Near East from the 1160s onwards, collecting information about the conditions of its Jewish communities. Perhaps his aim was to provide guidance to prospective refugees from the increasingly oppressive discrimination against the Jews of Spain after the recapture of Navarre for the Christian church in 1119. After much wandering, he found himself in Resen, near the Euphrates, a location mentioned in the Bible, but now lost to geography. 'Thence it is a day's journey to Babylon, which is the Babel of old,' he wrote in his travel diary.

> The ruins thereof are thirty miles in extent. The ruins of the palace of Nebuchadnezzar are still to be seen there, but people are afraid to enter them on account of the serpents and scorpions. Near at hand, within a distance of a mile, there dwell 3,000 Israelites who pray in the synagogue of the Pavilion of Daniel, which is ancient and was erected by Daniel. It is built of hewn stones and bricks. Between the synagogue and the palace of Nebuchadnezzar is the furnace into which were thrown Hananiah, Mishael, and Azariah, and the site of it lies in a valley known unto all.

Where the Jew led, others followed, though most travellers in the area, including Marco Polo, were happy to repeat hearsay and folklore rather than to investigate for themselves. By contrast, the Italian nobleman and adventurer Pietro della Valle did personally visit the ruins near Al-Hillah in 1616, correctly identifying them as those of Babylon. He is credited as the first European to recognize that the strange clusters of wedge-shaped marks on the bricks he found strewn over the nearby sands were not decoration but writing, and he furthermore somehow deduced that they were to be read from left to right. On his return to Italy in 1626 he was given a celebrity reception and appointed a gentleman of the bedchamber by the Pope. Yet for all that, it seems not to have been in Rome but in London that there was most keen interest in della Valle's revelations. So an unexpected discovery at the end of the nineteenth century tells us.

In 1886 a devastating fire destroyed the church of St Mary Magdalen and a row of old merchants' houses in Knightrider Street in the City of London, a narrow medieval passage not far from the river Thames, named for the fact that it was once the route for knights to make their way from the Tower Royal in Cannon Street to the tournament grounds at Smithfield. After clearing the charred remains, builders began to dig out the ancient foundations. In a layer deep underground they came across a number of fragments of black diorite stone inscribed with cuneiform characters. Sent for identification to the British Museum, they turned out to date, as the press delightedly reported, 'from the time of the oldest Babylonian kingdom as yet known'.

An expert from the British Museum, a Mr B. T. A. Evetts, noted that the houses from under which the stones were recovered dated back to the second half of the seventeenth century and were part of the rebuilding work undertaken after the destruction of the area in the Great Fire of 1666. Referring to the inscribed fragments, he suggested that 'there is hardly any reason to doubt that they were buried among the foundations when the street was afterward restored'. The Warsaw-born Jewish-American Orientalist Morris Jastrow Jr. concluded that more interest than previously supposed had been generated by della Valle's published letters, and the specimens of Babylonian brick that he brought back on his return.

> Learned men and societies began to take an interest in the subject, and since the surfaces of the mounds in Babylonia are commonly strewn with fragments of stone, bits of bricks and pottery, nothing is more likely than that, in consequence of the interest aroused by della Valle, a London merchant should have secured some specimens of these antiquities for his private collection of curios. The whereabouts of the bricks of della Valle above referred to being unknown, the British Museum now takes priority to the Louvre, the oldest piece in whose Babylonian collections was brought to Europe by Michaux, the botanist, in 1782.

The rivalry between London and Paris was real enough. Adventurers of many nationalities had, over the centuries, taken part in the exploration of the ancient Middle East. Towards the end of the Victorian era, just as European imperial powers were beginning the 'scramble for Africa', so also was there strenuous competition between them over the antiquities of the Levant, each striving to unearth and bring home the most impressive remains. By the end of the nineteenth century the field had shrunk to just three, Britain, France and Germany, each with political interests in the region. Britain was concerned to defend the trade routes to her Indian Empire; France was long established by treaty as protector of Catholic Christians in the Ottoman Empire; the newly unified German Empire was eager for support from the Sultan against perceived British attempts to keep her in her place. There were unedifying squabbles between them over the rights to excavation. Public interest was feverish; the spoils were spectacular; national pride was at stake. Magnificent displays were erected in the British Museum, the Louvre in Paris, and Berlin's Vorderasiatisches Museum. But while the astonishing antiquities from all over Mesopotamia were attracting visitors in ever greater number, the highest honour was reserved for whoever could bring the city of Babylon back to life in the public imagination.

Here Germany was definitely the winner. Her increasingly cordial relations with the fading Ottomans made it possible for Robert Johann Koldewey, an architect and art historian turned archaeologist, to unearth and export back to his homeland the entire ceremonial portal known as the Ishtar Gate, as well as part of the processional way leading to it, reconstructed from the original excavated multicoloured tiles. It seemed that very soon it would be possible to establish in fullest detail the whole history of Babylon from earliest times.

These hopes were, however, quickly to be dashed. While the objects transported to Berlin were undoubtedly spectacular, all too soon it was recognized that the Babylon of the excavations represented little more than the final centuries of the city's independent existence: the capital city of King Nebuchadnezzar's empire and of the Judaeans' exile. While beautiful, fascinating, and historically important in their own right, the ruins discovered by della Valle and his successors were not so very ancient at all, but belong to what, in Greece, would be considered part of the late archaic era – hardly very much older, in fact, than the buildings on the Athenian Acropolis. Nothing was found to date from much before the seventh or sixth century BCE. This was rather more than a thousand years after the establishment of the city as the major political player among the new polities founded by Amorite sheikhs in wake of the decline and collapse of the third dynasty of Ur.

The older layers of evidence could not be reached; they proved to be antediluvian in the strict meaning of the word. Through the course of millennia the water-table has inexorably risen, rendering all earlier occupation levels inaccessible to excavation. Thus, to the great chagrin of Assyriologists, we have no direct archaeological or documentary knowledge of Babylon City dating back to its earliest days. Nor are we ever likely to. We are forced to rely for our account of early Babylonian history on oblique hints and incidental references by others. It is like trying to establish the origins of the European renaissance had the city of Florence long ago been swept away by the river Arno.

The comparison is not as fanciful as it may seem. Many equally tumultuous events took place over the several centuries that separated the fall of the Third Dynasty of Ur from the establishment of Babylon as southern Mesopotamia's premier city, centre of the high-point of Mesopotamian civilization.

No King is Powerful Just on His Own

For a few hundred years the political kaleidoscope shook – all over Mesopotamia. Westerners, Amurru in Akkadian, arrived in an unstoppable flood. These were not all one nation; their names tell us that they spoke at least two different west-Semitic dialects. Other peoples entered from the east and the north. They frequently fought against each other. Dynasties rose and fell. Power rewarded intrigue and assassination. City strove against city for superiority. Great battles were fought. Kings took to the field. Some prevailed; some died.

And some found odder and more unusual ends. When the omens were particularly unfavourable it was the custom to spirit the monarch away to safety and temporarily place a commoner on the throne to receive whatever blow fate had in store for the man in the palace. Around 1860 BCE destiny spoke, probably in the form of a lunar eclipse, threatening the Sumerian King Irra-Imitti of Isin. 'That the dynasty might not end,' explains the later text that Assyriologists call the 'Chronicle of Early Kings', the sovereign 'made the gardener Enlil-Bani take his place upon the throne and put the royal tiara upon his head.' Thus legitimized, the pretend-ruler officiated in the temple rites and performed all other royal duties.

The usual course of events – which will be familiar to readers of the Victorian anthropologist Sir James Frazer, much of whose *The Golden Bough* concerns the late survival of this very practice into European history – would have been to wait until the danger had passed and then put the temporary monarch to death. But fate was not as blind as she is usually described and seems to have been perfectly able to distinguish the fake royal from the real: 'Irra-Imitti died in his palace after swallowing boiling broth. Enlil-Bani, who was upon the throne, did not relinquish it and so was established as king.' Enlil-Bani was remarkably success-ful, managing to maintain his rule for almost a quarter of a century, and being declared a god. Maybe the entertaining tale describing his acces-sion to power was merely a cover story for what really happened: a palace putsch – hardly an unusual occurrence in that violent century. A little later the city-state called Kurda was ruled by four kings in ten years, the city Shubat-Enlil the same, the city Ashnakkum saw five rulers in half that time. A palace official, writing from Mari City, confirms that during his period of office, 'No king is truly powerful just on his own: ten to fifteen kings follow Hammurabi of Babylon, as many follow Rim-Sin of Larsa, as many follow Ibal-pi-El of Qatna; but twenty kings follow Yarim-Lim of Yamhad.'

The state of Mari, the most north-westerly outpost of southern Mesopotamian culture, lying some 400 kilometres north of Babylon on the upper Euphrates, was ancient and glorious and boasted a palace that must have been the most splendid of its day. Its elaborately decorated throne room, audience chambers, reception and dining areas, with their frescoed depictions of Abrahamic daily life, must have been regularly thronged with a crush of exotically dressed visiting dignitaries: foreign kings coming to pay homage, vassals arriving with gifts, tribal sheikhs delivering tribute. An enormous entourage of slaves, servants, personal assistants, gentlemen- and ladies-in-waiting, the workforce that serv-iced the daily needs of the king and his several wives, would be pressing urgently through the narrow corridors of the royal private apartments, bearing baskets of clothes, trays of food, jugs of drink and boxes of docu-ments. The administrative block must have been a hive of activity, with its messengers, filing clerks, accountants and auditors, with its bustling secretaries, under-secretaries, assistant under-secretaries and deputy assistant under-secretaries, with its foreign envoys hoping to establish or cement political alliances, and its ambassadors recently returned home to be debriefed and receive fresh instructions.

In one section at ground level is a large scriptorium, where fair cop-ies were made from the scratch-tablets on which letters had been taken down by dictation. In another section the palace archive contains the files, records of correspondence between Mari's kings and officials, and the state's emissaries, enemies and allies, near and far.

All this busy and productive life came to a very sudden end when Mari was taken by Hammurabi, Amorite King of Babylon. Once the Babylonian garrison was in control and all resistance suppressed, the conqueror sent in an intelligence task-force to examine the files. Agents spent many weeks reading through the well over 25,000 documents, sorting them by author, subject and addressee, and placing each group in a separate container. Tablets with contents important to Babylonian national security – all letters from Hammurabi to Mari's ruler Zimri-Lim, for example – were packed up and shipped off by donkey caravan to the capital down south.

Some time later, perhaps after an attempted insurrection, Hammurabi had the entire palace cleared of people and burned to the ground. Workmen then demolished and levelled whatever walls were left standing after the fire. Mari's tragedy was archaeology's gain. The palace archive, its documents sorted into separate categories basket by basket, baked by Mari's final fire into everlasting permanence, were buried under the rubble, where they remained until dug up nearly 4,000 years later, starting in the 1930s, by a French team of Assyriologists led by André Parrot. The more than 23,000 tablets they recovered paint for us a remarkable picture of ancient life and times.

What is particularly striking, over and above the details of political machinations and ever-shifting alliances among the strongmen, warlords and mafia bosses who now dominated Mesopotamia, is that in their letters, you actually hear them talk. They do not couch their correspondence in some formal mode of expression but shoot from the hip and speak from the heart. These are authentic ancestral voices, and mostly they prophesy war.

> *This matter is not for discussion; yet I must say it now and vent my feelings. You are the great king. When you requested of me two horses, I had them conveyed to you. But as for you, you sent me just twenty pounds of tin.*
>
> *Undoubtedly, you could not be honourable with me when you sent this paltry amount of tin. By the god of my father, had you planned sending nothing at all, I might have gotten angry* [but not felt insulted].

Among us in Qatna, the value of such horses is ten pounds of silver. But you sent me just twenty pounds of tin! What would anyone hearing this say? He could not possibly deem us of equal might.

In other words, 'Show me some respect, man!'

But the whingeing ruler of Qatna had made the mistake of tangling with the King of Ekallatum, eldest son of Shamshi-Adad, a *capo di tutti capi* long remembered with great honour in later Assyrian history, who spread his tentacles of power out from his base in the city of Shubat-Enlil. The father's relations with his younger son, who ruled at Mari, read like dialogue from *The Godfather*. While the elder son was consistently praised for his lust for battle, the King of Mari was regularly scolded and denigrated: 'How long do we have to guide you in every matter? Are you a child, and not an adult? Don't you have a beard on your chin? When are you going to take charge of your house? Don't you see that your brother is leading vast armies? So, you too, take charge of your palace, your house.' Now the old mafioso wanted his younger son to teach the King of Qatna a lesson: 'While your brother here is inflicting defeats, you, over there, you lie about amidst women. So now, when you go to Qatna with the army, be a man! As your brother is making a great name for himself, you too, in your country, make a great name for yourself.'

Though we can read much of the correspondence of these gangster-like characters, as people we actually know very little about them. It is like coming to a radio play halfway through. We hear the words, but we do not know whether they are spoken by someone tall or short, fat or thin, old or young, trustworthy or mendacious, given to exaggeration or to understatement. Yet if we go on listening long enough, we can begin to recognize individual characters.

In his 1997 Presidential Address to the American Oriental Society, Professor Jack Sasson drew on a career-long study of correspondence written by Mari's last monarch, Zimri-Lin, who had grabbed the city from Shamshi-Adad's unfortunate younger son, to give us an informed thumbnail sketch.

Despite all the shortcomings, from these letters we were able to penetrate Zimri-Lim's personality. From witty or proverbial statements attributed to him we could decide that his sense of humour was more subtle than crude. We learned also that he was not without vanity, for he pestered his valets for specific cuts of garments and reacted with fury when feeling ignored. He was not without curiosity, for we have records of extensive visits beyond his kingdom. He had a large appetite for details of government, constantly soliciting answers to unsatisfied questions. But he also suffered well the internal bickering and scandal-mongering of bureaucrats vying for his attention. It is obvious, too, that Zimri-Lim was a pious, god-fearing man, prompting his staff to proceed with religious ceremonies and requesting to be kept abreast of the latest messages from the gods. Yet, he was not beyond whining, especially when asked for objects he did not wish to give up. He also seems to have had self-doubts.

How Zimri-Lim ended his life is unknown. But the event marks the close of that long, troubled interregnum between the Third Dynasty of Ur and a new, Babylonian, empire.

A New Social Order

When the Mesopotamian kaleidoscope was finally laid to rest, a novel stable pattern revealed itself – a pattern very different from the old. Centred on Babylon City, scholars call this the Old Babylonian era.

The reality of the new social order is illuminated by one of its best known relics. If King Hammurabi, the sixth ruler of the first dynasty of Babylon and the consolidator of the Old Babylonian Empire, is popularly known for anything, it is his law code, inscribed on a column of black diorite stone, recovered, not from Mesopotamia, but from Susa, the capital city of the state of Elam, now in western Iran. It had been looted as a spoil of war after the Elamite conquest of Babylonia in the thirteenth century BCE, half a millennium after the lifetime of its author.

Surmounted by an image of the king receiving the law from Shamash, sun god and patron of justice, this object probably once stood in a public court at a temple in Sippar. Other copies would have been found right across the king's realm, notably in the god Marduk's temple in Babylon, Esagila, the House with the Raised Head, cultic centre of Babylon City and therefore of the whole empire. In the text, Hammurabi himself describes purpose of the stele: 'Let the oppressed, who has a case at law, come and stand before this my image as king of righteousness; let him have read to him the inscription on this monument, let him hear my precious words; the inscription will explain his case to him; he will discover what is just, and his heart will be glad, so that he will say: "Hammurabi is a ruler who is as a father to his subjects."'

As with the earlier laws of Ur-Nammu, this is not a law code in our modern sense. It is not totally comprehensive; nor does it set out legal principles. Instead it provides a list of paradigms, records of model cases supposedly heard before the king but in fact probably representing long judicial tradition, rather like Anglo-Saxon common law, with its preference for precedent and case law, and its strong distaste for all-embracing schemes like the continental Code Napoléon.

The text does, nevertheless, cover a great range of eventualities. After a long preamble, praising Hammurabi as protector of the weak and oppressed, and detailing the regions over which he ruled, comes a list of some 280 judgements concerning the family, slavery and professional, commercial, agricultural and administrative law, including setting standard commodity prices and hirelings' wages. The section on family law is the largest, dealing with engagement, marriage and divorce, adultery and incest, children, adoption and inheritance.

Many of the judgements strike the modern reader as fair and reasonable. For example,

If a man wish to separate from a woman who has borne him children, or from his wife who has borne him children: then he shall give that wife her dowry, and a part of the income from field, garden, and property, so that she can rear her children. When she has brought up her children, a portion of all that is given to the children, equal as that of one son, shall be given to her. She may then marry the man of her heart.

If a woman quarrel with her husband, and says: 'You are not congenial to me,' the reasons for her prejudice must be presented. If she is guiltless, and there is no fault on her part, but he leaves and neglects her, then no guilt attaches to this woman, she shall take her dowry and go back to her father's house.

On the other hand Hammurabi's laws famously differ from those of Ur-Nammu, in that rather than specifying financial penalties, many judgements enshrine the principle of *lex talionis*, the law of retribution, otherwise known as 'an eye for an eye':

If a man put out the eye of another man, his eye shall be put out.
If he break another man's bone, his bone shall be broken.
If a man knock out the teeth of his equal, his teeth shall be knocked out.
If a builder build a house for someone, and does not construct it properly, and the house which he built fall in and kill its owner, then that builder shall be put to death.
If it kill the son of the owner the son of that builder shall be put to death.

It used often proposed that these apparently more cruel penalties expose a residual and irreducible savage barbarism intrinsic to the Semitic as opposed to the noble Sumerian mentality. There is a strong whiff of prejudice about such a judgement. Far more likely, Hammurabi's laws reflect the shock of an unprecedented social environment: the multi-ethnic, multi-tribal Babylonian world.

In earlier Sumerian–Akkadian times, all communities had felt themselves to be joint members of the same family, all equally servants under the eyes of the gods. In such circumstances disputes could be settled by recourse to a collectively accepted value system, where blood was thicker than water, and fair restitution more desirable than revenge. Now, however, when urban citizens commonly rubbed shoulders with nomads following a completely different way of life, when speakers of several west Semitic Amurru languages, as well as others, were thrown together with uncomprehending Akkadians, confrontation must all too easily have spilled over into conflict. Vendettas and blood feuds must often have threatened the cohesion of the empire. Just as today the sterner social system of the USA, with its abhorrence of collective provision of public services and commitment to the death penalty expresses its identity as a nation of immigrants and deportees from many countries and backgrounds, in contrast to the predilection for social market solidarity and justice tempered by mercy in continental Europe, until very recently a far more ethnically homogenous realm, so do the draconian Babylonian laws, like the similar legal provisions of the Hebrew Bible, both reflect and attempt to limit the potential for discord and violence that always haunts a fragmented society. The contrast with previous legal compendiums tells us that the rules of the game had changed, that radically different social arrangements had come into being.

Gone was the ancient perception of the land as divided into the spheres of influence of separate city-states, each with its own ruling divinity, the 2,000-year-old notion of city, land, people, crops and livestock as foundation and property of the gods. Hereon in the pattern would be one of large territorial states. Two major centres would emerge: Ashur, eventually controlling all the north, and Babylon, ruling over all the south.

Gone was the sense of unity, of an entire population sharing the same Sumerian–Akkadian ancestry, the same burdens, the same destiny. It could hardly be otherwise, when so many of the ruling class traced their origins to ancestors from elsewhere. An odd ambivalence of attitude towards the incomers persisted. At the same time as literary texts were showering the Amurru with contempt as primitive and hostile barbarians, Hammurabi of Babylon was still proudly calling himself King of the Amorites. But though the famous law code implies that individuals from different communities not infrequently locked horns with each other, there seems to have been no permanent legacy of general ethnic strife among the people. We do find hints at social divisions, though.

Hammurabi's laws tell us that there were three classes in Babylon: *awilum*, 'freeman' or 'gentleman', *mushkenum*, a member of the lower orders, and *wardum*, slave. The word *mushkenum* comes from a Semitic form, meaning 'that which is, or he who is, put in its place'. (The same Semitic root is still in use, nearly 4,000 years later, in some modern romance languages like French, where *mesquin* means base, shabby or wretched.) Though there is no actual evidence, it is tempting to interpret *awilum* as originally denoting a member of the incoming Amorite ruling class, and *mushkenum* as a native of the land now reduced to lower status. Whether that be true or not, it can certainly be said that the loss of ethnic uniformity led, as it has so often done at different times and in different places, to the disappearance of social solidarity. The longstanding Sumerian communal ideal was dead and buried.

Gone, therefore, was the Sumerian attraction to collectivism and central planning. From now on came an era of privatization and outsourcing

– there would be no such thing as society, just individual men and women and families, some wealthy, some poor, some weak, some powerful. Of course there remained the great temple and palace estates, but they shed most of their workforce, and with it their responsibility for those who serviced their needs, bureaucrats and craftspeople as well as ploughmen and stock-herders. Instead farmhands and artisans were hired and fired according to season, and independent entrepreneurs and tax-farmers were contracted to sustain the estates' monetary and commercial affairs.

The result was a financial system recognisably related to our own, featuring banking and investment, loans, mortgages, shares and bonds, trading companies and business partnerships. This was history's first experiment in mercantilist capitalism, with all its consequences, negative as well as positive.

The positive result was to make some people very rich. In his excavations, Leonard Woolley uncovered what has been called the financial district of Ur, separated from the palace and temple compound by the large canal that divided the town into two. This was not, as its alternative description as Ur's Wall Street might imply, a particularly splendid location where majestic buildings lined grand thoroughfares. Simple two-storied residences crowded against each other along a maze of twisting lanes and narrow alleyways, along which no more than a single donkey could pass at a time. To find any particular house, you would have to follow complicated directions of the kind satirized in a humorous anecdote of the period: 'You should enter by the Grand Gate and pass a street, a boulevard, a square, Tillazida Street, and the ways of Nusku and Nininema to your left. You should ask Nin-lugal-Apsu, daughter of Ki'agga-Enbilulu, daughter-in-law of Ninshu-ana-Ea-takla, a woman gardener of the Henun-Enlil gardens, who sits on the ground in Tillazida selling produce. She will show you.' Arriving at the address Woolley named Number 3 Niche Lane, there was the office, and perhaps home, of businessman Dumuzi-Gamil, an educated, cautious and thrifty merchant, who preferred to keep his records in his own idiosyncratic hand, disdaining to employ a scribe either because of the cost, the challenge to his self-respect or the desire to keep his affairs strictly confidential – hired scribes had a reputation for being unable to keep their mouths shut. The large number of documents found apparently buried under the floor

The aesthetic deprivation of the non-elite: Crudely moulded bevelled-rim bowls are found all over Mesopotamia, dating from the Uruk era – fourth millennium BCE.

The celebration of individual identity: The first known personal signature, of a scribe called GAR.AMA, dated to about 3000 BCE.

'The lips have no need to part for us to hear what she has to say': (*left*) André Parrot, Curator-in-Chief of the French National Museums describes the alabaster sculpture, probably of the goddess Inanna, known as 'The Lady of Uruk', created around 3100 BCE.

Not the goddess herself but the high priestess who represents her: (*below*) The worship of the Great Goddess of Uruk in around 3100 BCE from the upper register of the Warka.

Members of the dead king's court: (*above*) The royal cemetery known as the Great Death Pit of Ur, dating from about 2500 BCE and uncovered in 1928 by Leonard Woolley. The scene of human sacrifice as imagined by the *Illustrated London News*.

'They lay down and composed themselves for death.': (*below*) The scene in the great Death Pit, as shown in the *Illustrated London News*, after the royal servants and retainers had taken the poison draught but before the communal grave was filled in.

Ruler of the Four Quarters: (*left*) Life-size copper head, possibly depicting King Sargon of Akkad (reigned c. 2300 BCE), excavated in 1931 from the site of the Assyrian city of Nineveh.

Dignity, formality and serenity: (*below*) One of many votive statuettes of Gudea, Ensi (Governor) of Lagash in about 2120 BCE, dug up from the mound of Telloh, ancient Girsu, the major city of the state of Lagash.

'After kingship was lowered from heaven, the kingship was in Eridu': (*above*) The Weld-Blundell Prism inscribed with the Sumerian King List, written by an unnamed scribe in the city of Larsa in Babylonia in about 1800 BCE.

'Victorious in nine battles in a single year': (*above right*) King Naram-Sin's Victory Stele, celebrating his defeat, around 2200 BCE, of the Lullubi, a people of the mountains.

The bones of their attendants were strewn about the plain: (*right*) Fragment of the so-called Stele of the Vultures, named after these carrion-eaters carved on one side. The stele celebrated the victory of King Eannatum of Lagash over King Enakalle of Umma in about 2500 BCE.

'Let the oppressed, who has a case at law, come and stand before this my image as king of righteousness': From the preamble to Hammurabi's law code. The top the monument shows Shamash the Sun God, patron of justice, and Hammurabi King of Babylon (ruled c. 1700 BCE). The monument was looted from the city of Sippar and taken to Susa in Elam, where it was found by French archaeologists in 1901.

The Garden Party: Wall panel from the North Palace at Nineveh, unearthed by Austen Henry Layard in the mid-nineteenth century, showing Assyrian King Ashurbanipal and his Queen Ashur-sharrat dining in their garden some time around 645 BCE, with the head of the King of Elam hanging from a tree.

Shooting projectiles over the heads of the infantry: Assyrian archers and slingers in action at the siege of the Judean city of Lachish in 701 BCE. From a wall panel in Sennacherib's palace at Nineveh, according to the King a 'palace without rival'.

The lion hunt: (*above*) Assyrian huntsmen, from a seventh century BCE wall panel
in Sennacherib's palace at Nineveh. Assyrian horsemen fought sitting on a blanket,
secured only by breastband, girth and crupper.

Without saddles or stirrups: (*below*) Detail of above.

show him to have been a highly successful exponent of Old Babylonian commercial practice.

Not very long before Hammurabi succeeded in consolidating all Babylonia into a single imperial state, he and a business partner, Shumi-Abiya, borrowed a little over an ounce of silver from the businessman Shumi-Abum. They invested the money in bakeries that supplied the temples and palaces of Ur and Larsa with grain and bread. Woolley recovered a receipt issued by King Rim-Sin of Larsa, Isin and Ur, for a monthly supply of some 150 bushels of barley. The partners not only dealt with the great and the good. They lent much smaller amounts over much shorter terms to farm-workers and fishermen who needed emergency loans to pay their taxes. In turn, Shumi-Abum, who had advanced the partners the silver, sold the debt on to another partnership, Nur-Ilishu and Sin-Ashared. There was, it seems, an active market for bonds and what we now call commercial paper in Old Babylon. Dumuzi-Gamil's files similarly listed sums credited and debts owing to other merchants both in his home city and elsewhere. These records could be used as negotiable instruments, the original of our paper money. Investments made in overseas trading expeditions brought Babylonian merchants close to what we recognize as commodity futures.

In short, the financial system that flowered in Hammurabi's Babylon, had in place the very techniques which, when rediscovered several thousand years later, enabled first the Jews, then the Lombards and Venetians, to finance the expansion of the European economy during the Middle Ages. However, among the downsides of this proto-liberal economic revolution were the encouragement of debt, an ever-widening gap between the haves and the have-nots, and the reduction of many to penury and worse.

The term of Dumuzi-Gamil's silver loan was five years; the interest rate specified by law for silver was 20 per cent. That sounds very steep. But the cost of borrowing money was calculated differently in those days. Rates may not have been permitted to vary competitively, but as they were levied over the whole term of the debt and not calculated annually, varying the repayment date changed the equivalent annual rate. Twenty per cent interest over five years, as in Dumuzi-Gamil's case, is the same as something over 3 per cent a year: far more reasonable. Had the same been charged over two years, it would have equated just under 10 per cent per annum.

Dumuzi-Gamil's records show that when he made loans to workers and artisans, the repayment date was usually one or two months ahead. Over such a short time, the interest rate was the equivalent of up to 800 per cent APR: highly rewarding to the lender, but absolutely crippling to the debtor.

The privatized revenue agents and tax-farmers who preyed on the populace were relentless. Not only did they have to extract the cash owing to the tax-man, they also had to increase the obligation to ensure an income for themselves. Many of their victims were forced to sell themselves or members of their family into slavery because they simply could not pay. In the end the debt mountain grew to such colossal dimensions that something had to be done. Radical solutions were implemented that would have a long resonance in the history of finance.

Firstly, the law prescribed that debt slavery be limited to three years only. Hammurabi's law code specifies: 'If any one fail to meet a claim for debt, and sell himself, his wife, his son, or daughter for money or give them away to forced labour: they shall work for three years in the house of the man who bought them, or the proprietor, and in the fourth year they shall be set free.'

More dramatic yet, when the degree of general indebtedness grew so large as to threaten the financial, or even political, stability of the state, was the proclamation of general 'debt forgiveness', when all loans were declared null and void. Such edicts, often accompanying an amnesty for prisoners of the state, were the norm on the accession of a new ruler. But they were also sometimes promulgated mid-reign, such as when King Rim-Sin, a decade or so before his fiefdom fell to Hammurabi, suddenly declared all loans void, and in doing so completely wiped out Dumuzi-Gamil's cosy partnership, as well as much other business activity in Ur. There are suggestions that debt-remission was limited to short-term personal loans that funded consumption or tax-paying, and that borrowing for investment, as well as to pay fines and penalties, was excluded. That was not enough to rescue Babylonian business, which took many years to return to its previous levels of activity.

Perhaps the wild business-cycle enforced by such a crude method of control appeared less damaging to those who experienced it than it does to us. For the lesson was taken up many centuries later by the Hebrews, who in Deuteronomy 15 incorporated it into their religious law:

At the end of every seven years thou shalt make a release.

And this is the manner of the release: Every creditor that lendeth ought unto his neighbour shall release it; he shall not exact it of his neighbour, or of his brother; because it is called the Lord's release...

And if thy brother, an Hebrew man, or an Hebrew woman, be sold unto thee, and serve thee six years; then in the seventh year thou shalt let him go free from thee.

And when thou sendest him out free from thee, thou shalt not let him go away empty handed.

And finally, emphasizing the total political, social, and economic volte-face represented by the Old Babylonian Empire, gone were the last vestiges of Sumerian cultural dominance.

As a living language, Sumerian was finished. From now on Mesopotamia would be a land solely of Semitic everyday culture and Semitic everyday speech, though this would not be the western Semitic of the new ruling class, but a dialect of indigenous Akkadian that philologists call Old Babylonian. Nobody knows exactly when Sumerian stopped being heard in the streets. Perhaps some time towards the end of the previous Ur III era. Which is not to say that every use of the Sumerian language ceased. That would not happen until the final end of Mesopotamian civilization some 2,000 years hence. But it survived to be written rather than spoken, reserved for religion and scholarship rather than vernacular communication.

Such preservation of written Sumerian in later times is usually compared to the role of Latin as the language of learning in European history: from the fall of the western Roman Empire almost to the mid twentieth century, when the classics were finally abandoned by most schools. The analogy is slightly inaccurate because, of course, Latin never ceased to be spoken: following the usual processes of linguistic evolution, spoken Latin slowly turned into French, Italian, Spanish, Portuguese and the other modern languages of the Romance family. Written Latin on the other hand, as a language of scholars, stayed frozen at the stage it had reached in the first century of the Common Era.

A more useful comparison for Sumerian would be Hebrew. For more than 2,000 years after it stopped being spoken, replaced in everyday life first by Aramaic and later by the local languages of the Diaspora, Hebrew remained the religious, literary and scholarly language of the Jews, and the medium for teaching Jewish children to read and write. Whatever tongue ruled in the home and the workplace, the Hebrew alphabet was adapted to represent it. Eventually it would be the basis upon which spoken Hebrew was reinvented at the end of the nineteenth century. In a similar fashion Sumerian remained the basis of literacy for as long as cuneiform continued to be written.

What Sumerian, Latin and Hebrew all have in common is their role as touchstones, as symbolic markers, of their respective traditions. Command of Sumerian, at whatever level, would always be the entry ticket to taking part in the great and continuous cultural tradition that now in Babylonia, quite ignoring the continuous 'warfare, terror, murder and bloodshed' all around, was reaching the peak of its development.

The new masters of Mesopotamia used the Sumerian language and the Sumerian cultural tradition as a glue to hold together the now diverse populations of their realm. Just as in France citizens are taught fidelity to the Revolution and to *Liberté, Égalité, Fraternité*, and in the USA schoolchildren are taught loyalty to the flag, the constitution and to the ideals of the Founding Fathers, so in Old Babylon were the king's subjects, wherever their origin, taught to honour the ancient myths, legends and sacred stories, as well as the habits and the history, so far as it was known, of their Sumerian predecessors in the land. Religious beliefs remained largely unchanged, about the only innovation being the introduction to the pantheon of Babylon City's patron deity Marduk, who slowly took over the status and prerogatives of Enlil, former king of the gods. Distinguished scribes even adopted Sumerian names, just like those European scholars of the Middle Ages and even later, who classicized their identities, preferring be known, for example, not as simple Neumann but Neander, not as plain Schwartzerd but Melanchthon, and not as mere Philip von Hohenheim, but as Philippus Theophrastus Aureolus Bombastus – Paracelsus for short.

That made education of paramount importance. Indeed it was central to Babylonian civilization. No longer institutionalized in large and carefully regulated state-run academies, like those established in Ur III times by King Shulgi, but privatized like everything else in the new Babylonia, the education system none the less bequeathed us a huge legacy of documentary evidence: a small mountain of discarded written exercises and test-pieces. As a result we know more about what schooldays were like than many other aspects of life in ancient Babylon.

The Babylonian School

In Sumerian, school was called *E-Dubba*, in Babylonian *Bet-Tuppi*. Both names refer to the tablets on which documents were written. All education was based on reading and writing Sumerian and Babylonian text. From the résumé of a newly graduated student:

> *The total number of days I worked at school is as follows: I had three days of vacation each month: and since each month has three holidays when one does not work, I therefore spent twenty-four days in school each month. And it did not seem like a very long time to me!*
>
> *From now on I will be able to devote myself to recopying and composing tablets, undertaking all useful mathematical operations. Indeed, I have a thorough knowledge of the art of writing: how to put the lines in place and to write. My master has only to show me a sign and I can immediately, from memory, connect a large number of other signs to it. Since I have attended school the requisite amount of time I am abreast of Sumerian, of spelling, of the content of all tablets.*

Our graduate has not only mastered reading, writing and 'rithmetic, but has acquired many other office skills too.

> *I can compose all sorts of texts: documents dealing with measurements of capacity, from 300 to 180,000 thousand litres of barley; of weight, from eight grams to ten kilograms; any contract that might be requested of me: marriage, partnership, sales of real-estate and slaves; guarantees for obligations in silver; of the hiring out of fields; of the cultivation of palm groves; including adoption contracts. I can draw up all of these.*

All very impressive and maybe even true, although it sounds rather like an extract from a modern school brochure. Our graduate's account of his abilities undoubtedly paints an idealized picture of the deregulated Old Babylonian education system.

We receive a rather different impression, perhaps closer to the truth, from an anonymous writer – a sort of Charles Dickens or Thomas Hughes of ancient Babylon. This much-copied short story was called 'Schooldays' by its first translator and editor Samuel Noah Kramer, who pieced it together from more than twenty separate fragments lying in different museums, and it satirizes the randomness of the discipline, the corruption of the teacher and a risible lack of correspondence between praise and achievement. Not that the hero is much of a paragon of virtue.

The story begins with an account of a normal day's events. Our protagonist goes to school, reads out an exercise, eats his lunch, copies out further texts, returns home and shows off what he has learned to his father. His father is pleased with his progress, which the schoolboy takes as an excuse suddenly to turn into a little monster.

> *I am thirsty, give me drink!*
> *I am hungry, give me bread!*
> *Wash my feet, set up the bed!*
> *I want to go to sleep.*
> *Wake me early in the morning.*

All this serves as a contrast to what happens the very next day. At first everything seems normal enough. He gets up early, his mother gives him a packed lunch, and off he goes. Yet when he gets there, a supervisor stops him.

> *'Why are you late?'*
> *I was afraid, my heart beat fast.*
> *I went in and sat down, and my teacher read my tablet. He said 'There's something missing!'*
> *And he caned me.*
> *One of the monitors said 'Why did you open your mouth without my permission?'*
> *And he caned me.*
> *The one in charge of rules said 'Why did you get up without my permission?'*
> *And he caned me.*
> *The gateman said 'Why are you going out without my permission?'*
> *And he caned me.*

> *The keeper of the beer jug said 'Why did you get some without my*
> *permission?'*
> *And he caned me.*
> *The Sumerian supervisor said 'Why did you speak Akkadian?'*
> *And he caned me.*
> *My teacher said 'Your handwriting is no good!'*
> *And he caned me.*

Bewildered by the sudden turn in his fortunes, the boy goes home and hatches a plan. He suggests that his father invite the teacher to dinner. But not to protest at his son's treatment; the strategy is far subtler than that.

> *To that which the schoolboy said, his father gave heed.*
> *The teacher was brought from school.*
> *Having entered the house, he was seated in the seat of honour.*
> *The schoolboy took a chair and sat down before him.*
> *Whatever he had learned of the scribal art, he unfolded to his father.*
> *His father, with a joyful heart says joyfully to his 'school-father': You*
> *train the hand of my young one, you make of him an expert, show him all*
> *the finer points of the scribal art.*
> *Having cynically showered the teacher with praise, father and son pro-*
> *ceed shamelessly to lavish food, drink and presents on him.*
> *They poured out for him the good date-wine, brought him a stand,*
> *made flow the good oil in his vessel like water,*
>   *dressed him in a new garment,*
>   *gave him a gift, put a bracelet about his wrist.*

To which the teacher quite openly responds in the way expected of him.

> *Because you gave me that which you were by no means obliged to give,*
>   *presented me with a gift over and above my earnings,*
>   *showed me great honour,*
>   *may Nidaba [goddess of scribes], the queen of the guardian deities,*
> *be your guardian deity,*
>   *may she show favour to your reed stylus,*
>   *may she take all error from your hand copies.*

Of your brothers, may you be their leader,
of your companions, may you be their chief,
may you rank highest among all the schoolboys.'

If the word school conjures up in the mind the image of a large building with a playground and many pupils, that would be a mistake. Whatever the academies of Ur and Nippur set up by King Shulgi may have been like, in Old Babylonian days schooling took place in private dwellings, rather like the dame schools of the Victorian era, except that the instruction was undertaken by men. Also, though some archaeologists believed they had discovered schoolrooms, for example in the traces of a large chamber furnished with benches in the palace of Mari found by André Parrot, actually most learning must have taken place outside. Dealing with cuneiform text had to be largely an outdoor activity.

Writing, as we still do it today, with ink on papyrus, vellum, parchment or paper, depends for its readability on the contrast between the black, or at least dark, ink against a white, or at least pale, background. Though good light helps, it is not indispensable. The marks of cuneiform writing on clay are three-dimensional. There is no contrast in colour or tone between the sign and its substrate. To read or to write cuneiform demands excellent, and steady, illumination.

But ancient Mesopotamian interiors were dark. This is a very hot country for much of the year, boasting some of the highest temperatures to be found anywhere in the world. Every effort must be made to keep out the sun. In Babylonian houses windows were either entirely absent or heavily shuttered during the day. Literacy must have been learned – and indeed practised – in a courtyard under the open sky, either outside, within the house or perhaps on the roof.

Nevertheless, although the physical premises of a Babylonian and a nineteenth-century school may be quite different, the two still have much in common. The teacher in 'Schooldays', for example, is susceptible to bribery because he is a paid employee, rather than the equivalent of a master of apprentices. The monitors and supervisors who cane the protagonist may well have been senior boys, so-called 'elder brothers', constituting a kind of prefect system. And as in the nineteenth century, education seems to have been, in theory, open to all. We do not know whether Babylonian kings like Hammurabi could read and write, unlike King Shulgi of Ur who boasted of his education and his abilities as a scribe. But scholars believe that literacy was much more widely spread among the Old Babylonian population than at any time before or after in Mesopotamian history. The student body was not restricted to any particular caste, such as priests or bureaucrats. As in Victorian times, sending children to school was apparently open to any parents who did not need their offspring to contribute to household earnings – and for quite a long time, too, perhaps rather more than ten years. Ordinary families would have found this an impossibly great sacrifice. In one text, a father, complaining about his son's attitude to study, demands that his son show due appreciation:

Never in all my life did I make you carry reeds to the canebrake. The reed rushes which the young and the little carry, never in your life did you carry them. I never said to you 'Follow my caravans.' I never sent you to work to plough my field. I never sent you to work to dig my field. I never sent you to work as a labourer. I never in my life said to you, 'Go, work and support me.' Others like you support their parents by working.

We do not know how schooling was paid for, nor how much it cost. In any case, only better off families could have managed without their children's labour – although poor boys were sometimes adopted and sent to school. In common with many traditional societies to this day, reading and writing was a matter mainly for men, although there were female scribes too, some of whose names are known.

As in European schools until not so long ago, education was often in the hands of the clergy. Private schools were set up in the homes of temple officials, like Ur-Utu, a *kalamahhum*-priest in the city called Sippar-Amnanum, about 80 kilometres from Babylon, from whose residence several thousand student exercise-tablets were recovered. But the great difference between Mesopotamian religion and Christianity expresses itself in the apparent absence of explicit religious instruction. No texts discuss the nature of divinity, no tablets record meditations about the meaning of life; there are no documents laying down theological doctrine, nor prescriptions for the correct worship of the gods. Though ancient religious myths, and many hymns, were copied and recopied as writing exercises, the education that students received appears to have been largely secular, a great contrast with the education system in our own world, which has taken nearly 2,000 years to distance itself from the church, its original sponsor.

Babylonian schooling being restricted to the elite who were destined to fill all positions for which literacy was needed, the pupils received a general education with a broad curriculum. This was far from narrow vocational training. Students were taught not only the necessities for the future occupation of scribe, but they followed a liberal timetable that encompassed all the knowledge of the day. No doubt they would receive further instruction upon entering their final adult profession, whatever it may have been. Accountant, administrator, architect, astrologer, clerk, copyist, military engineer, notary, priest, public scribe, seal-cutter, secretary, surveyor, teacher are just some of which we know. But the foundations for all further study were laid in the schools.

It is clear from the recent graduate's résumé that arithmetic was as important to Babylonian education as reading and writing. A closer look at how the art of working with figures was taught and learned tells us much about how Babylonians approached all forms of knowledge.

To begin with, we must recognise that the ability to manipulate numbers was more advanced in that ancient era than at most times in European history. In his book *Beyond Numeracy*, the mathematician John Allen Paulos relates an anecdote about a medieval German businessman who inquired where he should send his son to be educated in mathematics. 'If you want him to master addition and subtraction,' was the reply, 'the local university will be adequate. But if you want him also to be able to perform multiplication and division, you will have to send him to Italy to study.' No such limitations applied to Babylonian schools. But they had an advantage. Their way of writing numbers was far superior to the Roman numerals that medieval Europeans were saddled with until early modern times. Here was the earliest known form of 'positional notation' – the 'hundreds, tens and units' that we learn as children. It differed from our modern system only in that, using so-called Arabic numerals, we make each place to the left ten times larger, while the Babylonians made it sixty times larger. What they wrote as 𒐕𒐕𒐕𒐕 (1111) represented, in our numerals, 216,000 + 3,600 + 60 + 1, which is 219,661. As is well known, we still preserve the Babylonian number system, based on multiples of 60 when we speak of 95,652 seconds as 26 hours, 34 minutes and 12 seconds, or when we write down the size of an angle as 26° 34' 12'. To Babylonians that number was 𒐀𒐀 𒐀𒐀 𒐀.

Two signs they lacked were zero and the decimal point. For zero they could have left a gap in the number – but mostly they did not. As a result, only context could differentiate between 26, 206, 2006, 260 or 2600. It would be several thousand years before the Arabs popularized the Indian notion that an empty place in a row of figures could be represented like any other number. (The Arabs used a point, '.', to represent it. Our 'o' actually comes from Rabbi Abraham ibn Ezra's book *Sefer ha-Mispar*, the Book of the Number, the earliest explanation of Indo-Arabic numbers to be published in Europe, written in Hebrew at Verona in 1146.) In fact Mesopotamians did eventually devise a way of marking a space in a number. But not until very much later, about 700 BCE perhaps. And not for use at the end of figures. Babylonian numbers were always true 'floating point': 26, 260, 2600, as well as 2.6, 0.26 and 0.026, were always represented identically.

Dealing with a number base as large as sixty, rather than base ten as we use today, was a stumbling-block to schoolchildren trying to remember their times tables. Up to ten is easy to learn by heart; a little more than ten is also possible. Before the decimalisation of British money, pupils had perforce to memorize multiplication tables up to twelve, since there were twelve pennies to the shilling. Dozens, too, were still in common use and every schoolchild knew that a dozen dozens was a gross. Early in the computer era, it was useful to write numbers based on multiples of sixteen, known as hexadecimal; six extra number signs had to be brought in: 1 to 9 was followed by A to F. Many computer enthusiasts knew multiplication tables up to sixteen by heart. But keeping in your head tables for every number up to sixty is too much to ask. So when passing a Babylonian school, we would probably not have heard the familiar sound of children chanting 'two ones are two; two twos are four'. And if we did, we would certainly not hear them go up to 'thirty-one fifty-threes are a thousand six hundred and forty-three'. Instead the Babylonians had recourse to multiplication tables written out on clay tablets.

Using such tables, the procedure to perform multiplication, even of very large numbers, was relatively straightforward. Division, however, was a problem. The Babylonians solved it with a method analogous to one that most people who went to school before the last third of the twentieth century would also recognize. Where we used to consult tables of base-ten logarithms, which made big calculations possible using only addition and subtraction, they used tables of reciprocals: one divided by the relevant number. (For example the reciprocal of two is ½ or, in our decimal system, 0.5. The reciprocal of 4 is ¼ or 0.25. The reciprocal of 5 is ⅕ or 0.2.) With reciprocal tables to hand, they were able to turn division into multiplication, because to divide by any number is the same as to multiply by its reciprocal – 12 divided by 4 is the same as 12 multiplied by 0.25.

Other tables were frequently put to use too: lists of squares and cubes as well as square and cube roots. With these, Babylonian students were expected to be able to solve really quite advanced mathematical problems. They had solutions for linear equations – a method similar, modern mathematicians note, to Gaussian elimination – for quadratic and cubic equations, for calculating the hypotenuse of right-angled triangles (Pythagoras's theorem), for deducing the areas of polygons, for working with circles and chords of circles – they called them bowstrings. Their approximation for π, 'pi', was 3⅛, which, at 3.125, is not so very far from the value we use, 3.14159 – closer, at any rate, than the value 3 prescribed in the Bible about a thousand years later.

If all the above looks fairly daunting, it is because it is expressed in the abstract language of modern mathematics. Babylonians educators put such problems much more accessibly. Like Victorian schoolbooks, they set them in entirely concrete, practical, situations. Just as our nineteenth-century ancestors were confronted with questions like 'if 8 men in 14 days can mow 112 acres of grass, how many men can mow 2,000 acres in 10 days?', so Babylonian schoolboys struggled over: 'With a volume of earth of 90 I shall capture the city hostile to Marduk. From the foot of the earth-ramp I went forwards 32 lengths. The height of the earth-ramp is 36: what is the length I have to advance in order to capture the city?'

Expressing maths in the form of apparently practical problems extended even to complex algebra. Where today we might ask a student to find the value of x in the quadratic equation $11x2 + 7x = 6.25$, a text from about 1800 BCE states: 'I have added seven times the side of my square to eleven times its area, and it is 6 15.' In Babylonian hexagesimal numbers, six and fifteen sixtieths represents our 6.25 or six and a quarter. The problem implied here is to find the length of the side. (It has been couched in terms of an imaginary geometry in which one can add a length to an area). Where a modern mathematician would apply the general quadratic formula, the Babylonian solution was reached this way:

> *You take 7 and 11. You multiply 11 by 6 15 and it is 1 8 45. You halve 7 and obtain 3 30. You multiply 3 30 and 3 30. You add the result, 12 15 to 1 8 45 and the result 1 21 has 9 as its square root. You subtract 3 30, which you multiplied by itself, from 9 and you have 5 30. The reciprocal of 11 does not divide. What shall I multiply by 11 so that 5 30 results? 0 30 is its factor. 0 30 is the side of the square.*

Typically for the Babylonians, the procedure for finding the solution is minutely described but never explained, and never reduced to a principle. One modern mathematician has suggested that such an approach will be quite familiar to anybody who remembers being 'subjected to an old-fashioned high school algebra course, where one learned of, say, quadratic equations by doing a large number of problems with varying coefficients instead of stating and proving a theorem which shows once and for all how to solve any quadratic equation that may arise.

Whether This is So, I Shall Ascertain

The preference for the concrete over the abstract, for practice over theory, for specific examples over general principles, extended into every area of Babylonian study, thought and intellectual life. It was one of the most significant characteristics of this high point of Mesopotamian civilization, indeed of all Mesopotamian civilization both before and long after, which may be one of the reasons why the Greeks, who favoured the opposite approach, have always been credited with the invention and discovery of much that was in reality inherited by them from Mesopotamia. For instance, Babylonian music-theory anticipated Pythagoras and Plato by more than a thousand years; but its concepts were expressed in the form of practical instructions for tuning a musical instrument's strings.

The foundations of science were laid long before Aristotle. At the root of all real knowledge stands observation and classification: taxonomy must precede zoology – a proper account of the way the living world is arranged must be established before a theory of evolution can be imagined. For every Charles Darwin, a Carl Linnaeus must come first.

Ever since the invention of cuneiform writing, training in literacy had been based on word tables – the so-called lexical lists. These were long tallies of plants and animals, rocks and stones, of human artefacts made of different substances, of verbal expressions and grammatical forms. Scribes learned to recognize and reproduce the many signs of cuneiform writing by copying out these lists – simple signs composed of few wedge-marks at first, more difficult spellings coming later. Naturally, if students were to become fully literate, the lists had to be comprehensive. In consequence most conceivable features of Mesopotamian life and the Mesopotamian environment were ultimately tabulated. The items listed were arranged according to the arrangement of their wedge-marks, their similarity of sound, or classified by function, or arranged by shape, or size or material composition.

It used to be claimed that here we had the beginnings of science, that in the ordering of the lists, the Mesopotamians were applying the first principles of taxonomy to the features of their world. However, scholars now recognize that if this was a science at all, it was a science, not of external reality, but just of writing. Even so, the recognition of the importance of regularity, of pattern and order, which the lexical lists show was part of the training of every educated Mesopotamian, must have had an influence on how they saw their world.

This is particularly noticeable in the other documents commonly found in Babylonian text collections: the omen tables – catalogues of events and the unusual occurrences that preceded them and were thought to predict or warn. To us the fact that one thing happens to have followed another does not necessarily mean that the first is in any way connected to the second. Yet, though fallacious, the belief in omens tells us something important about the Babylonians' outlook. They saw the world as based on laws and rules: if this occurs, then that is likely to follow. To them events did not take place, as some religious believers hold even now, because God or the gods arbitrarily decreed from moment to moment that they should. Babylonians did not think, as even modern

Kabbalists do, that the world only exists from day to day by a miracle. Rather they noted that there was an underlying order and logic to the universe, which careful observation had the power to disclose. Today we call that science.

Astrology, quintessentially Babylonian, is undoubtedly a science – a spurious one, maybe, one rejected by modern understanding of the universe, certainly. But that is merely the view of our time. Seeking the future in the stars was undeniably a study based on laws, on rules, on observation and deduction. And so were the omens sought in the livers of sacrificial animals, in the figures formed by pouring oil on water, in shapes seen in rising smoke, in unusual configurations in the night sky, in the patterns of storm clouds, in abnormal births of humans or animals:

If the foetus is male and female: it is an omen of Azag-Bau who ruled the land. [A former tavern-keeper who became a famous Queen of Kish around 2500 BCE.] *The king's country will be seized.*

If a foetus is male and female, without testicles, a son of the palace will rule the land or will assert himself against the king.

If it is a double foetus, the heads enclosed, with eight legs and only one spine, the land will be visited by a destructive storm.

Though we may now scoff at what we recognize as specious links, we must accept that the diviners themselves thought that they were working with empirical observations. They treated their evidence with a respect of which modern researchers would surely approve.

Omen: If a foetus has eight feet and two tails, the ruler will acquire universal sway.

A butcher, Uddanu by name, reported as follows:

A sow gave birth to a young having eight feet and two tails. I have preserved it in salt and kept it in the house.

Nor did investigators hesitate to state when they thought more research was needed. A report of the abnormal birth of two ass foals is interpreted as a favourable omen, but with the reservation: 'Whether this is so, I shall ascertain. It will be investigated according to instructions.'

Omen tables demonstrate one further step towards recognisable science.

Among the extensive lists of portents and predictions, we see how, though still always adhering to the concrete and the specific, augurs were beginning to systematize their discoveries and extrapolate from them to fill in gaps in their knowledge. We can best see this happening when the omen catalogues are extended to include purely theoretical, indeed impossible, phenomena, events which we know could not possible have ever been observed – for example lunar eclipses on nights when the sun and moon are aligned on the same side of the earth, so that the moon cannot be in our planet's shadow. The astronomers of the early second millennium may not have been aware that lunar eclipses are only seen on certain days of the month, but they surely did recognize that no Babylonian had ever experienced the following: 'If the sun comes out in the night and the country sees its light everywhere: there will be disorder in the country everywhere.'

Even those who insist on dismissing the investigation of omens as superstitious nonsense rather than science can hardly say the same of the Babylonian approach to medicine. The Greek historian Herodotus was guilty of an outrageous canard when he wrote, 'They bring out all their sick into the streets, for they have no regular doctors. People that come along offer the sick man advice, either from what they personally have found to cure such a complaint, or what they have known someone else to be cured by. No one is allowed to pass by a sick person without asking him what ails him.'

A charming and romantic idea perhaps, but very far from the truth. Of course there were doctors in Babylon. As a matter of fact there were two kinds: the *ashipu*, who specialized in omens and exorcism, and the *asu* who made physical diagnoses and prescribed remedies. Around the year 1800 BCE King Hammurabi's laws specified the fees to be paid to physicians, depending on the status – and therefore resources – of the patient. It also prescribed the penalties for a surgeon's failure.

Perhaps Herodotus did not recognize Babylonian doctors because, as Mesopotamians, they were far more interested in specifics and practicalities than the later Greek medical theorists, who concerned themselves with developing grand, overarching, but mistaken theories of disease. Their view that illnesses were caused by an imbalance of the four bodily humours – blood, black bile, yellow bile and phlegm – would bedevil the practice of medicine for more than two millennia. Contrast a letter from the King of Mari to his wife, which shows an understanding that would have bewildered most European practitioners before the late nineteenth century: 'I have heard that the lady Nanname has been taken ill. She has many contacts with the people of the palace. She meets many ladies in her house. Now then, give severe orders that no one should drink from the cup where she drinks, no one should sit on the seat where she sits, no one should sleep in the bed where she sleeps. She should no longer meet many ladies in her house. This disease is contagious.'

The authors of a collection and translation of Babylonian medical texts published in 2005 noted that that Mesopotamian treatments were often appropriate because they had evolved through hundreds of years of careful experimentation and observation: 'Some are still in use, such as surgically draining the pus that sometimes develops between the lungs and chest wall of pneumonia patients. Their precise instructions to "make an opening in the fourth rib with a flint knife" to insert a lead drainage tube, pretty well match present-day procedures.' Where it is hard to judge the efficacy of Babylonian treatments is where the names they gave to diseases mean nothing to the modern reader: 'If a man's eyelids thicken and his eyes shed tears, it is [the illness known as] "blast of the wind". If a sick man is relaxed during the day, but from dusk he is sick for the night, it is [the condition called] "attack of a ghost".'On the other hand, where the symptoms are accurately described, we can often recognize afflictions with which we are only too familiar. Arthritis, for example: 'If he has been sick for five, ten, fifteen, twenty days... the digits of his hands and his feet are immobilized and so stiff that he cannot open them or stand on them, [it is the condition known as] Hand of Ishtar.' Or senile dementia: 'His mind is continually altered, his words are unintelligible, and he forgets whatever he says, a wind from behind afflicts him; he will die alone like a stranger.'

Most treatments were, necessarily, herbal and dietary – pills and potions, rectal and vaginal suppositories, skin patches and plasters – but none the worse for it. Some even accord with modern medicine's prescriptions. 'A couple of tablets describe night blindness when a patient can see in daylight but is blind at night,' say the authors of the medical text collection,

'They talk about cutting off a piece of liver and having the patient eat it. Night blindness, we now know, is caused by Vitamin A deficiency, and liver is loaded with Vitamin A.' The Babylonians also seemed to have observed that date kernels contained what we now call oestrogen. Symptoms of the condition they called *Nahshatu* included abnormal uterine bleeding. To treat this, 'You char and grind date kernels, wrap them in a tuft of wool and insert the result into her vagina.'

In fact, much Babylonian medicine appears be good enough to raise the possibility of discovering some overlooked treatments for hard-to-treat conditions today. After all, many modern medications have been developed out of folk-wisdom and non-western medical traditions. It would not be surprising if in the course of 2,000 years and more of experiment and observation, the Mesopotamians had come across remedies as yet unknown to us.

The End of Old Babylon

There is nothing, in the enormous collection of documents that we have inherited from ancient times, which tracks in any detail the way in which the flourishing and extraordinary civilization centred on Old Babylon came to an end. Babylonian literary genres did not include history writing, and the decline and fall of the great City seems to come as a sudden surprise. Nor have we found any documents that reflect how the City's population felt to see their culture, which they knew to be outstanding, and their way of life, in which they felt so comfortable, threatened by radical change and ultimate dissolution.

In part this must reflect the lack of interest in expressing abstract, theoretical ideas so typical of Mesopotamian intellectual life. Yet to suggest, as many used to do, that the Babylonians had no interest at all in philosophy, in exploring the nature of human existence, is to do them very much less than justice. 'The Semite has been notoriously unproductive in the field of speculative thought,' wrote D. D. Luckenbill of the University of Chicago in April 1924: 'His early desert environment made him shrewd, self-reliant, selfish. As his chances for betterment in this world were slim, he was not likely to develop an optimistic view of the life beyond.... He is pessimistic as to the life beyond death, and the more he thinks about such problems as that of suffering, the deeper he plunges into the gloomy abyss.'

In fact, just as the mathematical exercises, the medical diagnoses and the omen lists clearly implied – though never overtly stated – that there did exist certain underlying general principles, so is part of the literature written in Old Babylon structured on notions that today we would recognize as philosophical. True, it is expressed in the usual Mesopotamian way, by the description of concrete situations. But that is hardly different from much of European literature. Who would today, after all, accuse the French Enlightenment philosopher Voltaire of being 'unproductive in the field of speculative thought', or share British historian Thomas Carlyle's view that he never had an original idea in his life, because in *Candide* he had couched his meditations in the form of a satirical novel?

One great difficulty is that, unfamiliar as we are with the Babylonian mindset, we cannot easily grasp what a writer is trying to say, even when it is clear that some kind of speculative thought is involved. It is even harder to deduce the historical circumstances that occasioned the work. Typical is one highly enigmatic text over which many scholars have ruminated: a short dialogue in which a vacillating master proposes various actions to his slave, and then immediately changes his mind. The servant, rather comically, always finds a way to endorse his master's decision.

Slave, listen to me!
  – Here I am, master, here I am!
Quickly! Fetch me the chariot and hitch it up. I want to drive to the palace.
  – Drive, master, drive! It will be to your advantage. When he sees you, the king will give you honours.

  O well, slave I will not drive to the palace!
    – Do not drive, master, do not drive!
    – When he sees you, the king may send you God knows where,
    – He may make you take a route that you do not know,
    – He will make you suffer agony day and night.

And so it goes on. The master first proposes, and then decides he does not want, to give a banquet, to go hunting, to get married, to go to court, to lead a revolution, to make love, to perform a sacrifice and more. Every time, the slave has something to say about each decision. The tale initially appears to be a satire on popular wisdom, as when we contrast proverbs like 'look before you leap' with 'a stitch in time saves nine'. Yet there are occasional moments when the slave demonstrates almost Hamlet-like profundity. The master turns against the idea of performing a public service:

> O well, slave, I do not want to perform a public benefit for my country!
> – Do not perform it, master, do not perform it!
> – Go up the ancient tells and walk about.
> – See the mixed skulls of plebeians and nobles.
> – Which is the malefactor and which is the benefactor?

In the final part of the dialogue, when the master contemplates suicide, the servant suddenly waxes mystical about the limits to human understanding, and then closes with an effective comic put-down.

> Slave, listen to me!
> – Here I am, master, here I am!
> What then is good? To have my neck and yours broken,
> Or to be thrown into the river, is that good?
> – Who is so tall as to ascend to heaven?
> – Who is so broad as to encompass the entire world?
> O well, slave, I will kill you and send you on first!
> – Yes, but my master will certainly not survive me for more than three days.

What can this strange little story really mean? Is it a just a joke? Or is it, like the very much later Ecclesiastes 1:14, a world-weary expression of the futility of all action and pointlessness of life? 'I have seen all the works that are done under the sun; and, behold, all is vanity and vexation of spirit.' The text is so terse and economical that without complete familiarity with the Babylonian world, we will probably never truly understand the writer's purpose. Yet purpose there must have been. Mesopotamian documents were not composed – and certainly not copied – in light-hearted moments of creative abandon. This story could not have been a mere *jeu d'ésprit*, thoughtlessly tossed off by some amateur intellectual in a few idle minutes. I think we should take this story as a reproach to those who have written off the Babylonians as incapable of profound thought, and an indication that, in their own way, and using their own modes of expression, ancient Mesopotamians were as interested in addressing the meaning of the human condition as any later thinkers.

There were five more kings after Hammurabi in the line of the First Dynasty of Babylon, each reigning for more than twenty years. Though Old Babylon lasted longer than the Third Dynasty of Ur, the great ruler's successors saw the territory ruled from his capital shrink. Serious rebellions broke out during the reign of his son, and, though largely militarily successful when he took to the field, he could not prevent important cities like Nippur slipping from his grasp. New peoples speaking new languages, Hurrians, perhaps originally from the Caucasus, and Kassites, from the Zagros Mountains, were penetrating the region and taking Mesopotamian territory for themselves.

Something else was happening too: in the heart of Mesopotamia people were on the move. As government failed, transport links ruptured and bureaucracy broke down, city life became unsustainable. Ur was largely deserted by its citizens; the priesthood of Uruk migrated away. People fled back to the countryside; the urban population fell to its lowest in a thousand years.

Finally, as often before, the *coup de grâce* came from a completely unexpected source. A new player in history, the Hittite kingdom of central Anatolia, populated by uncultivated speakers of a barbarian Indo-European tongue, sent a force south down the Euphrates Valley on an extended *razzia*. Perhaps they took the Babylonian military by surprise. In any event, they sacked the city and brought its illustrious dynasty to an end.

The Hittites had no intention of occupying a place so far from home and left immediately. Into the power vacuum quickly sprang a new ruling class of recent immigrants from the east, Kassites, who would maintained control for more than 400 years, another long period when the arts of civilization were not abandoned but, making little progress, went into suspended animation. To be sure, great efforts were made to collect and collate the literature of earlier ages, to compile translations of canonical works from Sumerian into Akkadian – not Kassite – and to provide new analysis and commentary. The minor arts of seal-cutting and jewellery-making were brought to new perfection. But Kassite Babylon remained a deeply conservative society, as if the incoming ruling nation felt its greatest obligation to be the preservation of what they found already in place when they arrived, and to ensure its continued survival.

For the next half millennium, the wellsprings of innovation and enterprise were to be found far north of the burning Babylonian plain, in the rain-watered homeland of the Assyrians, who would sustain the tradition of Mesopotamian civilization by giving it great clunking fists and the sharpest of teeth.

9

Empire of Ashur:
Colossus of the First Millennium

c.1800 BCE to 700 BCE

Model for All Future Empire-Builders

Near the centre of Baghdeda, a sprawling village not far from Mosul in the north of today's Iraq, surrounded by ugly concrete buildings from whose flat roofs television aerials and satellite dishes sprout like weeds, rises a tell of crumbled sun-dried brick some 8 metres high. A flight of stone steps leads up its side to an ancient church dedicated to Mart Shmoni.

There is nothing about the architecture of this church that particularly catches the eye: it is a squat, blank-walled building rendered in adobe, with a stumpy domed tower surmounted by a metal cross. But this unpretentious place of worship is a remarkably direct link with the very distant past, and offers a challenge to some of our easy assumptions about the history of the ancient world.

Nobody knows when the present structure was first erected, though a church has stood on this site certainly since the eighth century and probably since the fourth. The design suggests that before this it was a synagogue – a rounded apse at the end angled towards Jerusalem would have housed the *aron kodesh*, the curtained cabinet in which the Torah scrolls rest between their ceremonial outings. For Mart Shmoni was no Christian saint. She and her seven sons were martyrs in the Jewish battle against forced assimilation to Greek culture and religion in the second century BCE, a story told in II Maccabees. That Christians of this area honoured a Jewish heroine confirms accounts of large Jewish communities living across northern Mesopotamia in the early years of the first millennium CE. When Benjamin of Tudela visited Mosul as late as 1165, he still

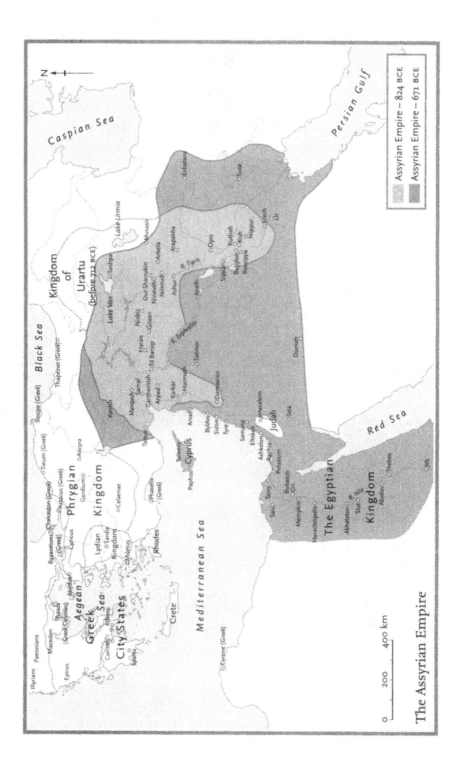

The Assyrian Empire

found 7,000 Jews at home there. The ten tribes of Israel, transferred to the heartland of Assyria in 722 BCE after the destruction of their kingdom by Emperor Sargon II, may not, it seems, have simply disappeared, as we have been taught to believe.

The history of the Mart Shmoni Church site takes us back even before then. The mound on which it stands shows us that here we have the accumulated remains of a series of successive temples and shrines, probably originally dedicated to Sin, the moon god, reaching as far back as 2000 BCE. In keeping with Mesopotamian tradition, none of these were swept away, but carefully levelled and then built over. To this day, unlike around other churches in the vicinity, no grave or well shaft may be dug in Mart Shmoni's precinct, to avoid desecrating what came before – even though it was a pagan deity who was originally honoured in this place.

It is not unusual for Christian buildings to be erected where older gods once ruled. Many English churches stand in what were once Anglo-Saxon sacred groves. Their names often make their debt to pre-Christian origins clear: Harrow on the Hill, for example, a harrow being a pagan holy site. But in most cases, evidence of the spot's earlier sanctity has been carefully erased.

Such amnesia would not, however, do for northern Mesopotamia, where it is not only buildings which acknowledge their antecedents. The worshippers attending services here are also proudly aware of their ancestry. They call themselves Assyrians, and see themselves as baptised Christian descendants of the citizens of the Assyrian Empire, the colossus of the early first millennium until its destruction in 612 BCE.

The name of their land, or part of it, has been retained too. After its conquest by Babylon, the western half of Assyria's domain was still called the province of Assyria – later, having lost its initial vowel, Syria. The Persian Empire retained the same name, as did Alexander's empire and its successor the Seleucid state, as well as the Roman Empire which was its inheritor. The late Assyriologist Professor Henry Saggs explained in *The Might That Was Assyria* that after the destruction of the Assyrian Empire,

> *descendants of the Assyrian peasants would, as opportunity permitted, build new villages over the old cities and carried on with agricultural life,*

remembering traditions of the former cities. After seven or eight centuries and after various vicissitudes, these people became Christians.

These Christians, and the Jewish communities scattered amongst them, not only kept alive the memory of their Assyrian predecessors but also combined them with traditions from the Bible. The Bible, indeed, came to be a powerful factor in keeping alive the memory of Assyria.

Such ancient identity has cost its bearers dearly. Their neighbours have, over the centuries, conducted vicious campaigns of discrimination and repression against Assyrian Christians, culminating in the genocide of 1914–20, when hundreds of thousands were murdered in the name of the Young Turk movement. They suffered grievously from the recent Gulf Wars, too, attacked by both Arab and Kurdish militias and even the Turkish air force from over the border. A huge number have been forced to flee their land into exile.

Can such very ordinary people, these shopkeepers, tailors, cobblers, doctors, engineers and university professors, really be descended from the people of ancient Assyria? If so, we need to adjust our view of that antique empire. For Assyria must surely have among the worst press notices of any state in history. Babylon may be a byname for corruption, decadence and sin but the Assyrians and their famous rulers, with terrifying names like Shalmaneser, Tiglath-Pileser, Sennacherib, Esarhaddon and Ashurbanipal, rate in the popular imagination just below Adolf Hitler and Genghis Khan for cruelty, violence and sheer murderous savagery. Most histories of Assyria quote the poet Byron's lines from 'The Destruction of Sennacherib'. I shall make no exception: 'The Assyrian came down like the wolf on the fold, And his cohorts were gleaming in purple and gold'.

Yet when one looks more closely at what is known about Assyria and its rulers, which is the story of how Assyria succeeded to Old Babylon's title as the centre of civilization, one finds a real paradox. The reputation for frightfulness that adheres to the Assyrian rulers and their military arm really does seem to be based on a truth. Which other imperialist would, like Ashurbanipal, have commissioned a sculpture for his palace with decoration showing him and his wife banqueting in their garden, with the struck-off head and severed hand of the King of Elam dangling from trees on either side, like ghastly Christmas baubles or strange fruit?

In truth, Assyrian warfare was no more savage than that of other contemporary states. Nor, indeed, were the Assyrians notably crueller than the
Romans, who made a point of lining their roads with thousands of victims
of crucifixion dying in agony, as after the slave revolt of Spartacus, when
as many as 6,000 bodies lined the Appian Way for years until they rotted
away. Not so very long ago in historical terms, the penalty in England for
treason was public hanging, drawing and quartering; thought-crime, or
heresy, witchcraft or belief in the wrong sort of religion, was punishable by
burning; the chopped-off heads of enemies of state were thought suitable
decoration for London's thoroughfares. Even in the twentieth century we
have found it acceptable to bomb defenceless villages from the air, incin-
erate whole urban populations by fire-storm, and drop atomic bombs on
Japanese cities.

And yet, at the same time as carrying out acts that now fill us with horror, the Assyrian Empire maintained and developed Mesopotamian art and
literature, theology, science, mathematics and engineering to new heights,
and oversaw the introduction of the age of iron into the Mesopotamian
world. Assyrian emperors advanced the welfare and equality of their subjects in ways no previous polity had ever attempted. Outside the Hebrew
Bible, the obligation to abstain from work every seventh day is first recorded in Assyria, while Finnish scholar Professor Simo Parpola writes that
'Assyrian religious beliefs and philosophical attitudes are still very much
alive in Jewish, Christian, and Oriental mysticism and philosophies.'

Assyrian rule served as a model for all future empire-builders: there is
direct continuity between the Assyrian, Babylonian, Persian, Hellenistic
and Roman empires. Moreover this empire was the conduit through
which much of Mesopotamian knowledge and culture was channelled to
Greece and points west, thus becoming part of our European inheritance.
The high point of Assyrian power coincided with what is known as the
orientalizing period in Greece, when Mesopotamian influence on art, literature and even law was the bridge over which the Hellenes passed from
their archaic to their classical era. One of Britain's most distinguished
classicists, Martin West, has shown 'that there is a substantial eastern element in the oldest stratum of Greek mythology, in some of the poetic
forms of the early archaic period, in the theology and natural philosophy of the seventh and sixth centuries.' He even suggests that the works

of Homer owe much to Mesopotamian epic, in particular to the story of Gilgamesh.

The people of Assyria were drawn from the same Semitic stock as those of Babylonia to the south, or so their languages suggest. Assyrian and Babylonian Akkadian were so closely related that philologists designate them as dialects of one and the same tongue. Assyrians' artistic and scientific traditions all derived from the mainstream of Mesopotamian culture. Their religion was more or less identical too, with the addition of their city god Ashur as a replacement or synonym for Babylon's Marduk in the otherwise universal Mesopotamian pantheon. Sin, god of the moon, was much worshipped here. The goddess Ishtar of Nineveh, mother, virgin and whore, whose planet was Venus, and whose symbol was an eight-pointed star, was famed throughout the Near East.

Some researchers have concluded that the Assyrian nation began when incomers from the southern city-states settled among and mixed with the indigenous inhabitants of the northern valleys, eventually asserting first their independence from, and then their superiority over, their original homeland. If true, then Assyria's inheritance of leading nation status from Old Babylon was rather like the USA's progression from British colonial possession to world-dominant power. The 'special relationship' between Assyria and Babylonia was extremely ambivalent, swinging between extremes of love and hate, alliance and enmity. On the one hand, Assyria derived almost its entire culture from Babylon, and could not help but recognize that debt. At the same time it was a fierce competitor and rival for trade and power. Assyria assaulted and wrecked Babylon City on a number of occasions – only to be quickly overcome by regret and to make attempts at restitution. It seems as if two powerful parties long vied for influence over Ashur's foreign policy: one strongly nationalist and anti-Babylon, the other traditionalist and pro-Babylon.

Such differences as separate Assyria from its southern neighbour resulted from living in a very different physical and political environment. Landscape and climate shape nations. Coastal peoples are not like steppe-dwellers, forest-folk are not like mountaineers. Those who sweat under the burning sun of the south have little in common with those who shiver among northern snows. Byron had something to say on that subject too, relating Britain's cloudy climate to 'our chilly women', and claiming that 'What men call gallantry, and gods adult'ry, / Is much more common where the climate's sultry'.

The heartland of what was once Assyria, near where today's Turkey, Syria and Iraq meet, is cradled in the curve of the great highland range, the Antitaurus, that links Turkey's Taurus Mountains in the west to Iran's Zagros in the south-east. Narrow valleys in the foothills run down to the wide plain that Arabs call Al-Jazireh, the Island. Across it, north to south, flows the Tigris, a swifter, deeper-cut, more dangerous river than its sister the Euphrates, which is here 400 kilometres off to the west, though both rise close to each other in the mountains and will join together again at the head of the Gulf.

Deserts stretch beyond the plain to the south and parched steppeland to the west, but much of the Jazireh itself shelters within the crucial 200 mm isohyet, the line that marks the limit behind which annual rainfall alone suffices for agriculture. So, unlike in Babylonia, Assyrian cultivators were not impelled towards constant collective action to keep water flowing to the fields; they did not know the ever-pressing need for collaboration to dig and maintain canals, dams, weirs, barrages, drains and sluices. Though later Assyrian emperors did indeed order the digging of aqueducts, canals and tunnels to lead water from the mountains to newly founded or expanded cities, these were prestige projects: luxuries rather than necessities.

From earliest times all over the south of Mesopotamia, particularly near the head of the Gulf, the demand for communal effort and a large labour force had led to cities with substantial populations springing up like mushrooms after rain, sometimes within sight of each other. The resulting sibling rivalry and fratricidal strife shaped history for millennia. Here in the north, by contrast, apart from ancient sacred sites like the goddess Ishtar's temple at Nineveh, which came to be surrounded by Assyria's most populous town, there was at first only one other fully-realized city, Ashur, with probably no more than 15,000 inhabitants. Protected in back by the cliffs above the Tigris and later in front by a massively high wall with eight huge gates and a 15-metre-wide moat, Ashur was at the same time the name of a god, the name of his city, and, ultimately, the name of the land and empire over which he presided. Outside these few urban centres Assyria was a country of individual farmers living in small independent settlements, which would eventually be welded together by political and strategic imperatives into an overarching proto-feudal system, as in the European Middle Ages.

The militarism for which Assyria is famous sprang from its location, which was extremely dangerous, making self-defence the necessary first principle of national survival – hence the monumental fortifications of Ashur City. Without natural protection, the area was always strategically vulnerable, lying as it did astride the major raiding and trading routes from the north and east that skirted the mountains to reach across Syria to the Mediterranean. Powerful barbarian kingdoms sprang up beyond Assyria's northern borders: Hittites, destroyers of the Old Babylonian Empire, who spoke an Indo-European language, and had their capital at Hattusas in central Anatolia; and Hurrians, perhaps from the Caucasus but with an Indo-Iranian ruling class, who set up a state called Mitanni which forced Assyria into prolonged submission.

However there were benefits, too, in both directions. The Hittites and Hurrians learned from Assyria the arts of civilization: most importantly how to write their languages, adapting Akkadian cuneiform to the task. In return the nations of the north led the way in technological developments that would greatly affect political history. From the Hittites, the Assyrians learned how to smelt iron and fashion it into weapons. From the Hurrians they learned horsemanship and acquired a device that would change the face of battle: the fast, lightweight, bentwood chariot with spoked rather than solid wheels.

But while the barbarian kingdoms to the north presented Assyrians with a source of novel ideas as well as a challenge that could be met on the battlefield and ultimately overcome, the Jazireh was also vulnerable to a second threat that was much harder to withstand. For it was ever open to infiltration and assault from the desert and steppe that lie to the west and the south. After the domestication of the camel in the second half of the second millennium, Assyria would have to contend with a new wave of Semitic immigrants: Aramaic-speaking bedouin from the deserts of what is now Syria. Though weak in battle, their numbers made them unstoppable. In time, they would change Assyria profoundly.

That very openness to the outside world in all directions offered an opportunity to the Assyrians which they took up from early times. Assyrian land was much less rich and fruitful than the great tracts of grain-growing alluvium from which Babylonia had benefited throughout her history. Much of the territory was suited only to raising sheep and goats. To supplement their national resources, Assyrians needed to trade, offering both woollen goods produced at home from their flocks, best quality textiles bought from neighbouring Babylonia, and commodities like metal ores originally sourced from the mountains to their east. Business served the Assyrians well. Like merchant nations of much more recent days, Belgians, British, Dutch and French, the demands of business changed the Assyrians slowly but surely from traders to empire builders.

The precise details of how this nation of roving merchants became, in the course of little more than a millennium, the most awe-inspiring and feared imperialist power of the ancient world, are not at all clear. Records are sparse. Archaeology has been able to open no more than a few narrow windows, at widely different times, on to the grand saga. But as luck would have it, we do have a view of the beginnings of the process, when international trading set the people of Ashur off on their historic adventure. We do not see Ashur City itself, nor even the land of Assyria; of both of these we know next to nothing in this era. Our window opens on to a place far from the Assyrians' home, deep in the heart of Anatolia.

Towards the end of the nineteenth century, large numbers of clay tablets written in the Old Assyrian dialect of the Akkadian language reached the international antiquities market. For a long time nobody knew where they were coming from. Eventually the site was tracked down to an unexpected location far from Mesopotamia: Kültepe, a mound in the highlands of central Turkey, close to a village named Karahüyük, near the watercourse known to Greeks as the Halys, and to Turks as Kızılırmak, the Red River. In 1926 the Czech scholar Bedrich Hrozný discovered that the tablets were actually being dug out of a subsidiary site about a hundred yards away. Closer study revealed that this was what remained of an expatriate enclave, a bonded settlement, within which Assyrian merchants were permitted to live and carry on business with the native community.

More recent trading empires would have called it a factory, like the first outpost of the English East India Company at Surat on the west coast of India. In Old Assyrian this one was called Karum Kanesh, Kanesh Port. It was far from being the only Assyrian factory on Anatolian soil: there were several others. However Kanesh was the headquarters for Assyrian trade everywhere in Anatolia, supervising and regulating all business activities and acting as the central communications hub between the widely dispersed trading-posts and Ashur itself – which they called simply 'The City'. It flourished during the early second millennium BCE: what has been called, for linguistic reasons, the Old Assyrian era.

Like the European 'nabobs' resident in India, the merchants of Karum Kanesh were a long way from home. Scions of the most prominent and wealthy Assyrian trading houses were sent out to look after their families' business interests: receiving consignments of goods shipped from Ashur and selling them on to the locals for silver, which they then dispatched back to base in the satchels of trusted runners. Over time some would go native, marry local wives and beget children. At the end of their expatriate years the law allowed that they could divorce these local women, as long as they paid appropriate compensation both to their temporary wives as well as to their offspring, before returning home.

Centuries earlier Sargon of Akkad had been celebrated for setting out to rescue the Mesopotamian merchants of Purush-khanda from the oppression of a local Anatolian ruler. In those days international business had been largely a matter of state. Now, in Old Assyrian times, private enterprise had taken over, creating the Levantine trading tradition which continues to this day. Indeed the role of Assyrian merchants in assisting the development of the Anatolian economy is strikingly reminiscent of that played by the Jews in opening up the interior of Europe during the Middle Ages. Perhaps that is unsurprising: Jewish culture and tradition, as minutely prescribed in the Babylonian Talmud, was itself largely forged in Mesopotamia.

For several generations the trading houses of Karum Kanesh flourished, and some became extremely wealthy – ancient millionaires. However not all business was kept within the family. Ashur had a sophisticated banking system and some of the capital that financed the Anatolian trade came from long-term investments made by independent speculators in return for a contractually specified proportion of the profits. There is not much about today's commodity markets that an old Assyrian would not quickly recognize.

Had we ourselves visited Karum Kanesh in the heyday of the expatriate merchant colony, sometime between the twentieth and eighteenth century BCE, we would have noticed everywhere scenes of intense commercial activity. In the courtyard of his warehouse we might perhaps have met young Puzur-Ashur, whom we know from his letters, supervising the unloading of caravans arriving here with merchandise: fifty donkeys or more, mostly carrying fine textiles and also a metal ore, *annukum*, which most scholars translate as tin, though others as lead. If tin, it was for use in making bronze; it has been calculated that over a span of some 50 years, at least 80 tons of the metal ore arrived here from the southeast, all on donkey-back, enough to make 800 tons of bronze. If, as others propose, it was lead, this was the necessary ingredient for refining silver by the process, still in use today, called cupellation. Silver was certainly available here in Anatolia. It was what the Assyrian merchants sold their goods for.

The animals and their drivers would have been exhausted after a difficult six-week journey that had first taken them up the Tigris to the foot of the mountains, then led them to skirt the highlands until they crossed the Euphrates, after which came the long and arduous climb up to the Anatolian plateau. Along the way they had not only to cope with the bad road surfaces and steep gradients, but also the danger of attack by the robbers and bandits who infested the wilderness; one route was actually called the Danger Road, *Harran Sukinim*, taken only by braver souls eager to avoid the customs office at Kanesh. A letter from a city merchant to his agent abroad reveals the kind of risk that travellers might run when passing through the domains of local rulers even quite close to home: 'Askur-Addu [King of Karana, a town less than fifty miles from Ashur] has allowed a caravan on to his land. From it fifty donkeys and their personnel have passed on to Kanesh. But the remainder have been retained at his court.' The fate of caravaneers could be yet more serious if they were caught transporting forbidden goods. Puzur-Ashur received a serious warning from his relatives back in the City.

The son of Irra sent his contraband to Pushu-Ken, but his contraband was caught, whereupon the palace seized Pushu-Ken and put him in jail. The guards are strong. The queen has sent messages to Luhusaddia, Hurrama, Shalahshuwa and to her own country concerning the smuggling, and lookouts have been appointed. Please do not smuggle anything. If you pass through Timilkia leave the iron which you are bringing through in a friendly house in Timilkia. Leave one of your lads whom you trust, and come through yourself. We can discuss it further when you get here.

Iron, *ashium* – at this time in history probably only available from meteorites – was a valuable and restricted commodity.

Assuming that they escaped all threats along the way, on the donkey trains' arrival at their destination the animals were sold together with the goods they carried, and the silver the traders earned was sent back home in the carrying bags of secure couriers. Perhaps these were the same messengers who took letters backwards and forwards between Ashur City and its merchant colonies.

Profits were high to reflect the risks involved: 100 per cent on metal ores and 200 per cent on Assyrian-woven textiles. The highest gains came from best quality cloth manufactured in Babylonia. But this was not always readily available, particularly when political events disturbed trade, as one Ashur trading-house had cause to explain to its Kanesh representative:

As to the purchase of Akkadian [i.e. Babylonian] textiles about which you wrote to me. Since you left, the Akkadians have not entered Ashur City. Their country is in revolt. If they arrive before winter and there is the possibility of a purchase which allows you profit, we will buy for you and pay the silver from our own resources.

In the absence of the real thing, every attempt was made to bring Assyrian production up to the same standard. Only recently Puzur-Ashur needed to write to his wife Waqqurtum back in the City:

Concerning the fine cloth that you sent me: you must make more like that and send it to me via Ashur-Idi. Then I will send you a half pound of silver. Have one side of the cloth combed, but not shaved smooth: it should be close-textured. Compared to the textiles you sent me earlier, you must work in one pound more of wool per piece of cloth, but they must still be fine. The other side must just be lightly combed. If it still looks fuzzy, it will have to be close shaved, like kutanu-cloth. *As for the* abarné-cloth *which you sent me, do not send me that again. If you insist, then at least make it the way I used to wear it.*

Not all textiles were woven in home workshops. Apparently Ashur also had a market where fabrics were on sale.

If you don't want to make the fine textiles yourself, then buy them and send them on to me; I have heard that they can be bought in quantity over there. One finished cloth, when you make it, should be nine ells long and eight ells wide [about 4 metres by 3.5].

Clearly, the merchants' wives back home in the City played a significant role in their husbands' trading enterprises: supervising the weaving of cloth, the loading of caravans, the dispatching of goods. Later Assyrian law would show a strong bias against women and their welfare. But, as in many societies where women would come to have *de jure* lower status than men, in practice at this time many were clearly willing and able to give as good as they got, never hesitating to criticize and complain:

Why do you keep writing to me: 'The textiles that you send me are always of bad quality!' Who is this man who lives in your house and criticizes the textiles that are brought to him? I, on the other hand, keep on striving to produce and send you textiles so that on every trip your business gains ten shekels of silver.

An often repeated complaint to their husbands from wives left behind in Ashur is that not enough money is getting back home, even for food. The consequences sound rather grave – though it seems that the husbands did not always take the protests as seriously as their wives intended.

You wrote to me as follows: 'Keep the bracelets and rings that you have; they will be needed to buy you food.' It is true that you sent me half a pound of gold through Ili-Bani, but where are the bracelets that you have left behind? When you left, you did not even leave me one shekel of silver. You cleaned out the house and took everything with you.

Since you left, famine has struck the City. You did not leave me a single litre of barley. I need to keep on buying barley for our food... Where is the extravagance that you keep on writing about? We have nothing to eat. Can we afford indulgence? Everything I had available I scraped together and sent to you. Now I live in an empty house and the season is changing. Make sure that you send me the value of my textiles in silver, so that I can at least buy ten measures of barley.... Why do you keep on listening to slander, and write me annoying letters?

Most of all, the correspondence demonstrates how little some things change over the millennia. Setting aside the exotic religious language, the sentiment expressed in the following letter by a wife required to excuse her husband's long absences from home by the need to earn money, is familiar:

Here we have asked the women who interpret oracles, the women who interpret omens from entrails, and the ancestral spirits. The god Ashur sends you a serious warning: 'You love money. You hate life.'

A Tetrarchy

In the end, the Assyrian wife got her wish. After three or four generations, the feverish money-making first faltered and then stopped altogether, and with it correspondence ceased to flow between Ashur and Anatolia. The reasons are, as usual, unclear. Perhaps new sources of metal ores were discovered locally. Maybe Assyrian and Babylonian textiles went out of fashion. All we know for sure is that our window on to the Old Assyrian world closes.

Most probably to blame were the great political changes that swept across the region near the beginning of the second millennium BCE. Back in northern Mesopotamia, the Amorite warlord Shamshi-Adad, long afterwards remembered as originator of the Assyrian state, had, with the help of his sons, taken control of the homeland. After no more than a few generations, most of his territory was lost and his line was extinguished. The subsequent confusion, during which time Karum Kanesh's trading activities came to an end, was expressed laconically in the list of Assyrian rulers compiled centuries afterwards. 'Ashur-Dugul, son of a nobody, who had no title to the throne; he ruled for six years. In the time of Ashur-Dugul, son of a nobody, the following six sons of nobodies ruled for periods of less than a year: Ashur-apla-idi, Nasir-Suen, Suen-Namir, Ipqi-Ishtar, Adad-Salulu, and Adasi.'

Up until now the Mesopotamian story could be told without much reference to other surrounding powers. Indeed for long ages the people of the Tigris and Euphrates Valleys could claim sole right to the title 'civilized'. However in the centuries following 2000 BCE other nations were making names for themselves on the international scene. Four states, a tetrarchy, jockeyed for power and influence. Egypt – not very much younger and far more long-lived than any Mesopotamian polity, as well as almost as advanced, although considerably more conservative in both religion and politics – was extending its power up the Mediterranean's eastern shoreline. There Egyptian forces faced resistance from the Hittites of Anatolia, relative newcomers but with knowledge of iron-working, who had grown powerful enough by around 1500 BCE to bring the Old Babylonian state to ruin. In turn the Hittites vied with the kingdom called Mittani, and also known as Khanigalbat, which had sealed off the Mesopotamian north all the way from near the sea in the west to the mountains in the east, from the area of Aleppo to the region of Kirkuk, reducing Ashur to vassalage in the process. In a long-remembered assault, the King of Khanigalbat sacked Ashur and took away a fabulous set of gold and silver doors to erect in his own palace. Meanwhile in central and southern Mesopotamia, Babylon, ruled by its Kassite dynasty, retained a recognized power seat at the concert of nations.

The small trading nation of Ashur was no match for such aggressively militaristic powers, with their novel iron weaponry and their battlefield horses and chariots. The humiliation of seeing their ruler forced into submission to Mitanni was a great blow. The consequent long economic depression visited on their home country taught the Assyrians a lesson that they would never forget: the need to keep trade routes and entrepôt towns, however distant, under their own firmcontrol. Otherwise they would be forever condemned to backwardness and poverty.

As a result the Assyrians came to see their world as a dangerous place, full of ruthless enemies who wished them nothing but harm. We know only too well from recent history how damaging such an attitude can be, and how it can lead nations to act in ways that are excessively savage. Great suffering does not always, or even often, make people gentler and kinder. Existential threats that are perceived to challenge a nation's very survival can drive it to act in ways that history will later roundly condemn. In Assyria's case we are fortunate in being able to follow the evolution of her political and strategic paranoia in the closest thing to popular culture that the ancient world has left to us.

Almost all art and literature unearthed from Mesopotamia comprise the works of the elite, representing the way in which the ruling class wished to be seen by their own subjects and by their foreign rivals and enemies. The principal aim was propaganda, the message was public. The works tell us little about how their makers really saw themselves and what they thought of their lives. One class of object, however, had a much more personal meaning: the cylinder-seal. These tiny, intimate sculptures were intended permanently to identify their owners with a particular image, and are, of course, elite items, too: only those who owned property that demanded identification, or who were in a position to issue instructions, needed seals. Yet even so, because they were so personal, they speak more of their users' true beliefs and feelings than any of the public arts of palace or temple.

The designs on seals used by the expatriate business community in Kadesh, our main record for the Old Assyrian era, show close continuity from their Babylonian, Akkadian and even Sumerian predecessors. They bore pictures of mythological scenes, of gods and goddesses, often depicting their owners as they present themselves to their deities and seek divine blessing. The tableaux were static, dignified, serene. They were usually accompanied by long screeds in Sumerian: hymns and prayers. Such a seal acted not only to identify its user, but also as an amulet or talisman with the power to ward off evil by virtue of the sacred image and text that, like a Tibetan prayer wheel, it both incorporated and endlessly reproduced.

After the disappearance of Karum Kadesh and the decline of Assyria's fortunes, the seals' thematic repertoire changed, and we see the first appearance of native Assyrian style. Inscriptions are far rarer. Physical energy and action become the keynote: the predominant theme is mortal combat, with great fights between wild beasts, savage monsters and evil demons. Two seals bearing the names of kings show horrible winged creatures overcoming smaller animals, the *Cambridge Ancient History* notes: 'Such winged apparitions... fill the Assyrian seals with a world of fantastic vigour which seems untrammelled with any purpose to tell a story but only to picture the clash of mythological terrors against daemoniac champions of human kind.'

The opportunity to reverse Assyria's weakness did not finally present itself until the late fourteenth century BCE. The Hittites sacked the Mitannian capital and its ruler was assassinated by one of his own sons in a palace coup. Khanigalbat fell into chaos. Hittites and Assyrians both reacted swiftly and moved to divide most of the Hurrians' territory between them.

With its newly acquired lands, Ashur, led by a vigorous ruler, Ashur-Uballit, could now claim its place as a player in the great game of Middle Eastern power politics. The Assyrian king lost little time before writing to the King of Egypt, the heretic Pharaoh Akhenaten, to announce publicly his new status.

> *Say to the King of Egypt, thus speaks Ashur-Uballit, King of the land of Ashur:*
>
> *May all be well with you, your household, your country, your chariots and your army.*
>
> *I have sent my envoy to visit you and to see your country. Until now my forefathers have not sent word. Today I have personally sent word to you. I have sent you as goodwill presents one fine chariot, two horses, and a date-shaped jewel of genuine lapis lazuli.*
>
> *As for my envoy, whom I have sent to visit you, do not detain him. Let him visit and then let him depart. Let him see your hospitality and the hospitality of your country and then allow him to leave.*

Akhenaten must have responded positively to the Assyrian's initiative, for later in his reign Ashur-Uballit wrote again to Egypt, calling the Pharaoh 'brother' – diplomatic code for a ruler of equivalent standing: 'Tell...the Great King, King of Egypt, my brother, thus says Ashur-Uballit, King of the Land of Ashur, Great King, your brother.'

That status of equality had to be fiercely defended. The Assyrian ruler was sensitive to any suggestion of a slight. Where lesser monarchs abase themselves before the Egyptian Pharaoh in their letters – 'At the feet of my lord the king, I prostrate myself seven times and seven times' – Ashur-Uballit adopts a straightforward, not to say impolite, tone, in his reaction to an Egyptian present he deemed unworthy.

> *Is it from a great king, a gift such as this? Gold is dust in your land – one simply gathers it up. Why should it linger before you? I intend to build a new palace. Send me enough gold for its decoration and its furnishing.*
>
> *When my ancestor Ashur-nadin-ahhe wrote to the land of Egypt, they sent him twenty talents of gold. When the King of Khanigalbat wrote to your father, to the land of Egypt, he sent him twenty talents of gold.*
>
> *Now I am equal to the Khanigalbatian king, but you send to me only… of gold* [unfortunately the crucial sum is illegible on the tablet]. *It does not even suffice for the expense of my messengers' journey there and back. If in good faith your intention is friendship then send me much gold.*

In his earlier letter Ashur-Uballit explicitly stated that there had previously been no contact between Ashur and Egypt. In this later message he was claiming that his ancestor had not only communicated with the Pharaoh of his day but had, in return, received a large gift of gold. He clearly felt that his position was now strong enough to play diplomatic games with the facts of history. In any case, there were more important things to concern him, such as the fact that his envoys had been made to stand out in the sun for long hours, apparently at danger to their lives. It may be that they had been made to participate in one of Akhnaten's sun-worship rituals. If so Ashur-Uballit was having none of it. His sarcasm was scathing.

> *Why should envoys be forced to stand constantly out in the sun and so die from sunstroke? If standing out in the sun brings some benefit to the king, then let him stand out in it and let him die right there from sunstroke – provided that there is some benefit for the king.'*

The Assyrians' striking new confidence did not go unnoticed by the surrounding powers. Indeed the sudden rise of this upstart nation so alarmed Kassite Babylon, Ashur's southern neighbour, that the Babylonian king dispatched an urgent note to the Pharaoh: 'The Assyrians are my subjects and it was not I who sent them to you! Why have they taken it upon themselves to come to your country? If you love me, let them conduct no business there, but send them back to me empty-handed.'

There is no indication that the Egyptian took the slightest notice.

But Babylon's Kassite ruler must have understood the new situation well enough. Soon after, he persuaded Ashur-Uballit to send one of his daughters south to be a wife for the Babylonian crown prince. Their half-Assyrian half-Babylonian son took the throne upon his father's death. However, after some time, a revolt by Kassite nobles resulted in the young man's assassination, whereupon the King of Assyria marched on Babylon, routed the conspirators, and put his own choice of ruler into the palace. The tables had turned. A Babylonian monarch was, for the first time, answerable to an Assyrian overlord. Babylon now stood in the shadow of Ashur.

The struggle for dominance between Assyria and Babylon would last for many centuries. The details of the unending conflict between them, not to mention the constant warfare with the surrounding powers, great and small, recorded later in interminable epics and annals full of boasts and dubious claims of victory, quickly become hard to follow and wearisome to relate. It is a relief when one of those powers leaves the stage, as does the Hittite Empire upon its collapse in the late twelfth century BCE, thus simplifying the picture. Enough to say that Assyria grew in territory, piece by piece, though with frequent reverses, to reach a first high point in the 1120s, when the king, Tiglath-Pileser I, crossed the Euphrates, captured the great city of Carchemish, and reached both the Black Sea and the Mediterranean, for the first time creating an Assyrian Empire.

It did not survive for very long. The entire Middle East was soon plunged, once again, into a period of great instability, when the incoming drift of Aramaic-speaking camel-herders from the west now surged into an overwhelming flood. The boundaries of the Assyrian king's territory were again pushed back. Ashur was again confined to its heartland for rather more than a century.

Yet, though Tiglath-Pileser's territorial gains were ephemeral, changes in attitude and religious faith were taking place in the City that would have profound and permanent consequences. The Assyrians, heirs to the long Mesopotamian cultural and philosophical traditions that had begun with the Sumerians millennia earlier, were quietly refashioning them into beliefs that would provide some of the foundations for the rest of history.

Misogyny and Monotheism

Among the best known relics of this Middle Assyrian era are lists of laws and palace decrees recovered during the extensive excavations of the Assyrian capital Ashur City, now called Qal'at Shergat, conducted by the Deutsche Orientgesellschaft between 1903 and the outbreak of European war in 1914. A number of legal tablets were found, dating from Tiglath-Pileser's time, though only three of the documents, labelled A, B and C, were in good enough condition to be deciphered and read. Tablets A and B deal with crime and punishment, property and debt.

The most immediately striking aspects of these laws are how harsh and cruel they seem compared even to Hammurabi's 'eye-for-an-eye' code, and how deep is the misogyny that they express. Punishments include severe beatings, horrific mutilations, and ghastly methods of capital punishment – flaying alive or impalement on a stake for instance, the original model for Roman crucifixions. This is prescribed as the punishment for a woman who procures an abortion: 'If a woman has procured a miscarriage by her own act, when they have prosecuted her and convicted her, they shall impale her on stakes without burying her. If she died in having the miscarriage, they shall impale her on stakes without burying her.'

For damaging a man's fertility the penalty is mutilation: 'If a woman has crushed a gentleman's testicle in a brawl, they shall cut off one finger of hers. If the other testicle has become affected along with it by catching the infection even though a physician has bound it up, or she has crushed the other testicle in the brawl, they shall tear out both her eyes.'

Adultery is either a capital offence or punishable by disfiguration: 'If a gentleman has caught another gentleman with his wife, when they have prosecuted and convicted him, they shall put both of them to death.... But if he cuts off his wife's nose, he shall make the gentleman into a eunuch and they shall mutilate his whole face.'

It must be admitted that we do not know to what extent such penalties were actually imposed in practice. Assyrian rulers energetically promoted their reputation for using appalling savagery – the historian Albert Olmstead called it 'calculated frightfulness' – as a tool of governance and a weapon of psychological warfare. An inscription of Tiglath-Pileser, comparing the king to a hunter, who 'set out before the sun rose and marched three days' distance before dawn', proudly claims that he 'cut open the wombs of the pregnant, he blinded infants'. Gruesome actions indeed, but closely matching those foretold to the Aramean king Hazael by the prophet Elisha in II Kings 8:11: 'their strongholds wilt thou set on fire, and their young men wilt thou slay with the sword, and wilt dash their children, and rip up their women with child.' So it is just possible that revelling in the barbarity visited upon women and children was a familiar literary trope rather than a truthful account of real events. After all, similar atrocity stories were told by both Entente and Central Powers during World War I, although this time intended to attract blame rather than praise. The savage provisions described in the Middle Assyrian Laws may have been intended more as a deterrent than as the glorification of cruelty.

However, even if the draconian punishments were theory rather than practice, their anti-female tone cannot be denied. Men could freely divorce their wives and turn them out of the house with nothing; wives had no right to divorce. Women were liable for their husbands' debts and were punished for their husbands' crimes; husbands had no responsibility for their wives' law-breaking. While no ancient society we know of could be truthfully described as a feminist paradise, Middle Assyrian regulations went far further in their oppression of women than any before. It is almost as if the other sex was regarded as another race, or even another species. Public separation of the genders was rigidly enforced. The earliest known requirement for women to wear what is now called the hijab is found here:

Neither wives nor widows nor women who go out on the street may have their heads uncovered. The daughters of noblemen... must cover themselves, whether it is with a shawl, a robe, or a mantle... When they go out on the street alone, they must cover themselves. A concubine who goes out on the street with her mistress must cover herself. A sacred prostitute married to a man must cover herself on the street, but one whom a man did not marry must have her head uncovered on the street; she must not veil herself. A harlot must not veil herself; her head must be uncovered. Harlots and maidservants who cover themselves shall have their garments seized, they shall be beaten with fifty blows, and shall have bitumen poured over their heads.

A slave-girl who had the temerity to veil herself would have her clothing taken from her and her ears cut off. Moreover, witnesses to any transgression of these rules must take action to report it, on pain of prosecution themselves:

He who has seen a harlot veiled must arrest her, produce witnesses and bring her to the palace tribunal; they shall not take her jewellery away, but the one who arrested her may take her clothing; they shall flog her fifty times with staves and pour bitumen over her head.

Not even upper-class men were immune from punishment if found guilty of dereliction of their civic duty:

If a gentleman has seen a harlot veiled and has let her go without bringing her to the palace tribunal, they shall flog that gentleman fifty times with staves; they shall pierce his ears, thread them with a cord, and tie it at his back. He shall do work for the king for one full month.

It must be said that the most fervent Wahhabi or severest Afghan Talib would probably have felt that the Middle Assyrian Laws went rather far in repressing women. The Palace Decrees went even further. Their subject was the royal women, their purpose circumscribing and limiting every activity of those who resided in the palace women's wing, as well as those who came into contact with them. This was the prototype for what we now know as a harem. Think of the women's quarters of the Ottoman Topkapı, 'Cannon Gate', palace in Istanbul, with its narrow twisting passageways, its secret doorways and grilled windows, its hidden courtyards and secluded chambers.

The Assyrian royal court's female apartments, in which the kings' wives and concubines spent their entire lives, were kept firmly locked at all times, to keep men out and women in. It was strictly forbidden for anyone to enter the women's area without the express permission of the palace commander. Going into any part of the palace from which the women could be observed, such as out on to a roof, was a serious crime. The restrictions even applied to the palace eunuchs, of whom there were apparently many.

When sent on business into the harem, the eunuch must, like everyone else, first apply for permission to the palace commander, who himself had to wait at the entrance to ensure that the eunuch came out again. And even when inside, a eunuch must be very careful of his behaviour: no eavesdropping on the women's conversations, no listening to the women singing. A eunuch who overheard the women quarrelling was condemned to have one of his ears amputated and to be beaten with a hundred blows. When required to speak to one of the women on official business, a eunuch might approach no closer than seven paces; if the conversation went on longer than necessary, even if the woman had initiated the conversation, the eunuch was flogged and his clothes were taken from him. For a man to engage in conversation with a palace woman, with no third party present as chaperone, was a capital offence. If anyone, a courtier or another palace woman, witnessed such a breach of the rules and failed to report it to the king, he or she was thrown into a hot oven – perhaps of the same kind as the 'burning fiery furnace' into which the Book of Daniel tells us that Shadrach, Meshach, and Abednego were cast.

The principles of extreme female seclusion developed here in ancient Assyria would be a model for many future societies. Indeed there is direct continuity from the harem of the Old Palace in Ashur, right through the Babylonian, Persian and Hellenistic eras, to the Byzantine royal court, from which imperial Islam in turn inherited so much of its preference for women's public invisibility. But Muslim teaching was intended to introduce social justice. The rulings were democratically extended to include *all* women, not just the nobility. In Assyria, as in Byzantium, lower-class women were strictly forbidden to cover themselves; in Islam there was to be no division between respectable and non-respectable females. Queens, princesses, noblewomen, wives, concubines, unmarried daughters, crafts-women, workers and slaves, all were to be modestly arrayed no matter what their social milieu. In its own eyes the Islamic demand for universal female reserve is seen not as restriction but as liberation.

*

It is no explanation to ascribe the anti-female flavour of the Middle Assyrian Laws and Palace Decrees, as some have done, to innate Semitic male chauvinism. The letters to and from Karum Kanesh had shown women playing an important role in Assyrian society, taking active responsibility for substantial aspects of their menfolk's business affairs. Even before then, women had been important in Mesopotamian religion. Ever since the time of Sargon of Akkad the eldest daughters of kings had been appointed to positions of the highest rank, such as high-priestess at the temple of the moon in Ur, the ruling house of all moon-temples. That women's lives were now so different is just one symptom of a profound and fundamental alteration in religious thinking, a radical shift in the way that Assyrians saw the powers that rule the world, and in consequence the place of men in the grand scheme of things.

This change in religious belief would have dramatic consequences for the world's history, the first stage in a revolution that has made our world of today what it is. It oversaw the move from faith in gods of immanence, spiritual representations of the forces of nature, deities who inhabit the world and wear the natural phenomena they represent like a suit of clothes, to gods of transcendence, deities outside, beyond and above nature rather than part of it.

We should not allow the fancy language – 'immanence', 'transcendence' – to obscure the enormous importance of that shift in religious perspective. Here was a new vision that would eventually lead most of humanity away from belief in a sacred earth, of which every feature – sky, land and sea, mountains, valleys and rivers, as well as the plants and animals that inhabit them all – is inspirited by supernatural powers, to faith in an unhallowed material universe which is controlled, as puppeteers manipulate the strings of their lifeless marionettes, by divine forces hidden behind the curtain of appearances that an anonymous medieval Christian mystic famously called the 'cloud of unknowing'.

In earliest Mesopotamian times the gods had been perceived as personifications, hypostases, of nature and her forces. Enlil, Lord Air or Lord Atmosphere – today we might call him Lord Biosphere – was overall ruler of the divine realm. His son, Enki, Lord Earth, later known as Ea, spirit of the sweet waters that well up to fertilize agricultural ground, was the purveyor of civilization to humanity. Anu was Lord Heaven; Nanna, later called Sin, was the moon; Utu, later Shamash, the sun. Inanna, whom Semites identified with Ishtar, was the adrenaline goddess, present whenever and wherever men fought or fucked. Even when new deities were introduced – as the Babylonians included the god of their city, Marduk, into the divine assembly – every attempt was made to integrate them into the old pattern. Thus Marduk was said to be son of Ea, Lord of civilization, with whom he ruled in harmony. According to his story in the *Enuma Elish*, he was awarded the competences, prerogatives and powers of Enlil, king of the gods.

Now in Assyrian days, on seals and sculptures, we witness the connection between the gods and nature first slowly stretched, then broken altogether. Previously, gods were represented in human form, wearing the horned crown of divinity, and surrounded by their attributes, as for example the scene of the investiture of the king of Babylon by Shamash the sun god, which adorns the top of the stele inscribed with Hammurabi's law code. But from now on the gods will first be represented as distanced from the world, positioned like idols on pedestals and podiums and finally not pictured at all, but replaced by symbols: a sun for Shamash, a moon for Sin, the planet Venus, pictured as a star, for Ishtar. A remarkable altar recovered from a temple in Ashur and now in a Berlin museum, presents Nusku, the messenger of the gods, in the form of a writing tablet and stylus, set on a stand as if waiting for the invisible power to inscribe upon it a blessing or a prophecy. Ashur appeared as a winged disc carrying the divine image hovering above the universe, a symbol later adopted by the Persians, whose Zoroastrian community still displays it today to signify the worship of their supreme god Ahura Mazda. Among the most striking imageless, an-iconic divine representations of all is the series of metre-long footprints of God – the sole earthly sign of an otherwise invisible presence – approaching the inner sanctum of a temple uncovered at 'Ain Dara, forty miles from Aleppo in Syria.

Belief in the transcendence rather than immanence of the divine had important consequences. Nature came to be desacralized, deconsecrated. Since the gods were outside and above nature, humanity – according to Mesopotamian belief created in the likeness of the gods and as servant to the gods – must be outside and above nature too. Rather than an integral part of the natural earth, the human race was now her superior and her ruler. The new attitude was later summed up in Genesis 1:26: 'And God said, Let us make man in our image, after our likeness: and let him have dominion over the fish of the sea, and over the fowl of the air, and over the cattle, and over all the earth, and over every creeping thing that creepeth upon the earth.'

That is all very well for men, explicitly singled out in that passage. But for women it poses an insurmountable difficulty. While males can delude themselves and each other that they are outside, above and superior to nature, women cannot so distance themselves, for their physiology makes them clearly and obviously part of the natural world. They bring forth children from out of their wombs and produce food for their babies from their breasts. Their menstrual cycles link them to the moon. In today's society the notion that, for women, biology is destiny is rightly regarded as abhorrent. In Assyrian times, it was a self-evident fact that debarred them from full humanity.

It is no accident that even today those religions that put most emphasis on God's utter transcendence and the impossibility even to imagine His reality should relegate women to a lower rung of existence, their participation in public religious worship only grudgingly permitted, if at all. It is well known that orthodox Jewish men pray every morning 'Blessed art Thou, O Lord our God, King of the Universe, who did not make me a woman.' Moreover, women's lowliness is, apparently, contagious, threatening to drag men down to their level, and especially emphasized at times when their physical nature is undeniable: immediately after childbirth and during menstruation, when according to the Middle Assyrian Palace Decrees, as to orthodox Jews and Muslims to this day, they are regarded as particularly unclean. No menstruating woman was allowed into the presence of the Assyrian king. Priests had to be particularly careful: all sexual contact even with their own wives required them to ritually purify themselves as soon as possible. Women were a danger to men's half-divine nature. The female sex would not begin to regain a measure of religious respect until Christians came to believe in a God who was born naturally, as a human being, into the physical world out of the womb of an earthly woman.

And this dislocation between the realm of the gods and the domain of nature had another, inestimably influential consequence. If different gods were no longer directly connected with aspects of the material universe, there was much less reason to imagine so many of them. And if the gods were now no longer thought of as embedded in nature and in particular sacred places where they could be worshipped in shrines, chapels and temples, they were freed to become omnipresent. One might pray to Ashur not only in his own temple in his own city, but anywhere. As the Assyrian empire expanded its borders, Ashur was encountered in even the most distant places.

From faith in an omnipresent god to belief in a single god is not a long step. Since He was everywhere, people came to understand that, in some sense, local divinities were just different manifestations of the same Ashur. Several scholars have noted that Assyrians tended to merge all the gods into a single figure for rhetorical effect. Others point out how Mesopotamian writings show that these ancients experienced one, universal deity as a distant presence behind each particular god they worshipped. As Simo Parpola put it in the introduction to his collection *Assyrian Prophecies*: 'all the diverse deities being conceived of as powers, aspects, qualities or attributes of Ashur, who is often simply referred to as (the) God.' Though Parpola's claim that much of Jewish metaphysics is rooted in Assyrian prophecy has been roundly rejected by his peers, even one of his sternest critics, Jerrold Cooper of Johns Hopkins University, agrees that 'for a Mesopotamian, 'the god' and 'the gods' were essentially the same divine power that determined destinies'. The foundations of the monotheism that the Hebrew tribes were to make the world's patrimony were being laid here in Assyria in the last part of the second millennium BCE.

That is not to say that the Hebrews borrowed the notion of a single omnipotent and omnipresent God from Assyrian predecessors. Just that their new theology was far from an utterly revolutionary and unprecedented religious movement. The Judaeo-Christian-Islamic tradition that began in the Holy Land was not a total break with the past, but grew out of religious ideas that had already taken hold of Late Bronze and Early Iron Age northern Mesopotamia, the world view of the Assyrian kingdom, which would spread its faith as well as its power right across western Asia over the course of the following centuries.

Ideology and Empire

Meanwhile Arameans continued to pour into Mesopotamia from desert and steppe, wresting away from Assyria imperial territory that had been so painstakingly acquired. It is not too hard for us of the twenty-first century to imagine how Assyrians felt about this.

There are times in history when it seems as if all the world is on the move; we seem to be living in such a period at present. According to the United Nations, 'Between 1960 and 2005 the number of international migrants in the world more than doubled, passing from an estimated 75 million in 1960 to almost 191 million in 2005'. Moreover nobody knows how many unrecorded and illegal migrations should be added to that total: perhaps as many as a quarter or a third more.

Such movements of groups and individuals are rather different from the historic migrations of entire peoples backed by military force, like the entry of Germanic-speakers into Europe in the middle of the first millennium CE, or the conquests in central and western Asia of Turkic-speakers in the first half of the second. Armed incursions can in principle be militarily opposed. Migration is in the end a more powerful force because it is ultimately irresistible: laws that nations introduce to limit it are ultimately unenforceable.

Assyria had no more prospect of halting the human flow than can the British government stop illegal entrants to the UK, although an effective natural moat surrounds the British Isles. There is little hope that the US Department of Homeland Security will have greater success with its border fence than did King Shulgi of Ur and his successors, whose 'wall to keep out the Amorites' failed to prevent the migrants' eventual takeover of all lower Mesopotamia and their founding of Old Babylon.

The region had always experienced regular waves of Semitic incomers from the steppes and deserts to the west. In very earliest prehistoric times, speakers of what would become the Akkadian language had arrived to join the Sumerians in exploiting the potential fertility of the alluvial Tigris and Euphrates plain. Later came the western Semites called Amurru, Amorites. In Assyria's day, it was the turn of the Arameans.

Mass migrations are the result of two forces: a push and a pull. Emigrants always have reasons for leaving their places of origin and they target destinations that are particularly attractive. In our own times people leave their homes because of unemployment and poverty, political, economic and religious oppression, social turmoil and war. Their aim is to reach places which offer better prospects for their future. Similar motives had probably propelled Semitic-speakers into the Fertile Crescent in a steady trickle from before the start of recorded history. But what confronted the Assyrians near the turn of the first millennium BCE was an influx at least an order of magnitude greater, a drive occasioned by a severe change in climate that made marginal lands uninhabitable.

There is much evidence that for two centuries or so from about 1200 BCE, east of the Mediterranean, rainfall decreased by approximately 20 per cent and average temperature rose by 2–3°. That would have been enough to cause widespread starvation among those who inhabited the steppelands and desert edges. It sent their tribes fleeing, desperate for survival, in all directions: northwards into Assyria, eastwards into lower Mesopotamia and westwards towards the Mediterranean coast, where they carved out petty sheikhdoms on lands taken from their previous inhabitants, who were themselves weakened by climate change famine. An Assyrian chronicle, written not long after, tells us that 'In King Tukulti-apil-Esharra's thirty-second year [1082 BCE], the famine was so severe that people ate one another's flesh... .Aramean clans plundered the land, seized the roads, and conquered and took many fortified cities of Assyria. Citizens of Assyria fled to the mountains... to save their lives. The Arameans took their gold and silver and their property.'

The picture looked similar even from the other side of the ethnic divide. It was during these centuries of drought, famine and population movement, when Arameans were flooding into the region, that the Bible has the Children of Israel laying claim to would become known as the Holy Land. Annually recited during the First Fruits Festival at the Jerusalem Temple were the lines from Deuteronomy 26: 'A wandering Aramean was my father, and he went down into Egypt, and sojourned there, few in number; and he became there a nation, great, mighty, and populous.' The Egyptian government took unkindly to what they perceived as a threat from a rapidly growing enemy within. 'And the Egyptians dealt ill with us, and afflicted us, and laid upon us hard bondage.' So, the Bible continues, the Hebrews were led by God out of Egypt and into the land of Cana'an, where they took advantage of the temporary weakness of the major regional powers to seize territory for themselves: 'And the Lord brought us forth out of Egypt with a mighty hand, and with an outstretched arm, and with great terribleness, and with signs, and with wonders. And He hath brought us into this place, and hath given us this land, a land flowing with milk and honey.' After several generations of tribal life under the rule of religious judges, a Hebrew kingdom was founded, according to Jewish tradition, by King Saul not long before 1000 BCE.

Scholars debate whether this is myth or history. But it is certainly true that the land of Cana'an began to take on its Israelite identity just at the time when Assyria was at its weakest and the texts were complaining of the movement of new peoples into the Fertile Crescent; at any other time it is most unlikely that the Twelve Tribes would have been allowed to set themselves up as masters of the Promised Land.

Once again, Assyria's borders were forced back to enclose an irreducible core. Much of what had for several centuries been Assyrian territory was now divided up among what they thought of as barbarian kingdoms. Once again, Ashur City had lost both much of its best hinterland as well as control of the international trade-routes that had underpinned its prosperity and afforded its luxuries. Ashur was reduced to near penury.

The moral that Assyrian rulers took from the disaster was that their only safety lay in possessing incontestable military power. War was too important to be left to the romantic heroism of kings and generals. If traditional fighting methods could not even hold off a swarm of camel-riding sheep-herders, Ashur's rulers would concentrate on designing and building a new kind of war-machine, one that nobody would be able to withstand. Moreover, the only sure way to stop people migrating into Ashur was to take over their homelands and rule them with a rod of iron. Empire was a necessity not a luxury. If that caused them unpopularity, so be it. As a well-known Latin tag, supposedly a favourite of the half-mad Roman Emperor Caligula, would later express it, *Oderint dum Metuant*: Let them hate, so long as they fear.

The process of creating an invincible army could not be achieved overnight. Apart from anything else, it would cost a lot of money, money that Ashur did not have, her base being too small and too poor. Her only recourse was to begin by exacting tribute from her neighbours using the forces already available to her. Initially at least, what the Assyrians lacked in military numbers, materiel and know-how, they would have to make up for by sheer ferocity.

Assyria soon discovered a painful truth: empires are like Ponzi schemes: financial frauds in which previous investors are paid returns out of new investors' deposits. The costs of holding imperial territory can only be underwritten by loot and tribute extracted by constant new conquests; empires must continue to expand if they are not to collapse. So, from the beginning of tenth century BCE, Assyria set out on the project of regaining her former territories, gobbling up the surrounding Aramean kingdoms and expanding her domain in stages up to the borders of her former possessions. And then surpassing them, to encompass a larger area than any empire ever before known. This was achieved by the eighth century, in the reign of King Tiglath-Pileser III. He is named Pul in II Kings 15:19, which may have been his personal rather than his throne-name, when he makes the first appearance of any Assyrian emperor in the biblical record: 'And Pul, the King of Assyria came against the land.'

The era of independent monarchy in Israel and Judah coincided with the era of greatest Assyrian imperial re-expansion, which is why most names of the rulers who dominated Assyria during its glory days are still known to us by their Biblical approximations. We have Shalmaneser for Shulmanu-Asharidu, '(the god) Shulmanu is the greatest'; Sargon for Sharru-kin, 'Rightful King'; Sennacherib for Sin-Ahhe-Eriba, 'Sin (the moon) replaced the brothers'; Esarhaddon for Ashur-Ahhe-Iddina, 'Ashur Has Given Me a Brother'; and Tiglath-Pileser for Tukulti-apil-Esharra, 'My trust is in the heir of Esharra', Esharra being the great temple of the god Ashur in Ashur City.

Tiglath-Pileser's assault on Israel took place some time around the year 740 BCE during the reign of Menachem, sixteenth ruler of the northern Hebrew kingdom. No stranger himself to savagery, Menachem had gained the throne by coup and assassination. In his struggle to consolidate his rule, the Biblical record – as ever pro-Judah and anti-Israel – attributes to him appalling atrocities: 'Then Menahem smote Tiphsah, and all that were therein, and the borders thereof, from Tirzah; because they opened not to him, therefore he smote it; and all the women therein that were with child he ripped up.' (II Kings 15:16) However even he would have been daunted by the sight of the Assyrian field army drawn up in full fighting array outside his capital city Shomron, not far from today's Nablus.

By now several generations of emperors had reformed the Assyrian military into the first truly modern fighting machine, a model for all future armies until the introduction of firearms and mechanization. The force would have been considerable, numbering between 30,000 and 50,000 men, equivalent to five modern divisions, a huge contingent by the standards of the day. King Menachem no doubt mounted to the top of the great ashlar masonry wall erected by his predecessor King Omri around the city's acropolis the better to observe the Assyrian battle-line which extended as far as 2.5 kilometres across and nearly 200 metres deep.

He would have seen, in the centre of the formation, the main body of infantry, compact phalanxes of spearmen, their weapon points glittering in the sun, each arranged in ten files of twenty ranks. He would have marvelled – and perhaps trembled – at the discipline and precision of their manoeuvring, a contrast to the relatively freewheeling manner of previous armies, for the reforms had introduced a highly developed and effective command structure. Infantrymen fought in squads of ten, each headed by an NCO, and grouped into companies of five to twenty squads under the command of a Captain, a *Kirsu*. They were well protected and even better equipped, for Assyria was fielding the very first iron armies: iron swords, iron spear blades, iron helmets and even iron scales sewn as armour on to their tunics. Bronze weaponry offered no real contest: this new material, which was cheaper, harder, less brittle, could be ground sharper and kept a keener edge for far longer. Iron ore is not found in the north Mesopotamian heartland, so every effort had been made to put all nearby sources of the metal under Assyrian control.

Assyrian spearmen were more mobile than their predecessors too. Rather than sandals, they now wore the Assyrian military invention that was arguably one of the most influential and long-lasting of all: the army boot. In this case the boots were knee-high leather footwear, thick-soled, hobnailed and with iron plates inserted to protect the shins, which made it possible for the first time to fight on any terrain however rough or wet, mountain or marsh, and in any season, winter or summer. This was the first all-weather, all-year army.

Behind the phalanxes of spearmen ranged archers and slingers, many of them foreign auxiliaries, also divided into companies, shooting their projectiles over the heads of the infantry. Archers were now equipped with a new weapon, the composite bow, another Assyrian innovation, constructed by glueing different materials together: wood, horn and sinew. Though suffering more from damp weather than traditional bows made of a single piece of wood, and demanding much greater strength to draw – according to some researchers, beyond modern sporting capabilities – and needing two men to string them, they could be made far more powerful and therefore deadly than the previous all-wooden weapon.

In the lead drove the shock-troops: formations of chariots, mobile missile platforms, the ancient equivalent of tanks. These were no longer drawn at a slow pace by asses, but by much faster, larger and more rugged animals: horses. Each chariot was powered by up to four of the beasts and manned by a driver who, as equestrian skills advanced, sometimes rode one of the horses and controlled the others with a system of traces, leaving room on the platform for the bowman and two shield-bearers to fight more freely. These men were also armed with spears, swords and axes, so that after the initial assault they could dismount and fight as heavy infantry while the charioteer returned his vehicle to safety.

Chariotry itself would have been no novelty to the Israelite king. Indeed the northern Hebrews excelled at the use of horse-drawn fighting vehicles. In the following century Israelite charioteers featured prominently in the roster of top officials and equestrian officers of the Assyrian army known as the Horse Lists. But another long-lasting battlefield innovation introduced by the Assyrians would have probably been unfamiliar to him: cavalry. If a driver could ride one of the chariot horses, then so could he ride a horse without a chariot attached. These fighters, wielding spears or bows, rode with bridles of modern style, but without saddles or stirrups, which had yet to be invented. Instead they sat on blankets anchored in place by breastband, girth and crupper, and they controlled their mounts by pressure from their heels. Horses were now so important to the Assyrian line of battle that they were imported from as far away as Nubia, the Land of Kush – ironically the Israelites were among the most important intermediaries in this trade – and the empire's borders had been redrawn and enlarged to include the best horse-breeding territories. Each province had an entire establishment of officials, *musarkisi*, dedicated to providing mounts for the army. According to documents recovered from the city of Nineveh they were able to secure some 3,000 animals a month, of which about 60 per cent were destined for the chariot corps, 30 per cent for the cavalry and the rest put out to stud. A century earlier the Assyrian Emperor Shalmaneser III claimed to have fielded a force of nearly 35,000 men, comprising 20,000 infantry, 1,200 chariots and 12,000 cavalry. The absolute numbers may well have been exaggerated for propaganda effect, but their relative ratios probably reflect the truth.

What Menachem would have seen from the top of his city wall was merely the tip of the iceberg. To assemble, provision and keep in the field a great fighting force such as this had required deep changes in Assyrian society, which by the time of Tiglath-Pileser III had been militarized through and through. The army had become the point – in every sense of the word – of the entire Assyrian nation. Each adult male had a duty to serve unless he sent a substitute or paid to be spared. The three highest military ranks, Commander in Chief, Commander of the Left and Commander of the Right, were also governors of provinces. Military officers were addressed in correspondence by their civilian titles and there seems to have been little or no distinction between the roles, just as in the European Middle Ages, when titles like duke, count, knight and esquire originally related to rank on the battlefield. And, as in medieval days, Assyrian aristocrats were granted lands by the king in return for military officer service: a proto-feudal system.

Much of this Menachem knew as he looked down at the Assyrian army in front of his city. He was also only too well aware of what happened to those who resisted, since the Assyrians always made quite sure that nobody could remain ignorant of the penalty. In accordance with the principle *Oderint dum Metuant*, Tiglath-Pileser's great-great-great grandfather had proclaimed to the world:

> *I built a pillar over against the city gate and I flayed all the chiefs who had revolted, and I covered the pillar with their skins. Some I impaled upon the pillar on stakes, and others I bound to stakes round the pillar... I cut the limbs off the officers... who had rebelled... Many captives... I burned with*

fire and many I took as living captives. From some I cut off their noses, their ears and their fingers, of many I put out their eyes. I made one pillar of the living and another of heads, and I bound their heads to tree trunks round about the city. Their young men and maidens I burned with fire... The rest of their warriors I consumed with thirst in the desert of the Euphrates.

Menachem felt that he could not risk defeat by such a brutal enemy and instead paid a generous indemnity. In any case, he thought the support of the world's superpower would strengthen his hand in retaining the throne of the Hebrew kingdom against all challengers – of whom there were many: 'And Menahem gave Pul a thousand talents of silver, that his hand might be with him to confirm the kingdom in his hand.' 'And Menahem exacted the money of Israel, even of all the mighty men of wealth, of each man fifty shekels of silver, to give to the King of Assyria. So the King of Assyria turned back, and stayed not there in the land.' (I Chronicles 5:26; II Kings 15:19)

The decision, and the huge cost, paid off. Thanks to Assyrian support, Menahem was the only Israelite ruler during this anarchic period who managed to retain his position and die naturally in his bed. The transaction is laconically confirmed in one of the Assyrian king's own inscriptions: 'I received tribute from Kushtashpi of Commagene, Rezon of Damascus, and Menachem of Samaria [spelled out in cuneiform as Me-ne-khi-im-me Sa-me-ri-na-a-a].'

For the moment the Kingdom of Israel, what the Assyrians called Samaria – or sometimes Omriland after Omri, the powerful founder of the fourth Israelite dynasty, father-in-law of Queen Jezebel, who had built Shomron as his capital – was included among the empire's client states rather than being incorporated bodily into Assyria proper. The empire's initial policy was to allow those whose loyalty was assured to retain their nominal autonomy, like the princely states that continued to survive during British Raj India.

Like the British East India Company, Assyria first grew by capturing and securing points of greatest strategic and economic importance, trade routes and entrepôts, and bypassing places of lesser significance as long as they offered no threat to Assyrian interests. Rather than a uniform solid block of possessions, the empire remained until quite late in its history more of an open web. As one historian of the period puts it: 'The empire is not a spread of land but a network of communications over which material goods are carried.'

For a long period there was a distinction between Assyria proper, a uniform territory centrally administered from the capital, known to its rulers and people as *Mat Ashur*, 'the land of Ashur', and outlying areas subservient to, but distinct from, Ashur's domain. Should a tributary ruler refuse his obligations, however, or, worse, conspire to attack or damage Ashur's interests, he would be summarily deposed, his kingdom annexed.

So, over time, the gaps in the network were filled in as resistance and rebellion by less than pliant client rulers led Assyrian emperors to bring more and more nominally independent kingdoms under their direct control, as happened when Hoshea, King of Israel, three reigns but only seventeen years after Menachem, stopped paying tribute and began plotting with the Egyptian Pharaoh to throw off the Assyrian yoke. As II Kings 18:4 recounts:

> *The King of Assyria found conspiracy in Hoshea; for he had sent messengers to So, King of Egypt* [probably Osorkon IV of the 22nd Dynasty], *and offered no present to the King of Assyria, as he had done year by year; therefore the King of Assyria shut him up, and bound him in prison.*
>
> *Then the King of Assyria came up throughout all the land, and went up to Samaria, and besieged it three years.*
>
> *In the ninth year of Hoshea, the King of Assyria took Samaria.*

Sargon himself recorded the event thus: 'I besieged and conquered Samaria. I led away 27,290 of its people; from among them I formed a contingent of 50 chariots. I made those remaining behind assume their social positions. I installed over them one of my officers and imposed upon them the tribute of the former king.'

It was the end of the northern Hebrew kingdom and – according to religious tradition – the ten tribes that were its inhabitants. Others were brought in from elsewhere to replace those deported. The territory itself was incorporated into Assyria proper and lost its identity. Assyrian royal annals were wont to express it this way: 'to the land of Ashur I added the land, to its people I added the people'.

Thus by the end of its days the Assyrian Empire had by accident or design become a single huge block of territory incorporating almost the whole of the Near East, stretching across and around the Fertile Crescent from the Mediterranean shore to the head of the Gulf, from Egypt to Elam, a domain in which every inhabitant was considered an Assyrian citizen, just as throughout the vast Roman Empire, after Emperor Caracalla, every free inhabitant could say *civis Romanus sum* (I am a Roman citizen). For empires cannot be permanently held by power alone. Subject populations will submit to naked military force for only so long. There must also be belief; there must also be principles. The Assyrian Empire rested upon a firm ideology, which has remained a model for imperialists throughout history.

There must be only one realm. Every Assyrian territory, no matter whether directly connected with the home country or separated from it by client states, was regarded as an equal province of 'the Land', as surely part of the national patrimony as Ashur City itself. Previous empires had allowed their separate possessions to retain a sense of ethnic identity and had ruled them through local elites co-opted into the imperial system; the slightest sign of weakness at the centre led to revolt and insurgency. The Assyrian Empire was a single unity, its constituent parts as much integral to the mother country as were modern France's overseas imperial possessions.

There must be only one people. All who lived in Assyria were Assyrians, no matter what language they spoke or what customs they followed. All were subject to the same benefits and burdens, the same taxation and conscription. Hence the best known of what are taken to be penalties imposed on conquered states: the deportation of the population and its replacement by other residents from elsewhere in the empire. From the Assyrian point of view this was no punishment. It was the Assyrian melting-pot, a way of ensuring that, over time, every ethnicity other than Assyrian and every allegiance other than to the empire would be forgotten. The disappearance of the Ten Tribes of Israel into the general Assyrian population demonstrates how well the policy worked, even with people as fiercely dedicated to preserving their identity as the Hebrews.

There can be only one leader. Previous Mesopotamian rulers had been hero-worshipped, idolized and several even deified. They presented themselves as the servants, as well as earthly representatives, of divine patrons, who were the real actors in history. Assyrian emperors were, by contrast, the ultimate expression of their nation: Assyria personified. The image of Assyrian emperors as despots of the worst order, indulging in vile cruelty and depraved luxury, as described by classical Greek authors, and depicted by orientalist painters like Eugène Delacroix in 'The Death of Sardanapalus', is about as far as can be from the account we find in Assyrian documents. 'To the Assyrians, a king immersed in revelries and cruelties would have been an abomination,' writes Simo Parpola, 'their kingship was a sacred institution rooted in heaven, and their king was a model of human perfection seen as a prerequisite for man's personal salvation.' Israel Finkelstein, professor of archaeology at Tel Aviv University, suggests that for a picture of what the Assyrian court was really like during the late eighth and seventh centuries BCE – the reigns of Tiglath-Pileser III to Ashurbanipal – one need only to look at the biblical Book of Kings and its depiction of King Solomon, his wealth, his wisdom, his wives. This, Finkelstein argues, has little to do with the reality of a rustic highland chieftain of the tenth century, but actually reflects 'a vision of Assyrian kingship as the ultimate ideal'. The ruler of the Land of Ashur was known as 'the perfect person', the very same expression to this day applied in Arabic, *al-Insan al-Kamil*, to the Prophet Muhammad.

There can be only one god. Ashur was omnipresent throughout the empire. He had just a single temple, the Esharra in his own home city, this too a model for the Hebrews of Judah, who 'removed the high places, and brake the images, and cut down the groves' (II Kings 18:4), and for the first time centralized their faith on God's temple in Jerusalem. Yet at the same time Ashur might be – must be – worshipped anywhere and everywhere: the first missionary divinity. Tiglath-Pileser wrote in an account of one of his victories, 'I imposed on them the heavy yoke of my empire. I attached them to the worship of Ashur, my Lord.' True, the old gods retained their followers. The rites of Ishtar continued in Nineveh; the worship of Sin, the moon, did not cease in Harran. But the whole empire was encouraged to share the understanding that these were somehow reflections, aspects, manifestations of a single, omnipotent, omnipresent universal Godhead, increasingly identified with Ashur. It was Ashur who provided the rationale of empire. Like the Christian God of the Byzantines and the Muslim God of the Khalifs, He had decreed that His service and His worship be spread throughout the region. And his earthly representative was the Assyrian emperor.

So we might, perhaps tendentiously, sum up Assyrian imperial ideology in the pithy phrase One Realm, One People, One Leader. It sounds more familiar in German: *Ein Reich, Ein Volk, Ein Führer.* However, though there may have been only one realm and only one leader, the infamous division of Hitler's subjects into *Arier* and *Untermenschen*, Aryans and Subhumans, would have been seen by Assyrians as a criminal betrayal. As the texts demonstrate, all Assyrians, whether foreign deportees, or of native ancestry like the *qinnate sha Ninua labiruti*, the 'old time families of Nineveh', were regarded as equal. Newcomers were carefully instructed in their duties. 'People of the four [ends of the world], of alien languages, diverse speech, inhabitants of mountainous regions and of the plains... at the order of Ashur, my lord, I made them as of one tongue and settled therein. I commissioned natives of Assyria, masters of every craft, as overseers and commanders to teach them proper conduct and to revere god and king.'

That this policy was successful is attested to by the foreign names that even high state officials bore. Girisapunu, governor of Rasappa, must have been a Phoenician, as was the famous Ahiqar, 'keeper of the king's signet and councillor of all Assyria' under Esarhaddon – his story would become a classic of Syriac, Arabic, Ethiopic, Armenian, Turkish and Slavonic literature. Provincial and district governors Gulusu, Arbaya and Adad-suri bore Aramean names. So did Hanunu, 'commander of the Eunuch's guard', Salamanu, 'commander of the Queen Mother's guard' and Abdi-ili from Ashkelon, 'third man on the chariot of the chief eunuch'. Qu'yah, Hilqi-yah, Giri-yah and Yah-suri, officials 'residing in fortresses', are shown by their names to have been Israelite worshippers of the Hebrew God.

However, this policy of inclusion and equality for all was to have profound consequences. New Assyrians, Aramaic speakers, soon came to greatly outnumber the old. Thus it was not very long before users of Assyria's original Akkadian dialect were reduced to a minority in their own land. Of course scholars and academics adhered tenaciously to their traditions, yet they could not stop the slow but inexorable progress of the new language, which became first an alternative official tongue, and finally the main chancellery medium of the empire.

So did imperial policy and high principle ensure that Aramaic would bring 2,000 years of civilization built on the Sumerian and Akkadian languages to an end. And yet, paradoxically, at the same time, it would also assure its immortality.

10

Passing the Baton:
An End and a Beginning

After 700 BCE

The Secret Weapon

An Assyrian scholar, writer of epics and annals for the royal household, like the compiler of the Chronicle of Tiglath-Pileser II that is inscribed on a reddish clay tablet the top part of which now lies in the British Museum, labelled K3751, steeped in the lore of Mesopotamia's past, convinced of his civilization's superiority over all other ways of life, and observing that Aramaic speakers were now promising to become a majority among the empire's population, might have consoled himself with the thought that this was nothing new. For thousands of years outsiders had entered Mesopotamia as either conquerors or immigrants: Gutians, Elamites, Amorites, Kassites and many others. Every one of these had eventually either been expelled or had become so totally absorbed that they vanished as identifiably separate ethnic groups, and instead had helped to carry forward their adopted Sumerian–Akkadian culture.

This time, however, with the naturalization of Aramaic speakers as Assyrian nationals, the outcome was to be very different. For the Arameans brought with them a secret weapon so overwhelmingly powerful that it was able to bring the long Mesopotamian tradition to a halt, eventually to crush it, and finally to cover over the remains so thoroughly as to make all direct evidence of the splendour of two and a half millennia vanish from the face of earth. And at the same time to begin the next wave of history, at the end of which we ourselves now live, by passing on to others the baton of civilization, and laying the foundations of the modern world. The weapon with that colossal achievement to its credit was an entirely

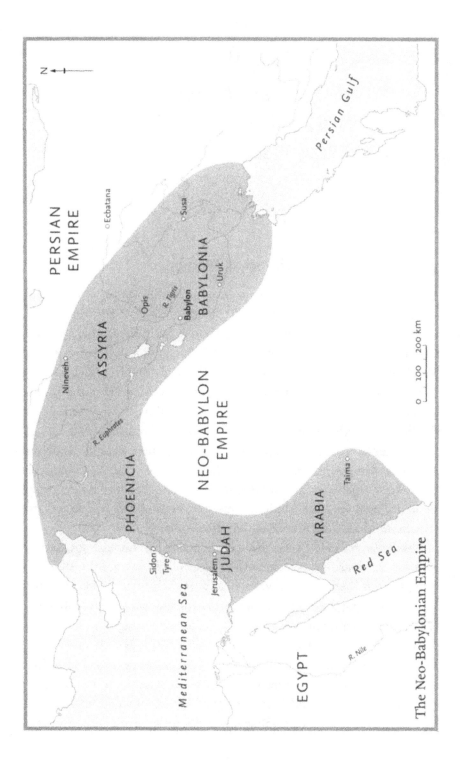

The Neo-Babylonian Empire

novel way of freezing evanescent speech in time: the alphabet. The letter 'K', written by the British Museum on to the top edge of Tiglath-Pileser's Chronicle symbolizes the victory of the new script over the old, and thus of the new world over the old.

While cuneiform was first invented, it is currently thought, by accountants, and developed by scribes and scholars, the alphabet seems to have had much more plebeian origins. The latest archaeological discoveries suggest that alphabetic writing was the brainwave of a group of expatriate Semitic workers resident in Egypt early in the second millennium BCE. Inspired by the pictographic Egyptian writing-system we call hieroglyphs – 'priest signs' – they dreamt up a shorthand to use with their own language. It was, said John Wilford, professor of Near Eastern studies at Johns Hopkins University, 'the accidental genius of these Semitic people who were at first illiterate, living in a very literate society. Only a scribe trained over a lifetime could handle the many different types of signs in the formal writing. So these people adopted a crude system of writing within the Egyptian system, something they could learn in hours, instead of a lifetime. It was a utilitarian invention for soldiers, traders, merchants.'

From such humble beginnings evolved every one of the alphabets and syllabaries (symbols that represent whole syllables rather than just individual letters) in use in the world today: from our own Latin alphabet, Greek and Russian, all the way to the scripts of India, Tibet and Mongolia. Naturally enough, on their way to becoming, say, the Greek or the Latin alphabet, many of the signs altered their forms – though not all. Our letter 'A', once representing a horned ox-head viewed full face, has turned upside-down, but is otherwise still recognizable; 'L', 'M' and 'N' have also changed relatively little. When we give the title alphabet to our list of letters, we are still recalling the Semitic words which began with the letters they named, the first referring to 'Aleph', ox, and the second to 'Bet', house.

The use of this workers' shorthand quickly spread among Semitic speakers along the eastern shores of the Mediterranean, Cana'anites and Phoenicians, whose far-flung trading empires carried it throughout the entire region, where each language adapted its principles to its own needs.

Aramaic writing was associated with ordinary working people while cuneiform was seen as the preserve of the educated and the elite; its relatively few signs – less than thirty – might be learned in a few weeks in contrast to the years of intense study demanded for the mastery of cuneiform; it could be written on almost any surface, inked on to potsherds, bones or leaves, chalked on to walls, scratched in the dust with a sharp stick, as well as formally calligraphed on to parchment or papyrus in contrast to cuneiform, which demanded some skill and experience even to prepare the clay for tablets. No wonder literacy spread rapidly and far more widely through society than was ever possible before.

The fact that Aramaic could be, and was, written ensured that it did not disappear like the speech of earlier immigrant groups. The fact that Aramaic speakers now so outnumbered Akkadian speakers ensured that the new language quickly established itself as a secondary national tongue, and ultimately as the principal official speech of the empire and the medium of government, as well as the lingua franca of the entire region, with Akkadian relegated to the role that Sumerian had once held: the language of diplomacy, scholarship and religion. The common analogy, by which use of the Sumerian language by Mesopotamians is compared to the place of Latin in medieval times, must now be changed. If Akkadian was the new Latin, then Sumerian itself became what Greek represented to the European Middle Ages.

For a long time, most educated Assyrians must have been fully bilingual, as much at ease in Aramaic as Assyrian. Scribes began to be represented on sculptures, wall panels and frescoes in pairs, side by side: one inscribing on a clay tablet, the other writing on leather or papyrus. These are not photographic records, of course; they may be more symbolic than realistic, and scholars differ over their interpretation. But as each kind of writing was restricted to its own language – Assyrian was always written in cuneiform, Aramaic always alphabetically – if cuneiform and alphabetic scribes ever did take dictation together, one of them must have been making a simultaneous translation of what was being dictated.

When the official languages of a state are replaced, profound consequences usually follow. In this case they affected not only the Assyrians of ancient times but modern archaeologists too: the change of language and writing spelled the imminent end of our rich inheritance of ancient texts. Clay tablets are all but indestructible, especially if fired to terracotta either purposely or in a conflagration, as so many were during the violent destruction of the buildings in which they were stored. Though abandoned for millennia, they still perfectly preserve the texts originally inscribed on them. Not so the organic materials, papyrus and leather, on which Aramaic records were set down. Even if not burned, such media decay and disappear, usually within a few decades, if not before. As a result, our knowledge of the last centuries of Mesopotamian civilization is limited. With few exceptions, we know only what the ancients chose to write down in what was even then becoming a language of scholars, clerics and antiquarians. To the Assyrians, that should have brought a warning of a devastating outcome: the loss to the world of their entire history.

There are no examples from modern times with which to compare and try to understand the implications of what was happening to Assyrian letters. The closest is the Turkish-language reform of the 1920s, introduced by Mustapha Kemal, later called Atatürk, founder and first president of the modern Turkish Republic that replaced the almost 500-year-old Ottoman Empire. In 1928, the use of Arabic script to write the country's language was prohibited and a modified form of the Latin alphabet substituted. Though there was resistance at first, the reforms were driven through in short order. Within a year, the use of Arabic writing became a criminal offence. Thus the entire country suddenly became illiterate. Atatürk himself travelled around Turkey with blackboard and chalk, setting up impromptu literacy classes in market squares and railway stations. Thereafter, with the establishment in 1932 of the *Türk Dil Kurumu*, the Turkish Language Society, the great number of Arabic and Persian words and expressions used in Ottoman times was weeded out and replaced by Turkish folk idioms and new coinages. All Turks had to relearn their way of speaking. Subsequent generations, who have been taught only the new letters and the new 'purified' language, can read no text written before 1928. The result has been to abolish the Turkish nation's entire past and eradicate all popular awareness of Ottoman times. That was, of course, for good or ill, Atatürk's intended purpose.

Could the Assyrians see such a situation coming in the future? As the Aramaic language made ever-greater inroads, could they imagine that all knowledge of the long history that lay behind their own achievements might one day be lost? It seems just possible that they did: a foreboding that the long Sumerian–Akkadian tradition, of which they were the proud inheritors, was for the first time seriously under threat.

The first sign of that fear, that the achievements of the past might be lost and even their very existence forgotten, was the royal library established at his palace in Nineveh by the last great Assyrian emperor, Ashurbanipal, who reigned form about 668 to 627 BCE. This was far from the first or only large collection of documents ever established in ancient Mesopotamia, but it does seem to have been an archive founded specifically for the sake of preserving the heritage of the past. The king's concern to conserve the literary riches of his cuneiform culture, that they might be read by scholars of the far future, is evidenced by the colophon associated with many of the tablets it stored: 'For the Sake of Distant Days'.

We do not know how many late Assyrian rulers were literate, able at least to read letters and dispatches without having to depend on secretaries to recite them aloud. This ability may well have been prized, not so much for its demonstration of the kings' superior education and mental prowess, but more for getting to the truth of what was really going on around them. It is easy to imagine scribes carefully filtering what they told the monarch. Many may well have feared to be the bearer of bad tidings, particularly if the monarch was irascible, given to explosions of ill-temper, and likely to punish the messenger for the message. That such censorship was hardly unknown is made explicit in this warning at the head of one letter addressed to the palace: 'Whoever you are, scribe, who is going to read this letter, do not conceal anything from the king, my lord, so that the gods Bel and Nabu should speak kindly of you to the king.'

Ashurbanipal went further than mere ability to read, and claimed complete mastery of all the scribal arts.

> I, Ashurbanipal, within the palace, understood the wisdom of Nabu [the god of learning]. All the art of writing... of every kind, I made myself the master of them all... I read the cunning tablets of Sumer, and the dark Akkadian language which is difficult rightly to use; I took my pleasure in reading stones inscribed before the flood.

He could not only read, but write, too.

The best of the scribal art, such works as none of the kings who went before me had ever learnt, remedies from the top of the head to the toenails, non-canonical selections, clever teachings, whatever pertains to the medical mastery of [the gods] Ninurta and Gula, I wrote on tablets, checked and collated, and deposited within my palace for perusing and reading.

(There may even be actual proof of his ability to compose cuneiform: some surviving tablets are marked 'Ashurbanipal, King of Assyria' in a notably unpractised hand.)

Assembling his library seems to have been no mere vanity project for this literate and well-schooled monarch. He wrote to all quarters of his empire instructing that whatever texts were locally available should be sent to him in Nineveh. We have, for example, his letter to the governor of Borsippa, an ancient city not far from Babylon: 'Word of the king to Shadunu: I am well, be of good cheer. On the day when you receive my tablet, you shall take with you Shuma, the son of Shum-ukin, Bel-Etir his brother, Apla, the son of Arkat-Ilani, and the expert from Borsippa whom you know; and you shall bring out all the tablets that are in their houses and those deposited in Ezida [the main temple of Borsippa's city god, Nabu].' He was concerned not just to amass as large a collection as possible, but to ensure that he had copies of every important work in the Mesopotamian canon. In the letter he goes on to list prayers, incantations and other texts, identified, as was usual in ancient times, by their first words. He wants the series of tablets called 'Battle', as well as 'Their blood', 'In the battle the spear shall not come near a man' and 'To rest in the wilderness and again to sleep in the palace'. In addition, he commands that Shadunu collect anything else that the palace library might lack.

You shall search for and send to me... rituals, prayers, stone inscriptions and whatever is useful to royalty such as expiation texts for cities, to ward off the evil eye at a time of panic, and whatever else is required in the palace, all that is available, and also rare tablets of which no copies exist in Assyria.

I have written to the temple overseer and to the chief magistrate that you are to place the tablets in your storage house and that no one shall withhold any tablet from you. And in case you should see some tablet or ritual text which I have not mentioned and which is suitable for the palace, examine it, take possession of it, and send it to me.

By a happy stroke of fortune, Ashurbanipal's aim of preserving in his archive the literary fruits of Sumerian–Akkadian culture 'for the sake of distant days' succeeded. His library was among the earlier discoveries made by the pioneers of Mesopotamian archaeology in the 1840s and 1850s, fulfilling the king's hope that one day the collection would help to restore to memory the intellectual riches of his civilization. Excavation of the site of ancient Nineveh, modern Kouyᵘnjik, provided a host of texts and fragments of texts, over 30,000 in all, representing many thousand individual documents – annals, myths, epics, prayers, incantations, glossaries, omen lists, mathematical exercises, astronomical tables, medical treatises – a boon to the scholars then working on the decipherment and translation of cuneiform. There was even a detailed acquisitions catalogue, noting the provenance of items in the king's collection. For example: 'One single-column tablet, anti-witchcraft, [written by] Mushezib-Nabu, son of Nabu-Shum-Ishkun, scribe of the King of Babylon. Two of 'Lamentations', one of the 'Dream Book', in all one hundred and twenty-five tablets, [written by] Arrabu, exorcist from Nippur.'

The downside to the early discovery of Ashurbanipal's library was, however, that the primitive excavation techniques and lack of proper record-keeping led to tablets from different buildings and even different excavations being irretrievably mixed together. The work of sorting out the jumble, of finding matches among the fragments and piecing them together, continues into the present.

The man credited with unearthing Ashurbanipal's library was Austen Henry Layard, a French-born British adventurer, diplomat and politician, whose explorations of the buried cities of Assyria, though they brought him international renown, in fact occupied little more than five years of his long and successful life. Most of the work was organized and supervised – and continued after Layard returned to his political career – by, very appropriately, an ethnic Assyrian; that is, a late descendant of Ashurbanipal's own people. Layard wrote appreciatively of Hormuzd Rassam in his account of the excavations: 'To Mr. Hormuzd Rassam, who usually accompanied me in my journeys, were confided, as before, the general superintendence of the operations, the payment of the workmen, the settlement of disputes, and various other offices, which only one as well acquainted as himself with the Arabs and men of various sects employed in the works, and exercising much personal influence amongst them, could undertake.'

No evidence there of the condescension and even contempt with which 'orientals', by definition oily, weak, and untrustworthy, were all too often treated by Europeans in the nineteenth century. Sir Henry Rawlinson, who played such an important part in the decipherment of cuneiform, had nothing but disdain for Rassam, and worked hard to have him excluded from taking any official role in the excavations. Layard, a future Under-Secretary for Foreign Affairs of the British Government, displayed a very different attitude to his Assyrian right hand man.

> *To his unwearied exertions, and his faithful and punctual discharge of all the duties imposed upon him, to his inexhaustible good humour, combined with necessary firmness, to his complete knowledge of the Arab character, and the attachment with which even the wildest of those with whom we were brought in contact regarded him, the Trustees of the British Museum owe not only much of the success of these researches, but the economy with which I was enabled to carry them through. Without him it would have been impossible to accomplish half what has been done with the means placed at my disposal.*

It is not hard to imagine the excitement the two must have felt as they and their team became the first people in over two and a half thousand years to explore the remains of the Assyrian emperors' sumptuous palaces, to discover passageways and great chambers guarded by colossal winged, human-headed bulls, *lamassu*, wearing the horned crown of divinity, and panelled with exquisite, if often gruesome, bas-reliefs. At the end of one tunnel they came upon two huge figures, of which only the lower half remained, yet which were none the less instantly recognisable as the fish-robed attendants of Eridu's god Enki or Ea, who had first taught humanity the arts of civilization. This was the historic moment when the glories of ancient literature were about to be introduced to the modern world.

The first doorway, guarded by the fish-gods, led into two small chambers opening into each other, and once panelled with bas-reliefs, the greater part of which had been destroyed. Layard first explains what was, in his day, a novel notion to the general public: that ancient Mesopotamians had used clay tablets as a medium for their writings, for this was still some time before the 1857 four-man challenge set by the Royal Asiatic Society to decipher cuneiform.

> *The chambers I am describing appear to have been a depository in the palace of Nineveh for such documents. To the height of a foot or more from the floor they were entirely filled with them; some entire, but the greater part broken into many fragments, probably by the falling in of the upper part of the building. They were of different sizes; the largest tablets were flat, and measured 9 inches by 63 inches; the smaller were slightly convex, and some were not more than an inch long, with but one or two lines of writing. The cuneiform characters on most of them were singularly sharp and well defined, but so minute in some instances as to be almost illegible without a magnifying glass.*

As so often, we owe the recovery of Ashurbanipal's collection of documents to a catastrophe: the destruction of the palace that housed it, the 'falling in of the upper part of the building' and its millennia-long burial under a mound of debris. But we do know what the reading room must once have looked like, because an archive dating from perhaps a century later – some 800 tablets, intact and preserved in the original extensive pigeon-holed shelving that lined the room's walls, carefully sorted and clearly labelled – was discovered in 1986 in the remains of the city of Sippar, a little north of Babylon. It contained few documents new to scholars, but their perfect state of preservation promised to fill in gaps in already known texts: 'the kind of discovery that one waits 100 years to see,' said the curator of the Yale University Babylonian Collection.

The nineteenth-century policy of shipping out such discoveries en masse to European museums having been long abandoned, the Sippar library was made part of Iraq's National Museum of Antiquities unparalleled tablet collection of more than 100,000 documents. This was looted after the fall of Saddam Hussein: the wooden boxes storing the collection were broken open and the catalogues recording their contents were burned. There is no great hope of getting much back. 'You put these things in the back of a truck and drive over a bumpy road,' lamented one archaeologist, 'and pretty soon you have a sackful of dust.'

Thus did Assyria's enemies ultimately fail to achieve their aim when they razed Ashur and Nineveh in 612 BCE, only fifteen years after Ashurbanipal's death: the wiping out of Assyria's place in history. The ancient destruction was so complete that when the Greek historian Xenophon and his mercenary army retreated past the location of Nineveh in 401 BCE, they were quite unaware of it. According to the satirist Lucian, an ethnic Assyrian who wrote in Greek, 'Nineveh is so completely destroyed that it is no longer possible to say where it stood. Not a single trace of it remains.' It was the almost inevitable consequence of the imperial policy of *Oderint dum Metuant*, let them hate so long as they fear. For when the fear is overcome, the hatred remains. An object lesson to states, even of the present day, who base their relations with their neighbours on the same principle.

A Terrible Defeat upon a Great People

The principal agent, and beneficiary, of the conquest of Assyria and the destruction of its cities was the land with which the northern imperialists had had such an ambivalent relationship for so long: Babylon. Assyrian rulers had tried everything to dominate and control their southern neighbour. Some, like Tiglath-Pileser III, imposed direct rule, creating a dual monarchy by nominating themselves King of Assyria and Babylon; others tried placing a close – and hopefully loyal – relative on Babylon's throne; yet others selected a native Babylonian as client–king. None of these choices was ultimately successful; rebellions and revolts were frequent, and were put down with great severity.

Assyria's difficulties were compounded by the fact that Babylonia had been just as subject to the flood of new immigrant Semitic nomads as Assyria. In the south, the principal incomers were a people related, but not identical, to the Arameans: the Kaldi, Chaldeans. Representing themselves as defenders of Babylon's independence, they fought strenuously against Assyrian domination. The convoluted, confused, and very violent political history of the time is exemplified in the tumultuous events which took place in the hundred years following Assyria's annexation of Israel in 721 BCE.

It all began in the days of Assyria's campaigning Emperor Sargon II. A Chaldean prince and leader of the Beit Yakin clan, called Marduk-Apla-

Iddina, known to the Bible as Merodach Baladan, had contrived to occupy
the Babylonian throne for some ten years, in defiance of attempts by the
Assyrian king to oust him. Eventually Sargon managed to drive him into
exile in Elam, and proclaim himself King of Babylon. But after Sargon's
death in battle, Marduk-Apla-Iddina immediately returned. Sargon's son
Sennacherib led his armies against this repeat offender, who retreated to
his base in the marshes around the head of the Gulf, while the Assyrian
king tried to assuage Babylonian sensitivities by appointing to the kingship a certain Bel-Ibni, a native Babylonian, albeit an aristocratic one who
had spent his childhood in the Assyrian palaces of Nineveh. But Bel-Ibni
also revolted against Assyrian hegemony and Sennacherib was forced to
replace him with his own son, Ashur-Nadin-Shumi. While the Assyrian
tried to drive Marduk-Apla-Iddina from his redoubt in the southern wet-
lands, the King of Elam, Mesopotamia's eternal enemy, took the opportunity to mount an attack on Babylon, impose a ruler of his own choice
and take away Sennacherib's son in chains – he was never heard of again.
Sennacherib returned to Babylon, captured the Elamite placeman, and
then set off east to punish the Elamites with an assault on their capital
Susa. But while he was thus engaged, yet another Chaldean prince clam-
bered on to the Babylonian throne. In a great rage, Sennacherib laid siege
to the city for fifteen months, and when he finally broke through the walls,
carried off the pretender, his family and other Chaldean notables into captivity, looted the palaces and temples of all their valuables, and dragged off
the statue of the god Marduk, protector and ruling deity of Babylon. He
then had canals dug right through the city centre and flooded the entire
urban area, so that nobody should ever live there again.

Or, at least, so he claimed in his inscriptions.

The city and its houses, from its foundation to its walls, I destroyed, I dev-
astated, I burned with fire. The wall and outer wall, temple-tower of brick
and earth, temples and gods, as many as there were, I razed and dumped
into the Arahtu-Canal. Through the midst of the city I dug canals, flooded
its site with water, and the very foundations thereof I destroyed. I made its
destruction more complete than by a flood. That in days to come, the site of
the city, its temples and gods, might not be remembered, I completely blotted
it out with floods of water and made it like a meadow.

Time and time again we read such accounts of the total destruction of great Mesopotamian cities, and yet after a relatively short interval they appear to have risen again as if nothing had happened. Babylon is a case in point. Utterly destroyed by the Assyrian emperor in 689 BCE, sixty years later, far from the site not being remembered, it was flourishing even more than before. How could this be? Is the truth that the devastation was never quite as great as we are led to believe?

Maybe we should remember our twentieth-century history. By the end of 1945 many European cities had been almost totally destroyed. Berlin was a sea of ruins; Minsk appears in photographs as no more than an ocean of pulverized rubble, square mile after square mile in extent; in Japan, Hiroshima and Nagasaki were utterly wiped out by the first atomic bombs. Yet within a few decades the damage had largely been repaired and the cities rebuilt, often reconstructed following the original architectural plans. Much the same seems to have taken place in Babylon.

After Sennacherib was assassinated in a palace coup and his son Esarhaddon took control, the new king allowed the deportees to return home, ordered the restoration of the gods' statues to their temples, and generally did his best to undo the damage his father had wrought. He tried to stabilize the relationship between Assyria and Babylon by designating his younger son, Ashurbanipal, as his successor to the Assyrian throne, and another son, Shamash-Shumu-Ukin, as King of Babylon.

But even this solution failed. Soon after Esarhaddon's death a bitter civil war broke out between the brothers, which ended only when Ashurbanipal besieged Babylon, broke through the gates and unleashed his forces on to the populace. Shamash-Shumu-Ukin died in his burning palace. Ashurbanipal installed a new puppet king and then turned on his rebellious brother's allies.

Here he made a grave political error, though he would not live to see its disastrous consequences. Elam had supported the Babylonian king against him, so in revenge, Ashurbanipal attacked Susa, the Elamite capital, and decided to make of it an object lesson: he stripped the palaces of everything of value, demolished the temples, destroyed the ziggurat, smashed the statues of previous Elamite kings and desecrated their tombs. Then he turned his attention to the Elamite hinterland. 'In a month of days I levelled the whole of Elam. I deprived its fields of the sound of human voices, the tread of cattle and sheep, the refrain of joyous harvest songs. I turned it into a pasture for wild asses, gazelles, and all manner of wild animals.' Susa city was eventually restored, but Elam would never regain its place as a major power in the region.

This was a tactical victory but a strategic blunder. In destroying Elam, Ashurbanipal had removed not only a barrier that protected Mesopotamia against attack from further east, but the power that had long prevented new peoples from establishing control over the Iranian plateau. With Elam humbled, semi-nomads from Central Asia could now take over: Medes and Persians, speakers of Indo-European languages, who had penetrated Iran through the passes over its northern mountains, quickly established themselves as the new strongmen of the Iranian highlands. The Medes, vigorous warriors, immediately began to challenge Assyrian power. In 612 BCE, a mere fifteen years after Ashurbanipal's death, with a succession of ever-weaker emperors allowing Ashur's borders to be pushed back yet further, Medean forces smashed through Assyria's defences and, supported by the Babylonian king, who cleverly arrived on the battlefield just too late to take part in the fighting, brought the state of Ashur to a sudden, unexpected, final and violent end.

After mopping-up operations that lasted several years, the Assyrian provinces were divided among the victors, the Medes ruling in Anatolia and the north-east, the Babylonians commanding the entire Fertile Crescent and the northern half of Arabia. In effect Babylon, led by its new king, a Chaldean sheikh who took the Akkadian name Nabu-Apla-Usur (Nabopolassar), meaning 'Nabu Protect the Heir', had taken over her longstanding rival's empire. What Assyriologists call the Neo-Babylonian Empire was born.

It did not last long: roughly three score years and ten, a single human lifetime, or the same as the USSR in the twentieth century, a shortness of span that is brought into remarkable focus by one of the great finds of recent archaeology.

In 1956, a British scholar, Dr David Storm Rice, was investigating a twelfth-century mosque in the ancient city of Harran, once city of the moon god, built on the orders of Saladin, the Kurdish general who retook Jerusalem from its Christian crusader occupiers in the year 1187. Rice was trying to confirm his belief that ancient paganism continued to reign in Harran until late in the Middle Ages. At each of the three entrances to the mosque, he uncovered large stone slabs that showed signs of being far older than the rest of the building. On turning them over he discovered carvings representing a Babylonian king in the act of adoring Sin, represented as a crescent moon. The stones had been placed face downwards so that the faithful would walk over them on their way in to pray, symbolizing the final victory of faith in Allah over the worship of the moon.

That was astonishing enough, but the cuneiform text accompanying the image named the king pictured as Nabonidus, last King of Babylon, and included a biography of his mother. In spite of the fabulous lengths of reign ascribed to the ancient kings of Sumer, and the impossibly long lives claimed for the patriarchs in the Bible, here we have the very first proper documented evidence for an ancient centenarian: 'I am the lady Adda-guppi, mother of Nabu-na'id [Nabonidus], king of Babylon'. She had lived 'From the 20th year of Asur-Bani-Apli [Ashurbanipal], king of Assyria, during whose rule I was born until the 42nd year of Asur-Bani-Apli, until the 3rd year of Asur-Etillu-Ili, his son, until the 21st year of Nabu-Apla-Usur [Nabopolassar], until the 43rd year of Nabu-Kudurri-Usur [Nebuchadnezzar], until the 2nd year of Amel-Marduk [Evil-Merodach], until the 4th year of Nergal-Sharu-Ussur [Neriglissar].' Furthermore, she remained in extremely good shape to the very end:

> Sin, the king of the gods, chose me and made my name famous in the world by adding many days and years of mental capacity to the normal span of life and thus kept me alive – from the time of Ashurbanipal, King of Assyria, to the 6th year of Nabu-Na'id, King of Babylon, the son of my womb: that is, for 104 happy years. According to what Sin, the king of the gods, had promised me, my eyesight was keen, my hearing excellent, my hands and feet in perfect condition, my diction well chosen, food and drink agreed with me... I was in good spirits.

The postscript reads:

> In the ninth year of Nabu-Na'id, King of Babylon, she died a natural death, and Nabu-Na'id, King of Babylon, the offspring of her womb, the favourite

of his mother, deposited her corpse in the coffin clad in fine woollen gar-
ments, shining linen,… precious and costly stones. He sprinkled her corpse
with perfumed oil. They placed the coffin in a secure tomb and, in front of
it, he slaughtered cattle and fat sheep, and assembled into his presence the
inhabitants of Babylon and Borsippa.

This amazing lady lived from the time of the height of Assyrian power to a mere six years before the final end of the Neo-Babylonian Empire, a century that would prove to be one of the most influential in all history. Why so? Because it was in the days of the second ruler of the Chaldean dynasty, Nabopolassar's son Nabu-Kudurri-Usur, 'Nabu preserve the first-born', whom we know from the Bible as Nebuchadnezzar, that the tiny client state of Judaea, after an inadvisable revolt, was finally fully annexed into Babylon's domains. The Jerusalem Temple was destroyed, King Zedekiah blinded, his heirs executed, the entire ruling class exiled to the imperial capital – and in a sweeping gesture of populist land reform, their estates given over to the common people. The most accurate report is probably not the politically and theologically motivated account in the Books of Kings and Chronicles, but the eye-witness testimony of the Prophet Jeremiah:

And the Chaldeans burned the king's house, and the houses of the people,
with fire, and brake down the walls of Jerusalem.
  Then Nebuzaradan the captain of the guard carried away captive into
Babylon the remnant of the people that remained in the city, and those
that fell away, that fell to him, with the rest of the people that remained.
  But Nebuzaradan the captain of the guard left of the poor of the people,
which had nothing, in the land of Judah, and gave them vineyards and
fields at the same time.(Jeremiah 39:8–10)

When the Neo-Babylonian Empire fell to the Persians less than fifty years later, and the Judaean nobility was permitted to return to Jerusalem and begin rebuilding the Temple, only those who had been exiled to Babylon were henceforth to be counted as Jews. Though the common folk who had been left behind in Judaea, 'the poor of the people', approached the returnees and begged to take part in the restoration work, they were told, in robust terms, to get lost:

*Ye have nothing to do with us to build an house unto our God; but we
ourselves together will build unto the Lord God of Israel, as King Cyrus
the King of Persia hath commanded us. (Ezra 4:3)*

In any case, only a minority of Judaeans wanted to resettle their provincial
and impoverished former homeland anyway. Most elected to stay on in
Mesopotamia, to continue enjoying the benefits of living in the heartland of civilization. For centuries, Babylonia and not Jerusalem housed
the largest Judaic communities anywhere. And it was in the Babylonian
academies that the Babylonian Talmud was created, the text that shapes
Judaism to this day. Without Nebuchadnezzar's conquest and deportation,
Judaism as we know it, and therefore Christianity and Islam in their turn,
could never have come to be.

Such profound and distant outcomes were of course never envisaged
by those like Adda-guppi' who lived through neo-Babylonian times. In
fact, few would have recognized that very much had altered at all when
Assyrian was replaced with Babylonian power. As so many times before in
Mesopotamian history, this was a takeover rather than a true conquest.

From the very beginning the story of Mesopotamian civilization is
reminiscent of one of those giant industrial enterprises of the modern
world, which may change ownership and shareholding but continue to
be the same company, promoting the same brands, generating the same
products, whoever actually draws the dividends and prepares the annual
financial reports. For those other than the city folk of Ashur and Nineveh
whose homes were erased from the map, for ordinary farmers, crafts
people, for traders outside the ruling class, not to mention slaves, little
may have appeared to have changed. The same bureaucrats stayed in place;
the same chancellery language, Aramaic, remained in use; the same literary culture was celebrated; the same music was played; the same prayers
were chanted; the same gods were worshipped – with the exception of
Assyria's patron deity Ashur, who lost everything. Indeed, Mesopotamians
may well have felt no more had occurred than that the leadership of
their traditions had been repatriated to its source. Observers like the
Greek historian Herodotus, who lived only a century after Babylon's glory
days, still recognized the empire as Assyrian, and Babylonian victory

as a mere change of the ruler's address: 'Assyria possesses a vast number of great cities, whereof the most renowned and strongest at this time was Babylon, whither, after the fall of Nineveh, the seat of government had been removed.'

Babylon, with its rather more than 1,000-year history, primary urban focus of the land of Akkad, heir to the Sumerian founders of civilization, was now the centre of its world once again. Nebuchadnezzar marked the city's regained status by raising it to its greatest prominence ever. He made it the largest, the most splendid, and in some eyes the most glamorous city the world had ever seen.

Herodotus again:

> *The city stands on a broad plain, and is an exact square, a hundred and twenty stadia in length each way, so that the entire circuit is four hundred and eighty stadia. While such is its size, in magnificence there is no other city that approaches to it. It is surrounded, in the first place, by a broad and deep moat, full of water, behind which rises a wall fifty royal cubits in width, and two hundred in height.*

Herodotus may well not have visited the place himself. His dimensions are impossibly large: a two hundred cubit-high wall would have towered to nearly 100 metres. And, since the remains of the city are still clearly visible on the ground, we know that, enormous as it was – about two and a quarter thousand acres – its circumference was not some 80 kilometres, as the ancient historian claimed, but just over 10.

The city as modern archaeologists have found it is mostly the result of Nebuchadnezzar's extensive and expensive rebuilding projects. But that does not mean that the city changed in any really significant way. Babylon's rebuilders were always careful not to alter what they believed to be her god-given form. Indeed, the archaeological layers piled one on top of another that scholars now use to determine the history of a site, is, in the Mesopotamian case, not so much the result of natural decay and restoration, as the fruits of a conscious policy of carefully preserving the old in the context of the new that goes all the way back to the building and rebuilding of sacred Eridu more than 3,000 years before.

Thus Nabopolassar, when restoring the defensive wall called Imgur-Enlil, 'Enlil is gracious', said that he had 'looked for its ancient foundation platform and found it'. He described himself as he who 'searches for the ancient foundation platforms... who discovers bricks of the past, who rebuilds... on the original platform.' Several decades later the last king of the dynasty, Nabonidus, rebuilt the temple to Ishtar of Agade, claiming that his brickwork was constructed directly 'above the original foundation... not allowing those foundations to protrude by one finger's breadth nor allowing them to recede by one finger-breadth'.

The exact replication of Babylon's ancient fabric when restoring and rebuilding was of paramount importance because the city symbolically represented the whole of Sumerian–Akkadian history. Approaching from any direction, the travellers would have first spied the gigantic walls and the towering ziggurat from afar. Coming closer, they would have seen that those walls seemed to rise out of a swamp, just as the ancient myths had described the creation of the land of Sumer and Akkad, as it emerged from the underground waters called the Apsu, home of the god of civilization Enki/Ea, far to the south in Eridu near the head of the gulf. 'Alongside Babylon great banks of earth I heaped up,' wrote Nebuchadnezzar. 'Great floods of destroying water like the great waves of the sea I made flow around it; with a marsh I surrounded it.'

Entering the double-walled inner city near the eastern bank of the Euphrates, through the heavily guarded gate named for the god Urash, and also known by the epithet 'the enemy is abhorrent to it', visitors quickly crossed a commercial district called Shuanna, and soon came to another gate, the Market gate. According to a contemporary topography of the city, 'from the Market Gate to the Grand Gate is called Eridu.' In the quarter bearing this ever-numinous name, representing the very origins of ancient Sumer, known to all as the very fount of civilization, stood the most important religious building in Babylon: E-Sagila, Sumerian for the 'House with a High Head'. the earthly residence of the god Marduk, Babylon's founder and protector as well as Prince of all the gods. E-Sagila was the very name borne by the sanctuary of Enki in Eridu. And, separated from it by a 75-metre-wide plaza, the most famous construction of all was Etemenanki, the 'House which is the foundation-peg of Heaven and Earth', the great 90-metre-high Ziggurat of Babylon, inspiration for the story of the Tower of Babel. The biblical author must have known its Akkadian name when he wrote, 'And they said, Go to, let us build us a city and a tower, whose top may reach unto heaven.' (Genesis 11:4) The not-always-reliable Herodotus described it as:

> *a tower of solid masonry, a furlong in length and breadth, upon which was raised a second tower, and on that a third, and so on up to eight. The ascent to the top is on the outside, by a path which winds round all the towers. When one is about half-way up, one finds a resting-place and seats, where persons are wont to sit some time on their way to the summit. On the topmost tower there is a spacious temple, and inside the temple stands a couch of unusual size, richly adorned, with a golden table by its side. There is no statue of any kind set up in the place, nor is the chamber occupied of nights by any one but a single native woman, who, as the Chaldeans, the priests of this god, affirm, is chosen for himself by the deity out of all the women of the land.*
>
> *They also declare – but I for my part do not credit it – that the god comes down in person into this chamber, and sleeps upon the couch.*

Yet Herodotus is not all we have to go on. When trying to imagine the building's appearance we do have one single apparently contemporary image. On a broken black stele, most of which is held in a private collection, is a representation of both the ziggurat's ground plan and its elevation, with King Nebuchadnezzar standing beside them, and an inscription stating: 'Etemenanki – I made it the wonder of the people of the world. I raised its top to the heaven, made doors for the gates, and covered it with bitumen and bricks'. The relief corrects Herodotus by showing not eight, but only six stages with a 'spacious temple' on top.

Today there is not even a ruin where Etemenanki once raised its top towards heaven. Alexander of Macedon, after his Asian conquests, intended to make Babylon the capital of his empire. Modelling his royal actions on Mesopotamian tradition, he determined to restore Babylon's ziggurat and began by dismantling the ageing structure in preparation for its reconstruction. He did not live long enough to achieve his ambition, so all we find today in what was once Babylon's Eridu quarter are the waterlogged foundations.

Beyond E-Sagila and Etemenanki, visitors to Babylon passed through another gate to enter the adjoining quarter: 'From the Grand Gate to the Ishtar Gate is called Ka-Dingir-ra', says the itinerary. Ka-Dingira is

Sumerian for the Akkadian Bab-Ilum, Babylon, interpreted as meaning Gate of God; perhaps this area was the original nucleus of the urban foundation. Thus Eridu, the original locus of Mesopotamian culture, and Babylon, its final and most glorious expression, were here symbolically united in facts on the ground.

The Ka-Dingir-ra quarter contained the most spectacular of Nebuchadnezzar's urban-renewal projects: his own magnificent palaces, the processional way, its walls magnificently decorated with glazed-tile lions, leading to the Marduk temple through the magnificent 18-metre-high Ishtar Gate with its crenellated bastions, their glittering blue façades adorned with bulls and dragons in white and ochre, and bearing a long inscription by the king himself:

> *This street of Babylon having become increasingly lower, I pulled down the gates and re-laid their foundations at the water-table with asphalt and bricks. I had them remade of bricks with blue stone on which wonderful bulls and dragons were depicted. I covered their roofs by laying majestic cedars lengthwise over them. I fixed doors of cedar wood trimmed with bronze in all the gates. I placed wild bulls and ferocious dragons in the gateways and thus adorned them with luxurious splendour so that Mankind might gaze on them in wonder.*

Fear of the Future

The concern to replicate the past and to ensure that the symbolism of Babylon City survived into the future might be seen as no more than a continuation of longstanding Mesopotamian tradition. But, just as Ashurbanipal's establishment of a library 'for the sake of distant days' reflected a new concern that the past might altogether disappear, so too did the rulers of first millennium Babylon seem to have similar concerns.

Most cultures either look forward to the future or look back towards the past. Rarely both. When the future is bright, when what is yet to come seems most exciting, history is usually left to fend for itself. Germanic settlers in western Europe left most Roman city centres to rot: thatched wooden shacks in the forum, animal pens in the circus, pigsties in the public baths. Medieval cathedral-builders showed little respect for the primitive chapels of their forefathers. Victorian architects in industrializing, modernizing Britain, with its rapidly developing science and its great feats of engineering, could hardly wait to pull down all those ghastly, old-fashioned neoclassical Georgian terraces. True, these were often replaced by buildings designed in a fantasy version of medieval style, but keeping the old in place was never on the nineteenth-century agenda.

As late as the 1940s, when Swiss art-historian Siegfried Giedion was researching the revolutionary period during which American industry pioneered the principles of mass-production, 'I myself visited a great factory outside Boston where clocks and watches were first assembled from standardized parts shortly after 1850. (This principle later found its most extensive use in the manufacture of automobiles.) The early products of this factory were mentioned by some European observers of the [eighteen-]seventies. I wanted to see examples of them and to study the early catalogues of the company. There were no old catalogues at all – the company destroyed them, on principle, when they were three years old – and the only old watches were those which had come in for repairs.'

By contrast, times that are obsessed with maintaining the past, with conservation and preservation, with genealogy, with investigating and unearthing prehistory, are usually those, like ours now, whose future looks uncertain, even threatening.

The mood of the mid-first millennium BCE must have had something in common with our own. Mesopotamians had always shown dedication to their ancestry and their traditions, but now a positive passion for deep antiquity came to the fore. Indeed Babylon in the seventh and sixth century can truly said to have invented the study of archaeology as we would recognize it. Professor Irene Winter, a distinguished historian of art at Harvard, has pointed out that most of the criteria by which we recognize modern archaeology were established by the rulers of the Neo-Babylonian Empire. They mounted field campaigns and made great efforts to expose architectural remains. Some of their records would not look out of place in the accounts of nineteenth-century explorers of Mesopotamia. Nabonidus went on an expedition to Agade and searched for the remains of the temple of Ishtar: 'I sought to rebuild this temple; and in order to do so, I opened up the ground inside Agade and looked for the foundation.' Elsewhere he writes, 'Kurigalzu, King of Babylon who preceded me, looked for the foundation of Eulmash [the Ishtar Temple] in Agade, which had not been known since the time of Sargon, King of Babylon, and his son Naram-Sin [actually his grandson]... but he did not find it. He wrote and set up an inscription which said: "I looked ceaselessly for the foundations of the Eulmash, but did not find them."' Nabonidus then credits Esarhaddon of Assyria, his son Ashurbanipal, and Nebuchadnezzar of Babylon with also having looked unsuccessfully for the building. 'As for Nebuchadnezzar, he called up his numerous work-men and looked ceaselessly... He dug deep trenches but did not find the foundations.' Finally, relentless perseverance paid off and Nabonidus was successful: 'For three years I excavated in the trench of Nebuchadnezzar... I looked to the right and left... to the front and rear of the trench ... Then a downpour occurred and made a gully... I said... "Dig a trench in that gully". They excavated in that gully and found the foundations of Eulmash.'

Like other neo-Babylonian rulers he also explored the ruins for ancient texts, which he then carefully studied: 'I looked upon the old foundation of Naram-Sin, an earlier king, and I read the tablets of gold, lapis and cornelian about the building of the E-Babbar [temple of the sun god].' Then he added his own new text and returned them all to their original locations. He also found a much damaged image of Sargon of Akkad, had it restored in his workshop, and then put it back in its place in the temple.

Other artefacts, of many different periods, were kept in the royal residence. Excavators have recovered from the ruins of Babylon's Northern Palace objects dating from the third millennium BCE to Nebuchadnezzar's time. Could they have constituted some kind of palace museum? Whatever their purpose, they demonstrate once more the neo-Babylonians' concern to preserve their past in the face of an increasingly uncertain future.

There is even a very late tradition, expounded by Berosos, Priest of Marduk, who earlier described the fish-god who taught humans the arts of civilization, and who was active around the beginning of the third century BCE, when Macedonians ruled in Mesopotamia, that Nebuchadnezzar himself had foreseen the fall of the Babylonian world. Berosos's own works are long lost, but are summarized in the writings of later authors, including the Church Father Eusebius of Caesarea, who lived from the third to the fourth century of our era, and who tells us that:

> *Nebuchadnezzar, having mounted to the roof of his palace, was seized with a divine afflatus, and broke into speech as follows: "I, Nebuchadnezzar, foretell to you, O Babylonians, the calamity which is about to fall upon you, which [the god] Bel, my forefather, and Queen Beltis are alike unable to persuade the fates to avert. A Persian mule will come, assisted by your gods, and will bring slavery upon you, with his accomplice, a Mede, the pride of the Assyrians."*

This is of course no more than 20/20 hindsight projected back on to the great Chaldean emperor. Nevertheless it does suggest that in Berosos's day, and long thereafter, it was believed that the last dynasties of Mesopotamia were given to intimations of imperial mortality, to the feeling that the glory and the dream were over; in short, that the Babylonian outlook on the future was far from sanguine.

It would be wonderful to know whether the neo-Babylonians were as subject to the effusions of prophets of doom and foretellers of disaster of the kind who regularly fill our newspaper pages today. Not to mention dishevelled men shambling along Tillazida Street bearing sandwich boards inscribed with the slogan 'The End is Nigh' – in cuneiform, of course. We have inherited such a tiny fraction of Babylonian writings – and none at all in their everyday language Aramaic – that we cannot tell. In any case, the ancients' familiar reluctance to express their ideas as theory and speculation rather than subtly and elliptically, in terms of tales of the gods and epic sagas, hides so much of their mentality from our matter-of-fact, less metaphorically inclined, modern minds.

Occasionally, however, a scholar does manage to part the cloud of unknowing. Some sixty years ago, the late Nels Bailkey, a professor at Tulane University, published an article provocatively entitled 'A Babylonian Philosopher of History', showing how intense study and close reading of a text can sometimes bring out its underlying message. The document in question is at first sight a typical Mesopotamian story of the gods, known variously as 'The Myth of the Pest-God Irra, The King of All Habitations', or 'The Dibarra Epic'. (Bailkey dated it to the time of Hammurabi or a little after. Scholars now are sure that it was written very much after that:

either in late Assyrian or neo-Babylonian days.) And it is, in fact, not typical at all.

The text tells us that a messenger from the god Irra-Nergal, Lord of plague, death and the ruler of the underworld, 'Revealed the poem at night [in a dream] to the author, Kabiti-Ilani-Marduk, son of Dabibu. When he arose in the morning he left no line out. Nor a single line did he add.' This, then, is not poesy but prophecy. Kabiti-Ilani-Marduk is not concerned, like others of his time, simply to reiterate ancient tales and preserve memories of the past. He has received a message for mankind, which foretells the future and, more importantly, explains it.

The poem is long: more than six hundred lines, falling into three acts. Act one tells of how the plague god intervenes in heaven, against some healthy opposition, to persuade the other gods to leave their places, abandon their protégés on earth, and allow Irra to wreak total devastation on the land of Sumer and Akkad. Previously Mesopotamians had ascribed the disasters that regularly befell them to the unpredictable actions of capricious gods. Kabiti-Ilani-Marduk, however, presents Irra's justification in words that would not, apart from the name of the divinity, seem out of place heard from the mouth of a Hebrew prophet: 'Because they have not feared my name and have rejected the word of Marduk, the Prince, and because they follow their own hearts, I shall challenge the Prince Marduk, cause him to arise from his throne, and crush mankind.' The destruction is not to be limited to Babylon, Marduk's own city; it will be as wide-reaching as the great Flood, that earlier disjunction in Mesopotamian history. 'Sea shall not spare sea, Subartu not Subartu, Assyrian not Assyrian, Elamite not Elamite,... land not land, city not city, house not house, brother not brother. They shall slay each other.'

In act two, after persuasive argument, Irra-Nergal gets his way. He unleashes his terrifying fury.

> *Open the way, I will take the road.*
> *The days are ended, the fixed time has passed. I will command.*
> *The splendour of the sun I will cut off;*
> *I will cover over the moon in the night…*
> *I will decimate the land and count it as ruin.*
> *The cities will I destroy and turn them to wilderness.*

The catastrophe is total. In passage after passage we see Irra destroy the cities, ruin the fields, reduce humanity to a remnant, wipe out civilization utterly. He calls the gods together and boasts:

> *Be silent, all of you, and learn my words....*
> *My heart raged so that I decimated the peoples...*
> *Like one who plants not fruit trees I weary not to cut down.*
> *Like a plunderer distinguishing not faithful and wicked I seize away;*
> *Like a devouring lion from whose mouth they seize not the corpse.*
> *And where one perished in fear a second shall not counsel him.*

Finally, in act three, we are shown the point and purpose of all this devastation. The world is to be rebuilt, humanity restored, the cities reconstructed, the fields and groves, the flocks and herds rendered fruitful once more. As the Hebrew Prophet Isaiah wrote in a different context: 'For, behold, I create new heavens and a new earth: and the former shall not be remembered, nor come into mind.' In the Babylonian seer's version, Irra-Nergal commands:

> *Thou shalt restore the gods of the land, who have become angered,*
>   *upon their thrones.*
> *The god of flocks and the grain-goddess shalt thou cause*
>   *to descend upon the land.*
> *Thou shalt cause the mountains to bring their produce*
>   *and the sea its tribute.*
> *The parched fields shalt thou cause to bear produce.*
> *The governors will have their heavy tribute brought to Babylon*
>   *from all their cities.*
> *The temples which have been destroyed,*
>   *like the splendour of the sun shall shine their censers.*
> *The Tigris and the Euphrates shall send their waters of fullness.*

So what was it for, all the terror and the agony? Was it pointless? No, Kabiti-Ilani-Marduk insists. The devastation was no wilful act of divine vandalism. Clearing the past away has allowed the future to grow anew. After destruction comes rebuilding. But what comes now is to be no mere reconstruction of an earlier golden age, for the new world is to be better than before. The aim of wiping out the past has been to allow a superior dispensation to take its place. In Professor Bailkey's words: 'The true nature and purpose of the destructive work of Irra-Nergal, the fact that change and progress are essential characteristics of human history, will now be realized by all and will be expressed in the form of praise to the god who has been given the leading role in the drama of history, making his initial appearance in the second act in the guise of a diabolical villain, but revealing himself finally in the third act as the far-seeing hero of the entire action.'

Kabiti-Ilani-Marduk is promoting a striking, almost Darwinian, even Nietzschean concept: that death and destruction, far from being the enemy of mankind, is the positive, creative force behind all history. That without it there can be no progress. And that change, progress, constant self-transcendence are the only true tasks of human existence. The Babylonian prophet is telling his hearers: 'Yes, the end is coming. Yes, the land you know and love will be destroyed. But from the ashes will rise a new and different world, one which will take the development of civilization on to its next stage.' In promoting this message, Kabiti-Ilani-Marduk is being true to that trust in the future, that Mesopotamian belief in unending development, which first made itself known among those who gathered, all those thousands of years before, around the miraculous sweet-water pool, dedicated to Enki god of progress, near the marshes around Eridu, far to the south by the side of the southern sea.

Mesopotamian independence survived Nebuchadnezzar by less than a quarter of a century. After he died of natural causes following a reign of forty-three years, he was succeeded by his son, who took the throne-name Amel-Marduk (Man of Marduk) – Evil-Merodach in the Bible. Two years of contentious policy-making led to his assassination and replacement by Nergal-Sharu-Ussur (O Nergal Protect the King), whom the Greeks called Neriglissar. On his death, his young son La-Abashi-Marduk (May I not be Destroyed, O Marduk) inherited the imperial rule. But he was soon eliminated – murdered in yet another palace coup d'état. A document known as the Dynastic Prophecy explained that he had been unable to exercise authority as he was a young man and had not 'learned how to behave'. Who killed him is not clear. The conspirators placed on the throne Nabu-na'id (Nabu be Praised), Nabonidus to the Greeks, who must have by then been in late middle age. He was assisted by his ambitious son Bel-Sharu-usur (Bel Protect the King), Belshazzar in the Book of Daniel.

Meanwhile the Medes, who had brought about Assyria's downfall had been, in their own turn, deposed as overlords of the Iranian plateau by their cousins the Persians, under the leadership of Cyrus, the Median king's son-in-law. Cyrus then turned his attention west. In 539 BCE, after a short campaign that saw city after city fall to Persian forces, Babylon herself was taken.

Several accounts of that momentous event have come down to us, so that we are able to reconstruct a picture of how it must have seemed to those who lived through it.

Babylon's Final Fall

On the 15th day of the Autumn month of Tashritu (12 October) in the greatest city on earth, the weather would have been pleasantly warm; the sky cloudless and blue – no longer yellowed, as throughout the summer, by sand lofted from the desert; the first tentative gusts of the *Ishtanu*, the winter wind from the north, lazily stirring the rubbish lying in the walkways between the houses, fluffing the fur of the clowders of hungry cats who patrolled the alleys and pounced on every wisp of straw or stem of reed blown in by the breeze.

The streets must have been unusually silent and deserted that day; wine bars and beer-halls unaccustomedly shut up; market squares strangely empty; fishmongers' and costerwomen's stalls folded and stacked back against blind khaki-coloured walls. Fast-food counters stood empty, their pots lidded over, no servers idling behind them waiting for custom. In the school for scribes, the *Bet Thuppi*, no young students chanted their reading exercises, or yelped as they received a sharp stroke of the cane for slapdash work, forgetfulness or daydreaming. It was a special day.

Yet the City was not totally quiet. Wherever you stood you would have heard the hubbub coming from the E-Sagila temple: the sound of thousands of voices raised in song and celebration, accompanied by the jangling and thrumming of hundreds of musical instruments. It was a festival day. The odour of sanctity, of butchered meat, wafted from the Temple precinct as sheep and oxen were sacrificed by the dozen; priests and ministrants scurried up and down the stairways of the Etemenanki ziggurat that dominated every view in the City.

The crossways boulevards, which ended at the towering niched and crenellated wall flanking the commercial quayside of the Euphrates River, which bisected the City, were also empty, the gates through the wall unmanned by guards or collectors of customs duty. Which is why nobody saw that the level of the stream had been falling rapidly for several hours, and that the water now reached to no more than halfway up a man's thigh.

The citizens would know it soon enough.

From both ends of the river, up and downstream, heavily armed fighters appeared, marching through the shallows, one platoon at a time to begin with, until they realized that the citizens were quite unaware of their presence and called to those behind to advance. Over half the army plashed its way along, the commander having earlier sent the other part upstream to open the sluices and divert the river into the huge reservoir, dug on an earlier Queen's command to protect the City from the spring floods. Bowmen and swordsmen climbed the quayside steps, advanced through the river gates, spread out into the streets and secured their line of retreat.

Herodotus: 'Had the Babylonians been alerted to what Cyrus intended, or had they noticed their danger, they would never have allowed the Persians to enter the City, but would have utterly destroyed them; for they would have secured all the street gates that gave on to the river, and would have mounted the walls along the sides of it, and so would have caught the enemy in a kind of trap. But, as it was, the Persians came upon them by surprise and so took the City.'

General Gobryas, former Babylonian governor of the province of Gutium (which stretched from the east bank of the River Tigris to the Zagros Mountains), had changed sides to become commander-in-chief of the army of Cyrus the Persian. Any ambition he may ever have nurtured must on this day have surpassed his wildest dreams. He had taken the greatest city on earth, the fount of civilization, the centre of the world. Without the citizens even noticing, says Herodotus. 'Owing to the vast size of the place, the inhabitants of the central parts (as the residents at Babylon declare) long after the outer portions of the town were taken, knew nothing of what had chanced, but as they were engaged in a festival, continued dancing and revelling until they learnt of their capture only too certainly.' Two weeks later Cyrus himself arrived and took King Nabonidus prisoner.

But Herodotus was born fifty years after the events he narrated. Those who were actually there at the time told different stories. A priest in the service of the Temple of Marduk, the official chronicler of Nabonidus's reign described an entirely peaceful occupation, greatly welcomed by a citizenry that was desperate for change after years of grotesque misrule by a scandalously impious and mostly absent monarch who, in any case, had stolen the throne by having its previous occupant murdered.

He showed no respect for the cult of Marduk, preferring to honour Ishtar, Shamash (the sun) and particularly Sin (the moon). He had absented himself for many years from his capital, residing instead at Tayma, an Arabian oasis town, which meant that the annual *Akitu* festival, the Assyrian New Year, the most important religious observance of the entire calendar, which demanded the presence and participation of the monarch, and on which the safety, security and good fortune of the Babylonian state depended, could not be celebrated. In his place he left his son and co-regent Belshazzar.

Cyrus, on the other hand, had promised to restore Marduk to his rightful place in the yearly round, and had indeed confirmed his intention to support the proper worship of all the gods. He was especially singled out for praise by the official chronicler – unlike our twenty-first-century conqueror of Iraq – for posting shield-bearers around Marduk's Temple, with its rich archives, irreplaceable libraries and precious antiquities, to prevent looting and theft in the chaotic aftermath of the occupation.

Even more positive about the great and gracious Cyrus was that temple priest who composed the romantic verse account of the conquest. He was utterly scathing about his former ruler:

> He muddled the rites,
> he confused the oracles.
> He ordered an end to
> the most important rituals.
> He looked at the sacred images in the temple of Esagila
> and uttered blasphemies.

All agreed that Cyrus was a worthy king, a paragon of virtue, a devout servant of God, who had captured the sacred City without a single act of violence.

On the other hand, a month after being incorporated into the Persian Empire, the city wall around the most vulnerable city gate was earmarked for swift restoration from damage incurred during the occupation. The destruction was extensive, the repair expensive. The contractor's receipt, signed by four witnesses, accounts for seven weeks of work

> *Nurea, son of Bel-iqisa, of the family of Nanaia the Priest, has received a payment of 19 shekels [about half a pound] of silver from Marduk-Remanni, son of Iddin-Marduk, of the family of Nur-Sin, for work carried out on the rampart of the Great Gate of Enlil from the 14th day of the month Tevet [18 December] to the 6th day of Adar [27 February].*

Cyrus had devoted great effort to psychological warfare. Months before his invasion – perhaps even years – his representatives had been busily spreading the word that the Babylonian king had proved himself a menace to his neighbours and an oppressor of his own people; that he must be deposed to restore freedom and justice to Babylonia. They proclaimed the Shahanshah's generosity and concern for basic rights. They sent secret letters to E-Sagila's management committee and its Shatammu, its head, reassuring them of Cyrus's firm intention to uphold the worship of Marduk and all the other deities sacred to the cities of Mesopotamia. To the leaders of the displaced peoples deported by Nebuchadnezzar they confirmed that it was Cyrus's intention to permit their return. To those in the court of the town called Nehardea, who served the sons of Jehoiakin, the last legitimate King of Judah, and to the major religious agitator and propagandist who would become known to posterity as the Second Isaiah, they promised Cyrus's revenge against the city that had humbled Jerusalem. Agents were dispatched to loiter in the bars and taverns to encourage the disaffected citizenry to abandon their loyalty to Nabonidus and to welcome a new ruler who would restore all the ancient traditions so neglected by the usurper of the immortal Nebuchadnezzar's throne, and deliver mercy and fairness to all.

To Babylonian grandees like the official chronicler dictating history in his temple office, the conquest of their city by the Persian represented no threat to their way of life, particularly given Cyrus's generous guarantees. It signified no more than another, and very welcome, change of management. In the course of her long history the land of Sumer and Akkad had been ruled by kings of many nationalities: Amorites, Kassites, Elamites, Assyrians, Chaldeans. All had assimilated to Mesopotamian culture and become more Akkadian than the Akkadians, more Babylonian than the Babylonians. Now the throne was to be occupied by an ethnic Persian. What difference could that make? It could not displace the country from its position – as the maps showed – at the very centre of the Universe, nor its role as the greatest engine of progress that history had ever known.

If he really thought that, then the official chronicler was wrong. The loss of confidence in the Mesopotamian future, first noted in Assyrian times, re-emphasized by the neo-Babylonian passion for antiquity, openly expressed by Kabiti-Ilani-Marduk, signalled that true change was on its way. For the first time ever, the new monarchs of the realm chose not to locate their capital in Babylon, but were content to rule from their original homeland, which meant from Pasagard, from Ecbatana (modern Hamadan), from Persepolis (modern Takht-e-Jamshid), and from Susa (modern Shush), former chief city of Mesopotamia's ancient enemy Elam. Somehow Babylon had lost its overwhelmingly glamorous allure.

Can we say then that it is here that we have reached the end of Mesopotamian civilization? The end of the great arc of development that had begun nearly 3,000 years previously in the rich alluvial soils around the northern end of the Gulf, risen to the first experiments in empire building under Sargon of Akkad and in central planning under King Shulgi of Ur, peaked in free enterprise Old Babylonian days, and experienced a last great surge, the template for the modern imperial state, under Assyrian rule?

Not really. A tradition more than 2,000 years old does not vanish overnight, in a year, in a decade, or even in a single century. For a long time yet, among the many peoples of what had been the Neo-Babylonian Empire, business would continue to prosper, the gods would continue to be served and lauded, the heavens continue to be observed, the omens to be read, the ancient texts to be studied, and the cities to be thronged by multinational, multilingual, multicultural crowds of Anatolians, Egyptians, Greeks, Judaeans, Persians and Syrians.

Though Mesopotamia was reduced to the status of a mere province – albeit retaining the still prestigious name Assyria – in an empire that now extended over four million square miles, the Persians never made any attempt to substitute their own traditions for those of their provincial subjects. How could they, when their own culture was by comparison so meagre, and their own history so short? In fact the traffic was mostly the other way. Persians adopted a form of cuneiform for creating inscriptions in their own, previously unwritten, language; they employed Babylonian Akkadian for scholarly and formal purposes; adopted Mesopotamian Aramaic – henceforth to be known as Persian Imperial Aramaic – as the language of diplomacy and commerce, even in the Persian homeland.

Yet the Babylonians were far from the only people from whom the new rulers of western Asia borrowed in order to enrich their civilization. Their architecture provides ample evidence that craftsmen from right across the wide Persian Empire were employed to beautify their cities: Babylonians, Assyrians, Anatolians, Egyptians, Greeks and all the other nations shown in exquisite detail bringing gifts on the sculptured panels that embellished the stonework of the Persians' new ceremonial capital, Persepolis. The famous autobiographical inscription of Darius the Great at Behistun that detailed his battle for the throne, and which provided the key for the decipherment of cuneiform, was illustrated by bas-reliefs of provincial Assyrian inspiration, but was written in Old Persian, Babylonian and Elamite, the language of the previous rulers of the Iranian lands. Persians had a wide choice in choosing their mentors.

For the Babylonian takeover from Assyria had masked a momentous change in the ecology of ancient civilization: Mesopotamia no longer stood alone as a beacon of development in a barbarian world. From every quarter new cultures challenged Babylon's central place in the history of progress. Other nearby states had caught up with the leader and were rapidly developing their own take on civilized development, in particular the Greeks, whose outlook on life, the universe and everything had started with a very different perspective and, from the eighth century BCE onwards, had taken them in a very different direction.

The contrast between the Persian and the Greek models of society quickly led to conflict: first intellectually on the page – with Greek authors setting up the Persian polity as the eternal future archetype for oriental despotism – and then physically on the battlefield. The conflict continued throughout the lifetime of the Persian Empire: a little over two centuries. The contending parties were too evenly matched for either to achieve easy victory over the other.

Just as it had taken unpolished incoming Amorites to establish the Old Babylonian Empire, and uncouth immigrant Arameans to carve out greater Assyria, so did it demand the barbarian energy and resourcefulness of a newcomer to Greek power, the kingdom of Macedonia, finally to tip the balance and win a decisive victory for the Greek, Hellenistic, way of life. Alexander of Macedon, by-named 'The Great' for these very victories, prevailed at the battles of Issus and Gaugamela, and chased Darius III, King of Persia from the heart of his kingdom, to meet his death at the knife-point of a kinsman. Alexander marked the historic moment by burning glorious Persepolis to ashes at the instigation, the Greek writer Diodorus of Sicily tells us, of an Athenian courtesan.

Had one to choose a day when the first half of all history ended and the second half began, when the original idea of how urban humanity should live was supplanted by a new and different vision, when the first ever civilization, which expressed itself in cuneiform writing, was overtaken by a second, which expresses itself through alphabets (and towards the end of which we ourselves live), then this date would be 1 October 331 BCE.

Of course, to repeat the point, longstanding ways of living do not disappear overnight. If one represents the arc of a civilization in a graph, the drawn line representing, say, its vitality over time, however measured, then the bell-shaped curve would rise first gradually from the base line, after that climbing increasingly steeply to the high point; at the end the curve would fall away, first sharply and then ever more slowly, before very gradually tailing away to nothing. When one civilization gives way to another, their graphs overlap, often by centuries, the decline of the one coinciding with the rise of the other. And so it was in this case.

Thus long before their millennial traditions fully disappeared, Mesopotamians had already begun their induction into an entirely new world, with new Hellenist cities springing up everywhere, with new kinds of public buildings under feverish construction: colonnaded temples, basilicas, gymnasiums; with a bewilderingly cosmopolitan population:

Persians, Indians, Greeks, Egyptians and Jews living cheek by jowl with Babylonians, Assyrians, Armenians and Scythians; and with entirely new classes of people, with no equivalent in the old order: shady entrepreneurs, charismatic adventurers, mercenaries, unattached thinkers and writers, freelance priests, religious revolutionaries.

Yet though the old style of life in the ancient cities still continued, change was inevitable. In her book *Babylonians*, Gwendolyn Leick tells us that:

> *Most of the documents from this period concern slave sales, sales of land and of temple offices, the last an apparently highly lucrative form of capital investment. However, when the Greek authorities decided to tax such activities, beginning initially with the sale of slaves, the temple administration was no longer in charge of recording such transfers and the new records were written on more perishable materials such as papyrus. Babylonian was no longer spoken in daily use, and cuneiform learning became increasingly specialized to deal with astronomical matters and divination. Those who practised these arts were known to the West as Chaldeans, magicians and astrologers, who belonged to a few prominent families of scribes. The last cuneiform tablets date to the first century AD and deal with astronomical observations.*

It is fitting that these final cuneiform records come from Uruk, where Mesopotamia's long and brilliant story of the inventing of civilization had first begun nearly 3,000 years earlier, after its principles, the *Me*, were brought there from Eridu.

We should not succumb to the belief that everything was now lost; that when the ancient cities finally sank below the sands in the succeeding age, their achievements were rendered to nought. That their people, in the words of Ecclesiaticus, 'which have no memorial, who are perished, as though they had never been, are become as though they had never been born and their children after them.' For the new civilization ushered in by the Macedonian conquerors was never pure Greek. Hellenism was a profoundly syncretic culture, borrowing much from the old as well as bringing in the new. Particularly here in Mesopotamia, Hellenism was always a complex brew of Greek, Assyrian and Persian culture. The greatest Hellenist bequest to the world, Christianity, had sprung from many sources: Mesopotamian Judaism, Hellenic paganism and Iranian Zoroastrianism.

Assyrian and Babylonian ideas, literary themes, philosophical notions, musical forms, astronomy and astrology, medicine and mathematics, had long travelled westward to be incorporated into the foundations of the new, alphabetic, civilization. And since a good case can be made that, in spite of the many subsequent changes in political mastership, Hellenistic culture survived – indeed survived magnificently – through Macedonian, Seleucid, Roman and Parthian times, in the end transforming itself into Byzantine civilization, which still, after so many centuries, distantly reflected the original Assyrian model of imperial management established by Tiglath-Pileser I in the twelfth century BCE, one could even say, only a little tendentiously, that the Mesopotamian way of the world lasted, one way or another, until 1453, when Mehmed the Conqueror finally took Constantinople into the Ottoman Empire. Or even – since the Ottomans themselves inherited so much from the Byzantines – until the founding of the modernist secular Turkish state in the 1920s.

So what do we learn from the long saga that we have followed from its beginnings before 4,000 BCE almost to the present? That it has a distinct shape and form.

The Italian systems analyst Cesare Marchetti has shown over a working lifetime of brilliantly argued papers and articles how statistical mathematics may be applied to social data, in particular equations first developed in the 1920s to model the relationship between population numbers of a predator species and its prey. Marchetti successfully used these to show that such disparate phenomena as the spread of the London plague, the history of the Catholic Church, the numerical strength of the British army and even the creative output of a whole series of artists, writers, musicians, scientists and inventors accorded with predictable mathematical patterns. By this means, for example, he was able to show that on his death at the age of thirty-five, Mozart had probably already composed almost everything that he would have written had his life lasted longer. Perhaps we scoff – until we remember that Rossini, born the year after Mozart died, had also completed his life's work by the time he was thirty-seven, though he lived on to the ripe old age of seventy-six.

When applying his insight to long-term phenomena like the growth and decay of empires, here too Marchetti found that the maths worked splendidly: 'The fact that the growth of an empire follows a single ... equation for hundreds of years suggests that the whole process is under the control of automatic mechanisms, much more than the whims of a Napoleon or Genghis Khan.' His results offer the exciting possibility that by following the rise and fall of the Mesopotamian civilization mathematically, we might learn something of the natural laws that shape all civilizations, including our own.

But Marchetti's results depended on amassing large datasets. For example, he plotted his Mozart curve by graphing the cumulative sum of the composer's works against the years of their composition, while his exploration of the vitality of the Catholic Church depended on the well-documented history, dates and numbers, of the canonization of saints and the building of cathedrals. So far no scholar has addressed the problem of selecting and accumulating anything like enough data to apply Marchetti's principles and processes to ancient Mesopotamian times.

But if Marchetti is right, and the rise and fall of civilizations, too, follow predictable mathematical laws, then they should also apply to our own civilization.

That should give us pause for thought, for we also live towards the end of an era. Many features of our own times are strongly reminiscent of the last centuries of Assyrian and neo-Babylonian rule. Our society too shows distinct signs of a loss of confidence in the future: an obsession with the past, an all-consuming zeal for preservation and conservation, a passion for museum culture, for genealogy and history – of which this very book is perhaps an example. We know that the way of life of the second half of all history, based as it is upon the unrestricted exploitation of the earth's resources, is not forever sustainable. We recognize that the world cannot survive if every Indian and Chinese peasant aspires to the lifestyle of the affluent west. We understand that continued population increase at the present exponential rate will certainly overwhelm the globe. And we perceive also that the 2,500-year-old alphabetic civilization, which has made us what we are, is for the very first time being seriously challenged by the first stirrings of a new dispensation – what we could maybe call the Digital Civilisation, which began with Hollerith's census-machine in the 1890s. As the composer of the 'Lamentation over the Destruction of Sumer and Ur' put it around 2000 BCE, 'Who has ever seen a reign of kingship that would take precedence for ever? The reign of kingship has been long indeed but had to exhaust itself.'

If that is so, then we might take some comfort from the moral first drawn by the philosopher Kabiti-Ilani-Marduk, composer of 'The Myth of the Pest-God Irra' back in Assyrian–Babylonian days: that ours is a world in which decline, collapse and destruction always presages some kind of rebirth; that without sweeping away the old, the new cannot be born. And that through all the ups and downs, nothing really worthwhile is ever permanently lost, even though its creators may be long forgotten. When, perhaps sooner, perhaps later, our civilization finally lies dying in the gutter, some of us will still be looking, as the ancient Mesopotamians taught us to do, at the stars.

FURTHER READING

When I first began to explore the history of ancient Mesopotamia, I sought academic advice. I was told, 'You could start with J. N. Postgate on early Mesopotamia, then look at the recent books by Marc van de Mieroop, with plenty of bibliography there to help you.' I cannot better that suggestion.

A History of the Ancient Near East, ca. 3000–323 BC, by Marc van de Mieroop, Professor of Ancient Near Eastern History at Columbia University, was published by Blackwell in 2004, with a second edition in 2007. No dry, academic textbook, but a very accessible narrative, it must rank as the standard work in the field for the lay reader, alongside the now slightly outdated *Ancient Iraq*, by Georges Roux, an independent scholar, the third edition of which was published by Penguin in 1992. For the widest possible perspective – though still lagging behind the most recent archaeological discoveries and perhaps burdened by an idiosyncratic footnote system – see the first three volumes of the second edition of *The Cambridge Ancient History*.

For cultural, economic and social history, *Early Mesopotamia: Society and Economy at the Dawn of History*, by J. N. Postgate, then reader in Mesopotamian Studies at Cambridge University, published by Routledge in 1994, can still not be bettered, though it does not cover the entire period. For a full account from the earliest days to the end of independent Mesopotamia, add Marc van de Mieroop's scholarly *The Ancient Mesopotamian City*, paperback edition published by Oxford University Press in 1999, and the enjoyable *Mesopotamia: The Invention of the City*, by Gwendolyn Leick, an independent scholar and cultural tour guide, published by Penguin in 2002.

The history of Sumerian art is fully laid out in the marvellous *Sumer: The Dawn of Art*, a volume in the Arts of Mankind series from French publisher Gallimard, English edition by Thames and Hudson. Though published as early as 1960, its superb illustrations and the text by André Parrot, then Curator-in-Chief of the French National Museums and a director of the Louvre, make it an indispensable resource for the study of ancient Mesopotamian sculpture and painting.

Further details of my sources follow in the next section. Note that many of the items are currently available online, in part or in whole, though certain journal collections require prepayment or membership of a participating library. An assiduous search will readily locate them.

BIBLIOGRAPHIC NOTES

Lessons from the Past

Several authors have written about Saddam Hussein and his concern to present himself as a successor to the monarchs of ancient Mesopotamia, notably a senior writer on the *New York Times*, Elaine Sciolino, *The Outlaw State: Saddam Hussein's Quest and the Gulf Crisis* (John Wiley, 1991), and John Simpson, *The Wars against Saddam: Taking the Hard Road to Baghdad* (Macmillan, 2003).

Saddam Hussein's claim to have been ordered by God to invade Kuwait is quoted in Umangh Harkhu, 'Does History Repeat Itself?': The Ideology of Saddam Hussein and the Mesopotamian Era', *Scientia Militaria: South African Journal of Military Studies*, 33 (2005). The account of George Bush's divine inspiration was in Norma Percy, Mark Anderson and Dan Edge's documentary film *Elusive Peace: Israel and the Arabs*, broadcast by the BBC on 10, 17 and 24 October 2005. Dan Cruickshank's critique of Saddam's restoration of Babylon is in 'Letter from Baghdad', *Architectural Review*, March 2003.

The story of the discovery of an unknown king of Uruk on a forgotten clay cone is told in the University of Minnesota College of Liberal Arts Newsletter (2008), online at <http://cla.umn.edu/discoveries/language.php?entry=138909>. Finnish Professor Simo Parpola has suggested that the Sumerians are in some way linguistically related to the speakers of Uralic languages like Finnish and Hungarian, who originated, so he believes, in the region of the northern Caucasus.

Owen Seaman's verses 'On the Instability of Things' were published in *Punch*, 18 July 1923.

Kingship Descends from Heaven

Reports of archaeological expeditions to ancient Eridu from which I quote can be found in H. V. Hilprecht, *Explorations in the Bible Lands during the 19th Century*, originally published in 1903; and H. R. Hall, 'The Excavations of 1919 at Ur, el-'Obeid, and Eridu, and the History of Early Babylonia', published in *Man: Journal of the Royal Anthropological Institute of Great Britain and Ireland*, 25 (January 1925). An excellent, up-to-date account of the uncovering of Eridu's many layers of habitation is in Gwendolyn Leick's *Mesopotamia, the Invention of the City* (Penguin, 2002).

Colin Tudge's remark about the harshness of the agricultural revolution is from *Neanderthals, Bandits and Farmers: How Agriculture Really Began* (Weidenfeld & Nicolson, 1998).

Anthony Donohue's case for Egyptian religious sites being located in places where they saw images of their divinities in features of the landscape was published as 'The Goddess of the Theban Mountain', *Antiquity*, 66 (1992).

The suggestion that a meteorite may have crashed into the marshland of southern Mesopotamia was put forward in S. Master, 'A Possible Holocene Impact Structure in the Al 'Amarah Marshes, near the Tigris–Euphrates confluence, Southern Iraq', *Meteoritics and Planetary Science*, 36 (2001).

Colin Renfrew presents his views on the connections between culture and social reality in *Prehistory: The Making of the Human Mind* (Weidenfeld & Nicolson, 2007).

Thorkild Jacobsen described the origins of the Capricorn at Eridu in *Towards the Image of Tammuz and Other Essays on Mesopotamian History and Culture* (Harvard University Press, 1970).

The passage beginning 'Enki, the Lord of abundance' comes from the epic *Enmerkar and the Lord of Aratta*, translated by S. N. Kramer and J. R. Maier in *Myths of Enki, the Crafty God* (Oxford University Press, 1989).

A fuller list of the *Me* is given by Diane Wolkstein and Samuel Noah Kramer in *Inanna, Queen of Heaven and Earth: Her Stories and Hymns from Sumer* (Harper, 1983): 'Shepherdship, kingship, the princess priestess, the divine queen priestess, the incantation priest, the noble priest, the libations priest, truth, descent into the underworld, ascent from the underworld, the *kurgarra*, the dagger and sword, the black garment, the colourful garment, the loosening of the hair, the binding of the hair, the standard, the quiver, the art of lovemaking, the kissing of the phallus, the art of prostitution, the art of speeding, the art of forthright speech, the art of slanderous speech, the art of adorning speech, the cult prostitute, the holy tavern, the holy shrine, the holy priestess of heaven, the resounding musical instrument, the art of song, the art of the elder, the art of the hero, the art of power, the art of treachery, the art of straightforwardness, the plundering of cities, the setting up of lamentations, the rejoicing of the heart, deceit, the rebellious land, the art of kindness, travel, the secure dwelling place, the craft of the woodworker, the craft of the copper worker, the craft of the scribe, the craft of the smith, the craft of the leather maker, the craft of the fuller, the craft of the builder, the craft of the reed worker, the perceptive ear, the power of attention, the holy purification rites, the feeding pen, the heaping up of hot coals, the sheepfold, fear, consternation, dismay, the bitter-toothed lion, the kindling of fire, the putting out of fire, the weary arm, the assembled family, procreation, the kindling of strife, counselling, heart-soothing, the giving of judgments, the making of decisions.'

The demography of ancient Oxyrhynchos is detailed in Peter Parsons, *City of the Sharp-Nosed Fish: Greek Lives in Roman Egypt* (Weidenfeld & Nicolson, 2007).

The lines expressing what happens when Inanna absents herself from the world, and describing the sexual laxity of the city, are translated in Stephanie Dalley, *Myths from Mesopotamia* (Oxford University Press, 1989). The story of Inanna's stealing of the *Me* from Enki is adapted from the epic *Inanna and Enki*, as translated in Oxford University's Electronic Text Corpus of Sumerian Literature, online at <http://etcsl.orinst.ox.ac.uk>.

The City of Gilgamesh

Alaric the Goth's burial at Cosenza in southern Italy was described by Edward Gibbon in *The Decline and Fall of the Roman Empire*: 'By the labour of a captive multitude they forcibly diverted the course of the Busentinus, a small river that washes the walls of Consentia. The royal sepulchre, adorned with the splendid spoils and trophies of Rome, was constructed in the vacant bed; the waters were then restored to their natural channel.' If the story is true, it is just possible that the treasure taken by Roman general (and later emperor) Titus from the Jerusalem temple might still be found somewhere beneath the waters of the river Busento. An account of the German expedition to investigate remains under the Euphrates is given in *Geophysical Research Abstracts*, 5 (2003).

André Parrot's reaction to the Lady of Uruk, aka the Warka Mask, is in *Sumer: The Dawn of Art* (Thames and Hudson, 1960).

Robert Marett developed his idea that all early religions involved an element of play-acting in *The Threshold of Religion*, first published in 1909.

G. H. Hardy's claim that scientific knowledge is useless comes from his best-known work, *A Mathematician's Apology* (Cambridge University Press, 1940).

Piotr Michalowski's claim that Uruk experienced revolutionary rather than evolutionary development is made in 'Tokenism', published in *American Anthropologist*, 95 (1993).

The references to lapis lazuli used to adorn city walls, temples and chariots are from the texts of *Lugalbanda and the Anzud Bird*, *Enki's Journey to Nibru*, and *The Building of Ningirsu's Temple*.

Thorkild Jacobsen's influential essay in which he introduced the idea of primitive democracy was entitled 'Primitive Democracy in Ancient Mesopotamia' and published in the *Journal of Near Eastern Studies*, 2 (1943).

David Wengrow's exploration of 'the aesthetic deprivation of the non-élite' is published as 'The Evolution of Simplicity: Aesthetic Labour and Social Change in the Neolithic Near East', in *World Archaeology*, 33 (2001). His article arguing that the Uruk civilization was the original inventor of the brand is 'Prehistories of Commodity Branding', *Current Anthropology*, 49 (2008). The view of Professor Andrew Sherratt (1946–2006) that the parallels between the Neolithic and the urban and Industrial Revolutions merit further study is quoted in the same essay.

The Royal Asiatic Society's full report on the decipherment of cuneiform, including the translations made by Fox Talbot, Hincks, Oppert and Rawlinson is, at the time of writing, available at <www.let.leidenuniv.nl/IAA/RAScuco.pdf>.

The reasoning behind the discovery that underlying the Akkadian writing system there had to be another, older language layer is adapted from Jean Bottéro, *Mesopotamia: Writing, Reasoning and the Gods* (University of Chicago Press, 1992).

The Danish scholar who proposed that Sumerian may have been a creole is Jens Høyrup. His suggestion is made in the article 'Sumerian: The Descendant of a Proto-Historical Creole?', published in AIΩN: *Annali del Dipartimento di Studi del Mondo Classico e del Mediterraneo Antico, Sezione linguistica, Istituto Universitario Orientale, Napoli*, 14 (1994).

The Flood

A splendid account of the significance of the Flood in the writing of history is Professor Emeritus Norman Cohn's *Noah's Flood: The Genesis Story in Western Thought* (Yale University Press, 1999).

A list of expeditions in search of remains of Noah's Ark appears online at <http://www.noahsarksearch.com/Expeditions.htm>.

The paper read to the Geological Society of America in 2003 on the breaching of the Bosporos by the Mediterranean Sea was titled 'Late Glacial Great Flood in the Black Sea and Caspian Sea', by Andrey Tchepalyga, Institute of Geography, Russian Academy of Science.

A brief but illuminating account of George Smith and his discoveries is given in Robert S. Strother, 'The Great Good Luck of Mister Smith', published in *Saudi Aramco World*, January/February 1971. The obituary of George Smith by the Reverend Archibald Sayce was published in *Nature* and reprinted in *Living Age*, 14 October 1876. I retrieved it from <http://cdl.library.cornell.edu/moa/browse.journals/livn.1876.html>. George Smith's own accounts of his work are to be found in *Assyrian Discoveries: An Account of Explorations and Discoveries on the Site of Nineveh, during 1873 and 1874* (1875) and *The Chaldean Account of Genesis* (1876).

The 'terrifyingly brilliant essay' by a fifteen-year-old schoolboy is 'To what extent can Sir Leonard Woolley be better described as an imperial orientalist than a scientific archaeologist?', by Jacob Gifford Head, City of London School, 2004.

The momentous changes that took place around 3000 BCE when the Uruk ideology collapsed are detailed in Petr Charvát, 'The Kish Evidence and the Emergence of States in Mesopotamia', *Current Anthropology*, 22 (1981), and in M. Staubwasser and H. Weiss, 'Holocene Climate and Cultural Evolution in Late Prehistoric–Early Historic West Asia', *Quarternary Research*, 66 (2006).

The recent expedition to the site of Hamoukar, in today's Syria, was undertaken by the University of Chicago and the Syrian Department of Antiquities. Their findings are detailed in 'Earliest Evidence for Large Scale Organized Warfare in the Mesopotamian World', University of Chicago press release, 16 December 2005.

The failure of the US-backed project to green the Helmand Valley by irrigation is described in Omar Zakhilwal, *The Helmand Valley Project* (Institute for Afghan Studies, 2004). I retrieved it from <http://www.institute-for-afghan-studies.org/Foreign %20Affairs/us-afghan/helmand_0.htm>.

Professor McGuire Gibson's explanation of traditional desalination techniques is in 'Violation of Fallow: An Engineered Disaster in Mesopotamian Civilisation', in *Irrigation's Impact on Society*, Anthropological Papers of the University of Arizona (University of Arizona Press, 1974).

Big Men and Kings

An example of the accounts, widely published on the internet, of the Iraqi cities of Al-Kut and Nasiriyah launching attacks on each other is at <http://en.wikipedia.org/ wiki/2003_invasion_of_Iraq>.

George Barton's comments on Sumerian onomastics can be found in 'Religious Conceptions Underlying Sumerian Proper Names', *Journal of the American Oriental Society*, 34 (1915).

Jean Bottéro's 1987 lecture to the American Oriental Society on ancient Mesopotamian cuisine was published as 'The Culinary Tablets at Yale', *Journal of the American Oriental Society*, 107 (1987). The recipe for poultry pie that Bottéro was able to decipher was cooked and photographed for a feature in the French magazine *Actuel*, no. 69–70 (June–July 1985).

Quotations from *The Farmer's Instructions* were retrieved from the Electronic Text Corpus of Sumerian Literature <http://etcsl.orinst.ox.ac.uk>.

Details of ancient Sumerian plumbing are given in W. Ludwig, 'Mass, Sitte und Technik des Bauens in Habuba Kabira Süd', in *Actes du colloque 'Le Moyen Euphrate, zone de contacts et d'échanges'*, ed. J.-Cl. Margueron (E. J. Brill, 1980); and in E. Strommenger, 'Habuba Kabira Sud 1974', in *Les Annales Archéologiques Arabes Syriennes*, 25 (1975), quoted in Jean-Luc Bertrand-Krajewski, *Short Historical Dictionary* on Urban Hydrology and Drainage (2006) at <http://jlbkpro.free.fr/shduhdfromatoz/habuba-kebira.pdf>.

The experiment to recreate ancient Mesopotamian beer is described by Miguel Civil, 'Modern Brewers Recreate Ancient Beer', *Chicago University Oriental Institute News and Notes* (1991), and by Gregg Glaser, 'Beer from the Past', in *Modern Brewery Age*, 31 March 2003.

The Sumerian drinking song was retrieved from the Electronic Text Corpus of Sumerian Literature <http://etcsl.orinst.ox.ac.uk>.

Professor Morris Silver's evidence for ancient markets is given in 'Karl Polanyi and Markets in the Ancient Near East: The Challenge of the Evidence', *Journal of Economic History*, 43 (1983).

Petr Charvát describes the Sumerian nouveaux riches in 'The Kish Evidence and the Emergence of States in Mesopotamia', *Current Anthropology*, 22 (1981).

Extracts from the *Enuma Elish* are adapted from the translation by L. W. King in *The Seven Tablets of Creation*, published in 1902.

Dwight W. Young proposes that the remarkable regnal lengths given in the Sumerian King List were derived from scribal school mathematical exercises, in 'A Mathematical Approach to Certain Dynastic Spans in the Sumerian King List', *Journal of Near Eastern Studies*, 47 (1988).

Details of the hundred years war between Lagash and Umma are given in Georges Roux's *Ancient Iraq*, Mark W. Chavalas, *The Ancient Near East: Historical Sources in Translation* (Blackwell, 2006), and *The Cambridge Ancient History*, vol. 1, chapter 13, 'The Cities of Babylonia'.

The description of slingstones falling like rain on to the walls of Aratta is from the epic that scholars call *Enmerkar and the Lord of Aratta*. A further classical description of slingshot warfare can be found in Diodorus Siculus, *Bibliotheca Historica*, Book XIX, 109. More detailed analysis of slingshot fighting can be found in K. G. Lindblom, *The Sling, Especially in Africa* (Stockholm: Staten Etnografsika Museum, 1940), and at <http://www.lloydianaspects.co.uk/weapons/sling2.html>.

Accounts of Woolley's excavations of the royal tombs of Ur are quoted in Richard L. Zettler, Lee Horne, Donald P. Hansen and Holly Pittman, *Treasures from the Royal Tombs of Ur* (University of Pennsylvania Museum, 1998), in Sir Leonard Woolley's own memoir, *Excavations at Ur* (Ernest Benn, 1954), and in Agatha Christie, *An Autobiography* (Collins, 1977).

Professor Bruce Dickson's article on theatres of cruelty is 'Public Transcripts Expressed in Theatres of Cruelty: The Royal Graves at Ur in Mesopotamia', *Cambridge Archaeological Journal*, 16 (2006).

'The food of the netherworld is bitter, the water of the netherworld is brackish' is a line from the epic known as *The Death of Ur-Nammu*.

The passages detailing Urukagina's reforms are adapted from *Iscrizioni Reali Dal*

Vicino Oriente Antico, translated by Giuseppe Del Monte (Università di Pisa Facoltà di Lettere e Filosofia, 2004), from <http://history-world.org/reforms_of_urukagina.htm> and from Samuel Noah Kramer, *History Begins at Sumer* (University of Pennsylvania Press, 1956).

The proverb about ancient lords, kings and tax assessors was retrieved from the Electronic Text Corpus of Sumerian Literature <http://etcsl.orinst.ox.ac.uk>.

Rulers of the Four Quarters

Time magazine's description of Saddam Hussein's fifty-third birthday celebrations appeared on 21 May 1990.

Sargon's boast, 'Now any king who wants to call himself my equal, wherever I went, let him go too!', is from the account known as *The Chronicle of Early Kings*.

The scholar who pointed out that 'Upon myself and my reign, what have I brought?' is like declaring 'The fault, dear Brutus, is not in our stars, but in ourselves' was Joan Goodnick Westenholz, in 'Heroes of Akkad', *Journal of the American Oriental Society*, 103 (1983).

Paul Treherne's study 'The Warrior's Beauty: The Masculine Body and Self-Identity in Bronze Age Europe' was published in the *Journal of European Archaeology*, 3 (1995).

The horse's 'arch-necked pride' and the reproof to the King of Mari for riding a horse rather than a mule are quoted in David W. Anthony, *The Horse, the Wheel, and Language: How Bronze-Age Riders from the Eurasian Steppes Shaped the Modern World* (Princeton University Press, 2007). The Sumerian king who compared himself to 'a horse of the highway that swishes his tail' was King Shulgi of the Ur III dynasty.

The extract describing the deification of Naram-Sin is quoted in Marc van de Mieroop's *A History of the Ancient Near East*.

The 'most recent translator' of Enheduana's 'Nin-me-sara', 'Lady of all the *Me*', is Dr Annette Zgoll. The different possible interpretations of the first lines are described in her *Der Rechtsfall der En-hedu-Ana im Lied Nin-me-sara* (Ugarit-Verlag, 1997).

The seal inscribed with the name 'Apil-Ishtar, son of Ilu-bani, servant of the Divine Naram-Sin' was found in Cyprus in the 1870s by American Civil War colonel, amateur archaeologist and first Director of the Metropolitan Museum of Art in New York, Luigi Palma di Cesnola.

Details of the guest list at the feast celebrating Manishtushu's purchase of several landed estates are given in *The Cambridge Ancient History*.

Marc van de Mieroop's impression that the material remains of the Sargonic period show 'skill, attention to detail and artistic talent' is stated in his *A History of the Ancient Near East*.

Official year names of the Akkadian Empire are quoted in J. N. Postgate's *Early Mesopotamia: Society and Economy at the Dawn of History*.

Sumerian-Akkadian compass directions are quoted from *The Cambridge Ancient History*.

The report of Yale University's expedition to Tell Leilan is in L. Ristvet and H. Weiss, 'Imperial Responses to Environmental Dynamics at Late Third Millennium Tell Leilan', *Orient-Express* (Paris), 4 (2000). Dr Weiss's link between climate change and the collapse of civilization was reported in the *New York Times*, 15 July 1993. His article 'Desert Storm' appeared in *The Sciences*, May/June 1996.

Sumer Resurgent

The details of Utu-hegal's conquest of the Guti come from the text known as *The Victory of Utu-hegal*. The Babylonian text ascribing the downfall of the Guti to their theft of Marduk's boiled fish is known as the *Esagila* chronicle and also as the *Weidner Chronicle*.

The irrelevance of the individual in ancient Sumerian society is described in Marc van de Mieroop's *The Ancient Mesopotamian City*.

Piotr Steinkeller's comparison between Ur III economics and the arrangements of the former Soviet bloc is taken from 'Towards a Definition of Private Economic Activity in Third Millennium Babylonia', in *Commerce and Monetary Systems in the Ancient World: Means of Transmission and Cultural Interaction*, eds Robert Rollinger and Christoph Ulf (Franz Steiner Verlag, 2004).

The Bala system of the Third Dynasty of Ur is described in Tonia M. Sharlach, *Provincial Taxation and the Ur III State*, Cuneiform Monographs, vol. 26 (E. J. Brill, 2004).

The state sheep-run near Lagash is described in *The Cambridge Ancient History*.

The document describing the work debt of a foreman of thirty-seven female cereal workers is detailed by Robert K. Englund of the Free University of Berlin in 'Hard Work – Where Will It Get You? Land Management in Ur III Mesopotamia', *Journal of Near Eastern Studies*, 50 (1991).

Wolfgang Heimpel's analysis of the administrative records of the 'industrial park' of Girsu is entitled 'The Industrial Park of Girsu in the Year 2042 B.C.: Interpretation of an Archive Assembled by P. Mander', *Journal of the American Oriental Society*, 118 (1998).

The description of the Ur III's standardization of weights and measures comes from the preamble to the *Law Code of Ur-Nammu*.

The account of the murder trial in which a woman was accused of not reporting the killing of her husband is adapted from Marc van de Mieroop, *The Ancient Mesopotamian City*, quoting Thorkild Jacobsen, 'An Ancient Mesopotamian Trial for Homicide', *Analecta Biblica*, 12 (1959), translation after J. N. Postgate, *Early Mesopotamia*. The alternative translation, in which the woman was acquitted, is in S. N. Kramer, *History Begins at Sumer* (University of Pennsylvania Press, 1956).

Article 103 of the 1936 Constitution of the USSR states: 'People's assessors function as "lay judges" with the power to decide guilt or innocence, but also have all the rights and powers of the professional judge, including the right to review all investigatory documents, call and question witnesses, examine evidence, set punishment, and award damages.' See Gordon B. Smith, *Reforming the Russian Legal System* (Cambridge University Press, 2008).

Trotsky's alarm at the consequences of Lenin's death is quoted in Nina Tumarkin, *Lenin Lives!: The Lenin Cult in Soviet Russia* (Harvard University Press, 1997). The verse, by A. O. Avdienko, praising Stalin as the one who 'who broughtest man to birth, Thou who fructifiest the earth' is quoted in Martin McCauley, *Stalin and Stalinism* (Longman, 2003). King Shulgi's praise poem, 'Hymn Shulgi B', was retrieved from the Electronic Text Corpus of Sumerian Literature <http://etcsl.orinst.ox.ac.uk>. Stalin's demand for skyscrapers in Moscow is attributed by Wikipedia to Хмельницкий, Дмитрий, 'Сталин и архитектура', гл.11, citing Khmelnitsky, Dimitry, 'Stalin and Architecture', available online at <http://www.archi.ru>.

The similarity between vernacular building style in modern Iraq and its Sumerian antecedents is described in Raymond P. Dougherty, 'Survivals of Sumerian Types of Architecture', *American Journal of Archaeology*, 31 (1927).

Woolley's reference to Abraham's grandson Jacob dreaming of angels going up and down Ur's ziggurat, and his praise for the subtlety of the ziggurat's architecture, is in Sir Leonard Woolley, *Excavations at Ur* (Ernest Benn, 1954).

The account of King Shulgi's run from Nippur to Ur and back is from 'Hymn Shulgi A', retrieved from the Electronic Text Corpus of Sumerian Literature <http://etcsl.orinst.ox.ac.uk>. Modern ultra-marathons are described in Deane Anderson Lamont, 'Running Phenomena in Ancient Sumer', *Journal of Sport History*, 22 (1995).

General Sharrum-bani's account of his building the wall called Muriq-Tidnum, 'It Fends Off Tidnum', and of General Ishbi-Erra's failure to bring grain to Ur, are taken from Mark W. Chavalas, *The Ancient Near East, Historical Sources in Translation* (Blackwell, 2006).

The description of Elam's destruction of Ur is taken from the text known as *Lament for the City of Ur*. The inevitability of the end of Ur's kingship comes from the *Lamentation over the Destruction of Sumer and Ur*.

The condemnation of the barbaric Martu is quoted in Georges Roux, *Ancient Iraq*.

Professor William Hallo's identification of the Amorites with the ancestors of the Hebrews is detailed in the *Encyclopedia Judaica*, in the entry on Mesopotamia.

Old Babylon

Peter Ackroyd's *London: A Biography* was published in 2000.

The Itinerary of Benjamin of Tudela, Critical Text, Translation and Commentary, by Marcus Nathan Adler, was published by Oxford University Press in 1907.

An extensive press report of the discovery of fragments of diorite found under Knightrider Street, 'from the time of the oldest Babylonian kingdom as yet known', by Morris Jastrow Jr., appeared in the *New York Times*, 11 January, 1891.

The letter from the Mari palace official beginning 'No king is truly powerful just on his own', the complaint of the ruler of Qatna to the king of Ekallatum, and the description of King Zimri-lin's personality as revealed in his letters, are taken from Jack M. Sasson, 'The King and I: A Mari King in Changing Perceptions', presidential address to the American Oriental Society, Miami, 1997. Shamshi-adad's criticisms of his younger son appear in Marc van de Mieroop, *A History of the Ancient Near East* and in Georges Roux, *Ancient Iraq*.

The directions for finding the way to a particular house in Ur, 'You should enter by the Grand Gate', are quoted in Adam T. Smith, *The Political Landscape: Constellations of Authority in Early Complex Polities* (University of California Press, 2003).

Details of Dumuzi-Gamil's business activities appear in Marc van de Mieroop, *Society and Enterprise in Old Babylonian Ur* (Dietrich Reimer Verlag, 1992), quoted in William N. Goetzmann, Financing Civilisation <http://viking.som.yale.edu/ will/finciv/ chapter1.htm>.

The extract from the résumé of a newly graduated Babylonian scribe is taken from Jean Bottéro, in Jean Bottéro, Clarisse Herrenschmidt and Jean Pierre Vernant, *Ancestor of the West: Writing, Reasoning, and Religion in Mesopotamia, Elam, and Greece*, translated by Teresa Lavender Fagan (University of Chicago Press, 2000).

The extracts from the story called 'Schooldays' by its first translator, Samuel Noah Kramer, are adapted from Steve Tinney, 'Texts, Tablets and Teaching: Scribal Education in Nippur and Ur', *Expedition*, 40 (1998). The complaint by a father that his son shows too little appreciation of his education is adapted from the text known as 'The Scribe and his Perverse Son', quoted in Karen Rhea Nemet-Nejat, *Daily Life in Ancient Mesopotamia* (Greenwood Press, 1998).

The problem set to Babylonian students, beginning 'With a volume of earth of 90 I shall capture the city hostile to Marduk', is adapted from J. N. Postgate, *Early Mesopotamia: Society and Economy at the Dawn of History*.

The modern mathematician who suggested that the Babylonian approach to mathematical problems would be familiar to those who remember old-fashioned high-school algebra courses was Asger Aaboe, in *Episodes from the Early History of Mathematics* (Mathematical Association of America, 1997).

The examples of abnormal births seen as omens are from Morris Jastrow Jr., *Babylonian-Assyrian Birth-Omens* (Alfred Töpelman Verlag, 1914).

The king of Mari's instructions to keep the Lady Nanname away from others because of her infectious condition is taken from Karen Rhea Nemet-Nejat, *Daily Life in Ancient Mesopotamia* (Greenwood Press, 1998). The authors of the collection of Babylonian medical texts published in 2005 told their story to William Mullen in 'Assyrian and Babylonian Medicine Was Surprisingly Advanced', *Chicago Tribune*, 24 October 2005.

Empire of Ashur

Henry W. F. Saggs's magisterial account, *The Might That Was Assyria*, was published by Sidgwick & Jackson in 1984.

Simo Parpola's somewhat controversial ideas on the transmission of Assyrian beliefs and philosophies to Jewish, Christian and Oriental mysticism are put forward in the introduction to *Assyrian Prophecies*, State Archives of Assyria, vol. 9 (Helsinki University Press, 1997). Jerrold Cooper's rigorous criticism of Professor Parpola's views was published as 'Assyrian Prophecies, the Assyrian Tree, and the Mesopotamian Origins of Jewish Monotheism, Greek Philosophy, Christian Theology, Gnosticism, and Much More', in the *Journal of the American Oriental Society*, 120 (2000).

M. L. West, Emeritus Fellow of All Souls College, Oxford, writes of the westward transmission of Assyrian mythology and poetic form in 'Near Eastern Material in Hellenistic and Roman Literature', *Harvard Studies in Classical Philology*, 73 (1968), and in *The East Face of Helicon, West Asiatic Elements in Greek Poetry and Myth* (Clarendon Press, 1999).

Extracts from the letters of the Assyrian merchants of Karum Kanesh and their wives are quoted from J. N. Postgate, *Early Mesopotamia: Society and Economy at the Dawn of History*, Marc van de Mieroop, *A History of the Ancient Near East*, and Amélie Kuhrt, 'The Old Assyrian Merchants', in *Trade, Traders, and the Ancient City*, eds Helen Parkins and Christopher John Smith (Routledge, 1998).

Quotations from the Middle Assyrian laws and palace decrees are adapted from James B. Pritchard, *Ancient Near Eastern Texts Relating to the Old Testament* (Princeton University Press, 1969) and from G. R. Driver and J. c. Miles, *The Assyrian Laws* (Clarendon Press, 1935).

Professor A. T. Olmstead coined the phrase 'calculated frightfulness' for the title of his article 'The Calculated Frightfulness of Ashur Nasir Apal', *Journal of the American Oriental Society*, 38 (1918). Tiglath-Pileser's inscription comparing the king to a hunter who cuts open women and blinds infants are detailed in Mordechai Cogan, '"Ripping Open Pregnant Women" in Light of an Assyrian Analogue', *Journal of the American Oriental Society*, 103 (1983).

The uncleanness of women in Assyrian custom and law is described in Elisabeth M. Tetlow, *Women, Crime and Punishment in Ancient Law and Society, vol. 1: The Ancient Near East* (Continuum International Publishing, 2005).

Figures for recent population movements are taken from the United Nations Department of Economic and Social Affairs, Population Division, *Trends in Total Migrant Stock: The 2005 Revision*. The flow of migrant Aramean nomads into Assyria is ascribed to climate change by J. Neumann and S. Parpola in 'Climatic Change and the Eleventh-Tenth-Century Eclipse of Assyria and Babylonia', *Journal of Near Eastern Studies*, 46 (1987).

That drawing a composite bow was beyond the ability of modern sportsmen is proposed in B. W. Kooi and c. A. Bergman, 'An Approach to the Study of Ancient Archery using Mathematical Modelling', *Antiquity*, 71 (1997).

The Assyrian Horse Lists, and the Israelite charioteers in the Assyrian army, are described in Stephanie Dalley, 'Foreign Chariotry and Cavalry in the Armies of Tiglath-Pileser III and Sargon II', *Iraq*, 47 (1985). The role of horses in the Assyrian military, and the arrangements for breeding and maintaining them, are detailed in Richard A. Gabriel, *The Great Armies of Antiquity* (Greenwood Press, 2002). Details of Assyrian military ranks are given by F. S. Naiden in 'The Invention of the Officer Corps', *Journal of the Historical Society*, 7 (2007).

The quotation from Ashurnasirpal (Tiglath Pileser's great-great-great-grand-father) detailing his punishment of a rebellious city is in Georges Roux, *Ancient Iraq*.

'The empire is not a spread of land but a network of communications over which material goods are carried' is quoted from M. Liverani, 'The Growth of the Assyrian Empire in the Habur/Middle Euphrates Area: A New Paradigm', *State Archives of Assyria Bulletin*, 2 (1988).

Simo Parpola's description of Assyrian kingship is from 'Sons of God: The Ideology of Assyrian Kingship', *Archaeology Odissy Archives* (December 1999).

The suggestion that the description in the Old Testament of King Solomon's court is really a reflection of Assyrian kingship as an ideal is in Israel Finkelstein and Neil Asher Silberman, *David and Solomon* (Free Press, 2006).

The principle that all Assyrians, even foreign deportees, were equal is stated in a letter to the Assyrian king found in Nineveh and in an inscription of Sargon II. These, and the details of foreign names borne by high officials, are quoted from Hayim Tadmor, 'The Aramaization of Assyria: Aspects of Western Impact', in *Mesopotamien und seine Nachbarn: Politische amd kulturelle Wechselbeziehungen im Alten Vorderasien vom 4 bis zum 1 Jahrtausend vor Chr*, ed. H.-J. Nissen and J. Renger (Dietrich Reimer Verlag, 1982).

Passing the Baton

The description of the invention of alphabetic writing as a 'utilitarian invention for soldiers, traders, merchants' is in John Noble Wilford, 'Discovery of Egyptian Inscriptions Indicates an Earlier Date for Origin of the Alphabet', *New York Times*, 13 November 1999.

The admonishment to a scribe not to conceal anything from the king, and Ashurbanipal's own claims to mastery of scribal skills, are quoted from Steven Roger Fischer, *A History of Reading* (Reaktion Books, 2004).

Ashurbanipal's letter to Shadanu, governor of Borsippa, instructing him to collect documents for his library is quoted from Roy MacLeod, *The Library of Alexandria: Centre of Learning in the Ancient World* (I. B. Tauris, 2004).

Austen Layard's praise of Hormuzd Rassam and his account of the unearthing of Ashurbanipal's library are taken from Austen H. Layard, *Discoveries among the Ruins of Nineveh and Babylon* (Harper & Brothers, 1853).

The curator of the Yale University Babylonian Collection, whose response to the discovery of the library of Sippar was reported in the *Washington Post*, 19 April 2003, is Benjamin Foster.

Ashurbanipal's boast of his destruction of Elam is quoted from *The Cambridge Ancient History*, vol. 1, chapter 21, 'Babylonia in the Shadow of Assyria'. The life story of Adda-guppi', mother of Nabu-na'id, is adapted from James B. Pritchard, *Ancient Near Eastern Texts Relating to the Old Testament* (Princeton University Press, 1969).

The accounts of the Babylonian rulers' archaeological researches are taken from Irene J. Winter, 'Babylonian Archaeologists of the(ir) Mesopotamian Past', in *Proceedings of the First International Congress of the Archaeology of the Ancient Near East*, eds P. Matthaie, Alessandra Enea, Luca Peyronel and Frances Pinnock (Dipartment di Scienze Storiche, Archeologiche e Antropologiche dell' Antichità, Università degli Studi di Roma 'La Sapienza', 2000).

Siegfried Giedion's visit to the Boston clock factory is described in his *Space, Time and Architecture: The Growth of a New Tradition* (Harvard University Press, 1941).

The priest Berosos's account of Nebuchadnezzar's prophesy of doom for Babylon is quoted in Eusebius, Προπαρασκευή Ευαγγελική (*Praeparatio evangelica, Preparation for the Gospel*). In turn, this is quoted in George Rawlinson, *The Testimony of the Truth of Scripture: Historical Illustrations of the Old Testament, Gathered from Ancient Records, Monuments and Inscriptions*, Boston, 1898. Rawlinson, quoting Eusebius, quoting Berosos, quoting Nebuchadnezzar: a perfect example of a quarternary source.

Nels M. Bailkey's article, 'A Babylonian Philosopher of History', was published in *Osiris*, 9 (1950).

The receipt for work done on the rampart of the Great Gate of Enlil is translated in P. A. Beaulieu, 'An Episode in the Fall of Babylon to the Persians', *Journal of Near Eastern Studies*, 52 (1993).

The equations modelling the relationship between the population numbers of a predator species and its prey were developed by Alfred Lotka and Vito Volterra, after whom they are named; they express an s-shaped function known as a logistic curve. An archive of most of Cesare Marchetti's publications is accessible online at <http://cesaremarchetti.org>. Well worth seeking out are the papers 'Action Curves and Clockwork Geniuses', from 1985; 'Looking Forward – Looking Backward: A Very Simple Mathematical Model for Very Complex Social Systems', from 1996; and 'Is History Automatic and Are Wars à la Carte? The Perplexing Suggestions of a System Analysis of Historical Time Series', from 2005. I am indebted to the late Rex Malik for introducing me to Dr Marchetti's work.

Internet

Weblinks for images of some events, sites, artefacts, people and buildings described in the text:

The Burning of Susa: http://en.wikipedia.org/wiki/File:Susa-destruction.jpg

The Site of Eridu: http://www.atlastours.net/iraq/eridu.html

The Warka Vase: http://oi.uchicago.edu/OI/IRAQ/dbfiles/objects/14.htm

Ancient Tracks around Tell Brak: http://www-news.uchicago.edu/releases/03/oicorona/oi-corona-02.jpg

The Standard of Ur: http://commons.wikimedia.org/wiki/File:Standard_of_Ur_-_War.jpg

Slingshot Projectiles: http://www.newscientist.com/data/images/ns/cms/dn8472/dn8472-1_650.jpg

Enheduanna, Sargon's Daughter: http://www.arth.upenn.edu/smr04/101910/Slide2.19.jpg

The Great Ziggurat of Ur: http://farm1.static.flickr.com/29/46769923_a35c9ac3b5.jpg

Fresco from Mari Palace: http://commons.wikimedia.org/wiki/File:Mari_fresco_Investiture_Zimri_Lim_0210.jpg

Mart Shmoni Church, Baghdeda: http://www.atour.com/education/20040419a.html

Symbol of the God Ashur: http://en.wikipedia.org/wiki/File:Sumerian_symbology.jpg

God's Footprint at the Ain Dara Temple: http://commons.wikimedia.org/wiki/File:SYRIE_294.jpg

Assyrian Scribes: http://www.aina.org/images/scribes1.jpg

Nabonidus, Last Ruler of Babylon: http://commons.wikimedia.org/wiki/File:N

INDEX